ROYAL HISTORICAL SOCIETY
STUDIES IN HISTORY
New Series

POVERTY, GENDER AND LIFE-CYCLE UNDER
THE ENGLISH POOR LAW
1760–1834

Studies in History New Series

Editorial Board

Professor John Morrill (*Convenor*)
Professor Barry Doyle (*Economic History Society*)
Dr Emma Griffin (*Literary Director*)
Dr Rachel Hammersley
Professor Michael Hughes (*Honorary Treasurer*)
Professor Daniel Power
Dr Bernhard Rieger
Professor Alec Ryrie
Dr Selina Todd (*Past and Present Society*)

This series is supported by annual subventions from the Economic History Society and from the Past and Present Society

# POVERTY, GENDER AND LIFE-CYCLE UNDER THE ENGLISH POOR LAW 1760–1834

*Samantha Williams*

THE ROYAL HISTORICAL SOCIETY
THE BOYDELL PRESS

© Samantha Williams 2011

*All Rights Reserved*. Except as permitted under current legislation no part of this work may be photocopied, stored in a retrieval system, published, performed in public, adapted, broadcast, transmitted, recorded or reproduced in any form or by any means, without the prior permission of the copyright owner

The right of Samantha Williams to be identified as the author of this work has been asserted in accordance with sections 77 and 78 of the Copyright, Designs and Patents Act 1988

First published 2011
The Royal Historical Society, London
in association with
The Boydell Press, Woodbridge

Paperback edition 2013
The Boydell Press, Woodbridge

ISBN 978 0 86193 314 3 hardback
ISBN 978 1 84383 866 1 paperback

Transferred to digital printing

The Boydell Press is an imprint of Boydell & Brewer Ltd
PO Box 9, Woodbridge, Suffolk IP12 3DF, UK
and of Boydell & Brewer Inc,
668 Mt Hope Avenue, Rochester, NY 14620–2731, USA
website: www.boydellandbrewer.com

A CIP catalogue record for this book is available
from the British Library

The publisher has no responsibility for the continued existence or accuracy of URLs for external or third-party internet websites referred to in this book, and does not guarantee that any content on such websites is, or will remain, accurate or appropriate.

This publication is printed on acid-free paper

TO HAMISH

# Contents

| | |
|---|---|
| List of figures | viii |
| List of tables | ix |
| Acknowledgements | xi |
| Abbreviations | xiii |
| Map | xiv |
| Introduction | 1 |
| 1  People, place and poverty | 21 |
| 2  Policy and paupers | 35 |
| 3  Paying for poverty | 69 |
| 4  Gender, life-cycle and the life-course | 101 |
| 5  Work, unemployment and the makeshift economy | 131 |
| Conclusion | 160 |
| Bibliography | 167 |
| Index | 181 |

# List of Figures

1. A typical family reconstitution form: William Newman and Lucy Townsend, married 1771 — 32
2. Annual expenditure on the poor in Campton (1767–1834) and Shefford (1794–1828) — 37
3. Growth in the number of pensioners and all paupers, Campton and Shefford, 1760s–1830s — 37
4. Distribution of weekly pensions, Campton, 1760s–1830s — 40
5. Distribution of weekly pensions, Shefford, 1790s–1820s — 41
6. Payments in kind in Campton, 1760s–1830s — 45
7. Payments in kind in Shefford, 1790s–1820s — 46
8. Poor relief expenditure in Bedfordshire, 1814–47 — 67
9. *Per capita* poor relief spending in Bedfordshire, 1834–47 — 67
10. Rental values of ratepayers in Shefford, 1803–20 — 74
11. Rental values under £5 of ratepayers in Shefford, 1803–20 — 76
12. Pauper careers of William and Elizabeth Newman — 117
13. Pauper careers of Steven and Mary Thompson — 118
14. Pauper careers of Thomas and Esther Merryweathers — 119
15. Number of unemployed men and boys, Campton and Shefford, 1800–34 — 133
16. Cash payments to the unemployed and for make-work schemes, Campton and Shefford, plus receipts for work done in Shefford, 1800–34 — 135
17. Ellard's and Kelynge's charity expenditure, Campton, 1726–87 — 151
18. Number of recipients of Ellard's and Kelynge's charity, Campton, 1726–87 — 152

## Map

1. Bedfordshire, c. 1834 — xiv

## List of Tables

1. The scale of poverty in Bedfordshire and England and Wales, numbers and proportion of the population, 1803, 1813–15 — 28
2. Recipients of poor relief in the hundreds of Bedfordshire, 1802–3 — 30
3. Spending on the poor *per capita* and *per pauper*, Campton and Shefford, 1801–31 — 38
4. Clothing and footwear items provided by Campton's overseers (1767–1834) and Shefford's overseers (1794–1828) — 43
5. Proportion of the population benefiting from poor relief in Campton and Shefford, 1801–31 — 54
6. Number of pensioners in each family category by decade in Campton and Shefford, 1760s–1830s — 57
7. Trends in rate-paying in Shefford, 1803–20 — 70
8. Proportion of ratepayers, non-ratepayers and paupers in Shefford, 1803–20 — 72
9. Occupations of male ratepayers in Shefford, 1803–20 — 79
10. Minimum and maximum proportions of annual expenditure to the non-resident poor in Campton and Shefford, 1760s–1830s — 84
11. Non-resident pensions as a proportion of total non-resident expenditure in Campton and Shefford, 1760s–1830s — 85
12. Age distribution of elderly pensioners at the start of their pension, Campton and Shefford, 1760s–1830s — 114
13. Numbers of the unemployed and unemployment expenditure, Campton and Shefford, 1800s–1830s — 134
14. Ages of the unemployed in Shefford, 1800–34 — 141
15. Three case histories of Shefford's older 'unemployed' in the early nineteenth century — 142
16. Duration of Ellard's and Kelynge's charity payments, Campton, 1726–87 — 153

Publication of this volume was aided
by a most generous grant from the
Girton College, Cambridge, Fellows' Publication Fund

# Acknowledgements

I owe my biggest debt to Professor Richard M. Smith who has accompanied me on the long journey of investigating the poor in Campton and Shefford. He has been extremely generous with his time and advice and has offered me his unfailing support over many years. My interest in the history of poverty was sparked by Mark Jenner and Steve Constantine. I benefited enormously from being a member of The Cambridge Group for the History of Population and Social Structure. It had a rich intellectual atmosphere with plenty of coffee and I have been extremely lucky to be able to chat about the history of poverty with Tony Wrigley, Roger Schofield, Richard Wall, Peter Laslett, Jim Oeppen, Ros Davies, Leigh Shaw-Taylor, Alice Reid, Gill Newton, Peter Kitson, Chris Briggs and Max Satchell, among many, many others. Discussions with Susannah Ottaway have been invaluable, as has her friendship. Eilidh Garrett has been wonderfully supportive on an academic and a personal level, and is now godmother to my own little Eilidh.

At the Royal Historical Society Nigel Goose has provided a great deal of support and academic advice, while Christine Linehan has been invaluable with assistance on the presentation of the manuscript. I would also like to thank my colleagues at the Institute of Continuing Education, particularly Liz Morfoot, Clare Kerr, Heather Falvey, Rebecca Lingwood and Adrian Barlow, and my fellow Girtonians, Ben Griffin, Alastair Reid, Danielle van den Heuvel, Jenny Blackhurst, Peter Sparks and Frances Gandy, for stimulating conversations over lunch.

I have received financial support from a number of sources: the Wellcome Trust; the Faculty of History, Cambridge, Ellen McArthur, Prince Consort and Thirlwall Fund studentships; and from the London School of Economics, an Eileen Power and Michael Postan Studentship. In addition, Girton College Fellows' Publication Fund has made a most generous grant towards publication costs.

Earlier versions of chapter 2 appeared in the *Economic History Review*, the *Historical Journal* and the *American Historical Review*.

I am indebted to Sue Hall for a friendship and interest in the poor of Campton and Shefford that has lasted since our days at Oxford, despite our living on different continents.

Finally, I also owe a big debt to my husband Hamish, who has been there throughout, and to our girls, Morag and Eilidh.

Samantha Williams<br>July 2011

# Abbreviations

| | |
|---|---|
| AgHR | *Agricultural History Review* |
| A&S | *Ageing and Society* |
| C&C | *Continuity and Change* |
| EcHR | *Economic History Review* |
| EHR | *English Historical Review* |
| HJ | *Historical Journal* |
| IRSH | *International Review of Social History* |
| LPS | *Local Population Studies* |
| JBS | *Journal of British Studies* |
| JEcH | *Journal of Economic History* |
| P&P | *Past and Present* |
| SH | *Social History* |
| TRHS | *Transactions of the Royal Historical Society* |
| | |
| BHRS | Bedfordshire Historical Record Society |
| BLARS | Bedfordshire and Luton Archives Service |
| FRF | Family reconstitution form |
| JP | Justice of the Peace |

Map 1. Bedfordshire, c.1834

# Introduction

'The poor of the parish crowded upon us.'[1]

This book is about the poor and their families during the last three decades of the eighteenth century and the first three and a half decades of the nineteenth, the final seventy years of the old poor law. This was a period of long-drawn-out crisis for the relief of the poor which resulted in an overhaul of welfare legislation in 1834 and the introduction of the New Poor Law. At its core is a micro-history, providing detailed case studies of poor relief and the makeshift economy in the two communities of Campton and Shefford in Bedfordshire. It may even be termed 'micro-cosmic' history, in that the local is the site for the consideration of much wider issues; it is a testing ground for research questions that can only be answered accurately by detailed analysis at the parochial, familial and individual level.[2] However, it is also possible to move beyond the locality to the broader regional and national framework. Campton and Shefford can be placed in the much wider geographical area of south-eastern England, a largely agrarian region characterised by high poor law spending, effectively the heartland of the 'poverty problem'. It was concern primarily about spiralling relief costs in this region that prompted the Poor Law Amendment Act of 1834.

A number of issues within current historical scholarship are pertinent to this study: the implementation and growth of the poor laws, the 'mixed economy' of social welfare and the related concept of the 'economy of makeshifts', and the economic impact of the poor laws, as well such wider questions as the 'politics of the parish' and the gendered and life-cycle nature of poverty.

---

[1] The quotation, dated 1800, is from William Holland, a Somerset parson, and is cited in P. King, 'The rights of the poor and the role of the law: the impact of pauper appeals to the summary courts, 1750–1834', in R. M. Smith and S. King (eds), *Poverty, poor relief and welfare, 1650–1929*, Woodbridge 2011.
[2] On microhistory as a methodology see B. Reay, *Microhistories: demography, society and culture in rural England, 1800–1930*, Cambridge 1996, ch. ix. On the concept of microcosmic history M. M. Postan comments that 'Unlike the macrocosmic subjects of the general sociologist and the microscopic subjects of the antiquarian, those of the historican are microcosmic ... The microcosmic method of a scientific historian implies a recognition of the need for making his investigations relevant to the wider issues of social science and a yet further recognition of the special difficulties and peculiar shortcomings of social investigation': *Fact and relevance: essays on historical method*, Cambridge 1971, 20–1.

## The old poor laws

The 'old poor law', codified with the acts of Elizabeth I of 1598–1601 (39 Eliz., c.3, 39 Eliz., c.4, 43 Eliz., c.2), established a clear legal obligation for parishes to deal with three broad classes of applicants for relief: the impotent poor, 'the lame ... the old, the blind, and such other among them being poor and not able to work', such as orphans, widows, the sick and the elderly, were to be relieved; poor children and orphans were to be apprenticed; and the able-bodied, 'all such persons (married or unmarried) as having no meanes to maintain them, use no ordinary and daily trade of life to get their living by', were to be set to work.[3] Those refusing to work – such as rogues, vagabonds and sturdy beggars – were to be whipped or otherwise punished, and then returned to their place of birth or dwelling. 'Wandering and begging' was prohibited unless approved by overseers of the poor,[4] who were to be appointed to raise funds (the poor rates) 'by taxing inhabitants and occupiers of land in the parish' and were then to dispense them to the deserving poor.[5] Responsibility for poor relief thus fell at the parish level and eligibility for relief was negotiated through legal settlement (which identified the parish which was legally responsible for an individual), enshrined in legislation of 1662, 1685, 1691 and 1697–8.[6]

The pace of implementation of the Elizabethan poor laws differed by locality and region.[7] Some communities, particularly urban ones, embraced parish-centred relief even before it became mandatory. Rating was widespread in Kent in the 1590s, was beginning in Lancashire in the 1620s and in Sussex, Lincolnshire and Warwickshire in the 1630s, but was much slower

---

[3] E. M. Leonard, *The early history of English poor relief*, Cambridge 1900, repr. London 1965, 140; M. J. Daunton, *Progress and poverty: an economic and social history of Britain, 1700–1850*, Oxford 1995, 449; G. Taylor, *The problem of poverty, 1660–1834*, London 1969, 4; P. A. Fideler, *Social welfare in pre-industrial England*, Basingstoke 2006, 99–101.

[4] P. Slack, *The English poor law, 1531–1782*, London 1990, ch. iii, and *Poverty and policy in Tudor and Stuart England*, London 1988, ch. v; A. L. Beier, *Masterless men: the vagrancy problem in England, 1560–1640*, London 1985; J. P. Huzel, 'The labourer and the poor law, 1750–1850', in J. Thirsk (ed.), *The agrarian history of England and Wales*, VI: *1750–1850*, Cambridge 1989, 755–810 at p. 756; Fideler, *Social welfare*, 100.

[5] Slack, *Poverty and policy*, 126–8; Fideler, *Social welfare*, 100. L. A. Botelho emphasises that churchwardens, who had played a crucial role in the relief of poverty before the Elizabethan poor laws, continued in that role long after the establishment of overseers: *Old age and the English poor law, 1500–1700*, Woodbridge 2004, 24.

[6] K. D. M. Snell, *Parish and belonging: community, identity and welfare in England and Wales, 1700–1950*, Cambridge 2006, 85–6. For how settlement was gained see chapter 1 below.

[7] Slack, *Poverty and policy*, 114; S. Hindle, *On the parish? The micro-politics of poor relief in rural England, c. 1550–1750*, Oxford 2004, 21–3; Fideler, *Social welfare*, 103, 105. See also P. Slack, *From reformation to improvement: public welfare in early modern England*, Oxford 1999, 66–7.

to start in Northumberland and Durham.[8] It has been estimated that by the end of the seventeenth century perhaps 80 per cent of parishes were implementing a parish rate.[9] Paul Slack has asserted that this 'machine of social welfare' was well established by the later seventeenth century and was still expanding. This was, he states, 'a general phenomenon of major importance'.[10] Given that relief was administered at the parish level and that there were around 15,000 parishes, the old poor law was highly decentralised and policy varied from locality to locality.[11]

The growth of social welfare[12] – with an increasingly extensive and 'generous' poor law system – has been documented for the later seventeenth and eighteenth centuries.[13] There was a significant increase in poor law expenditure due to the increase in the size of parish pensions (regular weekly or monthly relief to all categories of the poor, not just the elderly), some expansion in the numbers of pensioners, and also by increasing spending on 'casual' poor relief in the urban centres of York, Exeter, Norwich, Salisbury and Bristol.[14] Far more charitable relief was available in urban centres than in rural areas and London in particular generally spent far less *per capita*, partly due to alternative sources of welfare assistance and its younger age profile.[15] In the London suburb of St Martins-in-the-Fields, for example, the number of pensioners did not keep pace with the increase in population but there was

---

[8] S. Hindle, *State and social change in early modern England*, Basingstoke 2000, 153–5; *The birthpangs of welfare: poor relief and parish governance in seventeenth-century Warwickshire* (Dugdale Society Occasional Papers xl, 2000), 1–32, and *On the parish?*; Fideler, *Social welfare*, 109, 140; J. Healey, 'The development of poor relief in Lancashire, c. 1598–1680', *HJ* liii (2010), 551–72.

[9] Fideler, *Social welfare*, 140.

[10] Slack, *Poverty and policy*, 182.

[11] A. Kidd, *State, society and the poor in nineteenth-century England*, Basingstoke 1999, 13; Botelho, *Old age*, 20; J. Broad, 'Parish economies of welfare, 1650–1834', *HJ* xlii (1999), 985–1006 at p. 986.

[12] Slack notes that the term 'social welfare' was first used in the Victorian era: *Reformation to improvement*, 1.

[13] Hindle, *Birthpangs*; Slack, *English poor law*; T. Wales, 'Poverty, poor relief and the life-cycle: some evidence from seventeenth-century Norfolk', in R. M. Smith (ed.), *Land, kinship and life-cycle*, Cambridge 1984, 351–404; S. King, *Poverty and welfare in England*, Manchester 2000.

[14] Slack, *Poverty and policy*, 178–82. For the eighteenth-century urban experience see A. Tomkins, *The experience of urban poverty, 1723–82*, Manchester 2006; R. Dyson, 'Who were the poor of Oxford in the late eighteenth and early nineteenth centuries?', in A. Gestrich, S. King and L. Raphael (eds), *Being poor in modern Europe: historical perspectives, 1800–1940*, Oxford 2006, 43–89; and S. King, 'Friendship, kinship and belonging in the letters of urban paupers, 1800–1840', *Historical Social Research* xxxiii (2008), 249–77.

[15] Slack, *Poverty and policy*, ch. viii. See also the research on London by D. R. Green: *Pauper capital: London and the poor law, 1790–1870*, Farnham 2010.

an upward trend in average pensions.[16] There is evidence that in rural areas, particularly in the south and east, poor relief became more comprehensive and markedly more generous after the middle of the seventeenth century.[17] Tim Wales has charted a rise in pension payments in rural Norfolk from around 6d. a week in the first half of the seventeenth century to around 1s. a week in the second half, a sum which could maintain an individual living alone and which might provide a standard of living that compared favourably with that of families of day labourers in work. Moreover, pensions were increasingly supplemented with relief in kind, such as fuel, rent and medical care.[18] During the seventeenth century the majority of the aged poor in Aldenham, Hertfordshire, and Norfolk received more and more as the parish became their principal, and in many cases their sole, source of support.[19]

Vestries which sought to set the under-employed to work faced persistent problems. Some parishes still had stocks of materials which could be used for this purpose in the eighteenth century, but they were few in number.[20] Early in the eighteenth century concern at the cost of poor relief resulted in the permissive legislation of the Workhouse Test Acts of 1722, which recognised Corporations of the Poor in fourteen provincial towns and the City of London. If the act were adopted by a parish, all paupers were to enter the house. In East Anglia, Corporations of the Poor were also founded, offering 'houses of industry', and outdoor relief was cut back.[21] Many workhouses could not achieve even partial success, however, once population, prices and rural unemployment started rising again after 1760. The concentration on arable farming in the east produced large-scale seasonal demands for labour in the summer and autumn, but left a large reserve of labour not fully employed for more than half the year.[22] Opinions were shifting and Gilbert's Act of 1782 reflected the turning tide of opinion and recognised the problem of un- and under-employment. If parishes adopted the act, they were only to house the impotent poor inside workhouses. The able-bodied were to be found employment outside, and supported from the rates if wages were

---

[16] J. Boulton, 'Going on the parish: the parish pension and its meaning in the London suburbs, 1640–1724', in T. Hitchcock, P. King and P. Sharpe (eds), *Chronicling poverty: the voices and strategies of the English poor, 1640–1840*, London 1997, 19–46.
[17] Wales, 'Poverty, poor relief and the life-cycle'; W. Newman Brown, 'The receipt of poor relief and family situation: Aldenham, Hertfordshire, 1630–90', in Smith, *Land, kinship and life-cycle*, 405–22; Botelho, *Old age*, ch. ii.
[18] Wales, 'Poverty, poor relief and the life-cycle', 354–7, 360, 364–5, 374, 387–8.
[19] Newman Brown, 'The receipt of poor relief', 414; Wales, 'Poverty, poor relief and the life-cycle', table 11.1 at pp. 362–4.
[20] Slack, *English poor law*, 39.
[21] Ibid. ch. iii; Daunton, *Progress and poverty*, 453; T. V. Hitchcock, 'The English workhouse: a study in instututional poor relief in selected countries, 1696–1750', unpubl. DPhil. diss. Oxford 1985.
[22] J. D. Marshall, *The old poor law, 1795–1834*, 2nd edn, Basingstoke 1985; K. D. M. Snell, *Annals of the labouring poor: social change and agrarian England, 1660–1900*, Cambridge 1985, ch. i.

insufficient or employment could not be found. By the eve of the New Poor Law, 924 parishes had combined themselves into 67 Gilbert Act unions, all of which were in the east, south-east and Midlands.[23]

Total nominal expenditure rose continually during the eighteenth century, while, in real *per capita* terms, spending grew steadily between 1696 and 1803.[24] Historians have attempted to estimate the generosity or otherwise of the old poor law during the long eighteenth century,[25] Keith Snell, for example, suggesting that 'one can be surprised by the generous and widely encompassing nature of relief … to settled inhabitants rural parishes were indeed "miniature welfare states", and before about 1780 relief policy was usually generous, flexible, and humane'. After 1780, however, parishes came under increasing pressure, with rising expenditure brought on by structural unemployment, population growth and agricultural depression after 1813.[26] Research by Richard M. Smith, Mary Barker-Read, Susannah Ottaway and Steven King has reinforced this general picture: they have shown that pensions in the south and east were most likely to be 'generous' in the first half of the eighteenth century, since pension sums were rising while wages were static and prices falling. In the later eighteenth and early nineteenth centuries, however, not only did pension sums fail to keep pace with inflation, but a greater proportion of the welfare budget was allocated to irregular relief.[27] John Broad largely confirms this chronology, arguing that in southern England before 1780 assistance to the poor facilitated a 'generally humane approach to the treatment of poverty and misfortune', but that from the late eighteenth century the poor became an increasingly dependent group.[28] However, as Steven King has demonstrated, a very different system operated in the north and west, with fewer people relieved and less generously.[29]

---

[23] Slack, *English poor law*, 39–45; A. Brundage, *The English poor laws, 1700–1930*, Basingstoke 2002, 21–2; S. A. Shave, 'The welfare of the vulnerable in the late eighteenth and early nineteenth centuries: Gilbert's Act of 1782', *History in Focus*, Special Theme 'Welfare' (on-line journal), 2008, http://www.history.ac.uk/ihr/Focus/welfare/articles/shaves.html, last accessed July 2010. The act is reproduced in A. Aspinall and E. Anthony Smith (eds), *English historical documents, 1783–1832*, viii, London 1959, repr. 1996, 285–90.

[24] Slack, *English poor law*, 30–1.

[25] For the problems with the concept of 'generosity' see King, *Poverty and welfare*, chs iii–iv.

[26] Snell, *Annals of the labouring poor*, 104–7.

[27] R. M. Smith, 'Ageing and well-being in early modern England: pension trends and gender preferences under the English old poor law, c. 1650–1800', in P. Johnson and P. Thane (eds), *Old age from antiquity to post-modernity*, London 1998, 64–95; M. Barker-Read, 'The treatment of the aged poor in 5 selected West Kent parishes from settlement to Speenhamland (1662–1797)', unpubl. PhD diss. Open University 1989; S. R. Ottaway, *The decline of life: old age in eighteenth-century England*, Cambridge 2004; King, *Poverty and welfare*, ch. vi.

[28] Broad, 'Parish economies of welfare', 985–6.

[29] King, *Poverty and welfare*, ch. vii.

Another way to assess the generosity of the old poor law – in the south and east at least – is to compare provision under the old system with that under the New Poor Law. Given the cuts that followed 1834, such an approach would make even the 'crisis' period of the old poor law appear relatively generous.

It is increasingly recognised that there was a 'mixed economy' of social welfare in the seventeenth, eighteenth and nineteenth centuries that went beyond the poor law.[30] Assistance to the poor of a parish included charity in terms of bequests, benefactions and privately-funded charities, as well as 'face-to-face charity, the gifts of bread and beer at back gates and kitchen doors'.[31] L. A. Botelho argues for seventeenth-century Suffolk that too much emphasis has been placed upon the role of poor law pensions and that this has obscured the continuing importance of charity.[32] Similarly, John Broad has shown that in three southern communities during the later seventeenth and eighteenth centuries parish elites drew upon the total available resources, which not only included poor relief, but also customary rights and charitable funds. He argues that non-rate-based resources should not be seen as separate from parochial assistance, but rather as a complement to it. There were many 'parochial economies of welfare'.[33] Arguing that the old poor law was the most striking example of the state and community interacting creatively, Paul Slack suggested that the poor law formed the backbone of a whole web of provision for public welfare.[34] Yet by the later eighteenth century both customary rights and charity were under considerable pressure. The scale of poverty had increased to such an extent that the contribution of charity was proportionately reduced and marginalised when compared with the contribution from the poor law.[35] Such a situation was evident, for example, in

---

[30] G. Finlayson, *Citizen, state and social welfare in Britain, 1830–1990*, Oxford 1994, 6; Kidd, *State, society and the poor*, ch. i.
[31] Fideler, *Social welfare*, 103, 105, 111, 192–3; Botelho, *Old age*, 19. Other research of relevance here includes Joanna Innes, 'The "mixed economy of welfare" in early modern England: assessments of the options from Hale to Malthus (c. 1683–1803)', in M. Daunton (ed.), *Charity, self-interest and welfare in the English past*, London 1996, 139–80; M. B. Katz and C. Sachsse (eds), *The mixed economy of social welfare*, Baden-Baden 1996; S. King and A. Tomkins, 'Introduction', in S. King and A. Tomkins (eds), *The poor in England, 1700–1850: an economy of makeshifts*, Manchester, 2003, 1–38; and Hindle, *On the parish?*, chs i, ii, iv.
[32] Botelho, *Old age*, 19.
[33] Broad, 'Parish economies of welfare', passim.
[34] Slack, *Reformation to improvement*, 163–4.
[35] Broad, 'Parish economies of welfare'. See also D. Eastwood, 'The republic in the village: the parish and poor at Bampton, 1780–1834', *Journal of Regional and Local Studies* xii (1992), 18–28; King, *Poverty and welfare*; King and Tomkins, *The poor in England*; J. Humphries, Enclosures, common rights, and women: the proletarianisation of families in the late eighteenth and early nineteenth centuries', *JEcH* l (1990), 17–42; P. King, 'Customary rights and women's earnings: the importance of gleaning to the rural poor, 1750–1850', *EcHR* xliv (1991), 461–76.

Colyton, Devon, where charitable relief provided proportionately more in the seventeenth century than in the eighteenth, but by the second half of the eighteenth century parochial officers spent far more than the feoffees.[36] However, 'legal charity' (the poor law) did not crowd out 'voluntary charity'.[37] The mixed economy of welfare was important in the nineteenth century, particularly after the introduction of the New Poor Law, and philanthropic activity continued to increase. In the Victorian period state action and voluntary charity were seen as particularly inter-dependent.[38]

Another related and overlapping theme is the concept of the 'economy of makeshifts', a term first coined by Olwen Hufton in relation to the family economies of the poor in eighteenth-century France.[39] The poor employed a wide range of survival strategies which included any self-provisioning activity, income in cash and kind from the parish, local charities and friendly societies, additional payments in kind by employers, and by-employments. The concept of the makeshift economy is similar to that of the mixed economy of social welfare; both include poor relief, charity in all its forms and customary rights. It extends further by incorporating a much wider range of activities to generate income and resources and it places the poor themselves at its centre. Steven King and Alannah Tomkins have defined the makeshift economy as 'the use of numerous, often local, resources by the poor over time to ensure the survival of individuals and families'.[40] Nevertheless, these concepts are remarkably similar. The makeshift economy extends to credit, loans and debts, selling and pawning goods, barter, friendly societies, baking one's own bread and making one's own clothes, as well as kinship and neighbourhood networks and co-residence. Less legitimate activities included begging, vagrancy, squatting, defrauding the poor law, petty theft, poaching, petty unlicensed brewing, prostitution and receiving stolen goods.[41] By the Victorian period there was a strong emphasis upon 'self-help' and mutual aid.[42] Steven King has highlighted the differential access to elements within the economy of makeshifts between the south and east and the north and west. In the former, poor relief became an increasingly central component in the family economies of some of the labouring poor and the economy of makeshifts weakened, while in the north and west poor relief was more

---

[36] P. Sharpe, *Population and society in an east Devon parish: reproducing Colyton, 1540–1840*, Exeter 2002, ch. vi.
[37] Innes, 'Mixed economy of welfare', 144.
[38] Kidd, *State, society and the poor*, ch. i.
[39] O. H. Hufton, *The poor of eighteenth-century France, 1750–1789*, Oxford 1974.
[40] King and Tomkins, 'Introduction', 13.
[41] King and Tomkins, *The poor in England*, passim. See also J. Humphries, 'Female-headed households in early industrial Britain: the vanguard of the proletariat?', *Labour History Review* lxiii (1998), 31–65, and 'Enclosures, common rights, and women'; King, 'Customary rights'; Ottaway, *The decline of life*, 209–18; and I. K. Ben-Amos, *The culture of giving: informal support and gift-exchange in early modern England*, Cambridge 2008.
[42] Kidd, *State, society and the poor*, ch. iv.

peripheral to family economies and northerners resorted more frequently to assistance from friendly societies, charity and kin.[43] Jane Humphries has emphasised that women and children played a key role in the makeshift economy and that contraction within it therefore had important negative implications for them.[44]

By the later eighteenth century a 'crisis' in the management of poverty was developing. Nationally, poor law expenditure rocketed, as did the numbers being relieved. In 1776 the total poor relief expenditure in England and Wales was £1.5 million (£0.21 *per capita*), by 1803 it had reached just over £4 million (£0.44 *per capita*), in 1813 it was £6.6 million (£0.63 *per capita*), and thereafter fluctuated between £5 million and £7 million (£0.44–£0.68 *per capita*).[45] Many reasons may be advanced to account for this rise: rapid population growth had resulted in a youthful population and a high dependency ratio; there were severe harvest failures in the 1790s and early 1800s; the Napoleonic Wars of 1793–1815 resulted in a significant number of men being enlisted, some of whom deserted their wives and children, and there was rapid price inflation.[46] After 1815 there was demobilisation, post-war depression and widespread structural unemployment in the south and east. There was a weakening of support for the old poor law. Intellectuals, politicians and other contemporaries heatedly debated the state of the poor and possible reforms of the poor laws. The poor were increasingly problematised, pauperised and stigmatised as reformers geared up to the radical overhaul of the law in 1834 which brought in the 'New Poor Law'. The labouring poor, however, increasingly regarded parish relief as an entitlement.[47] Paul Fideler has described the period between the later eighteenth century and 1834 as one in which 'the parish-centred social welfare system itself was on its last legs, unable to cope with population expansion, rising prices, industrial

---

[43] King, *Poverty and welfare*, chs vi–vii; 'Reconstructing lives: the poor, the poor law and welfare in Calverley, 1650–1820', *SH* xxii (1997), 318–38; and 'Making the most of opportunity: the economy of makeshifts in the early modern north', in King and Tomkins, *The poor in England*, 228–57. However, charitable provision *per capita* was much lower in much of the north at least by the 1860s (personal communication with Nigel Goose).

[44] Humphries, 'Female-headed households', and 'Enclosures, common rights, and women'. See also King, 'Customary rights'.

[45] D. Eastwood, *Governing rural England: tradition and transformation in local government, 1780–1840*, Oxford 1994, table 6.1 at p. 135.

[46] E. A. Wrigley and R. S. Schofield, *The population history of England, 1541–1871: a reconstruction*, 2nd edn, Cambridge 1989, 215–19, 228–36, table A.3.1 at pp. 528–9; Brundage, *English poor laws*, 25–7; D. A. Kent, '"Gone for a soldier": family breakdown and the demography of desertion in a London parish', *LPS* xlv (1990), 27–42.

[47] Fideler, *Social welfare*, 134, 146–51, 166–71, ch. vi passim; T. Hitchcock, P. Sharpe and P. King, 'Introduction: chronicling poverty: the voices and strategies of the English poor, 1640–1840', in Hitchcock, King and Sharpe, *Chronicling poverty*, 1–18 at pp. 10–12; P. Sharpe, '"The bowels of compation": a labouring family and the law, c. 1790–1834', in Hitchcock, King and Sharpe, *Chronicling poverty*, 87–108 at p. 87.

development in the north, and the loss of agricultural and proto-industrial employment in the south'.[48]

There is a substantial secondary literature on the subject of the economic impact of the old poor law during this long-drawn-out crisis. In part it seeks to establish the accuracy of the Poor Law Commissioners' conclusions which were published as the *Poor law report* in 1834 (and the questionnaires, 'Rural and town queries', published in the appendices), as well as the evidence published in other parliamentary papers, most notably the 1824 *Select committee on labourers' wages*. This literature has focused on the belief that escalating expenditure on poor relief was the result of a new type of assistance to young families, in the form of child allowances and allowances-in-aid-of-wages (the allowance system). Lagging wages and increased food prices meant that many more families were unable to make ends meet, even with the male heads of household in full employment. After 1815 male un- and under-employment became an increasing problem.[49] Allowances-in-aid-of-wages were intended to subsidise the weekly income of labourers' families, adjusted according to the prices of bread and (sometimes) the number of children in the family. The most famous example of such a scale was adopted by the magistrates at Speenhamland in Berkshire in May 1795, which was a scale of relief to top up local wages to a minimum amount based upon the number in a family and the price of bread.[50] Typically child allowances were paid to labourers' families with four or more children.[51] George Boyer has identified a further four methods of maintaining able-bodied labourers from 1780 to 1834: payments to seasonally unemployed labourers, the roundsman system, the labour rate and the workhouse system.[52] He argues that the major function of poor relief in rural parishes from 1795 to 1834 was the first of these four – the payment of unemployment benefits to seasonally unemployed agricultural labourers. The roundsman system and the labour rate were two variants on unemployment relief. Under the first, unemployed labourers were offered to farmers at reduced rates of pay ('going the rounds'), with the parish making up the difference between earnings and subsistence. Under the labour rate, a ratepayer could either hire labourers at the (subsistence) wage set by the parish or pay a labour rate to the parish. Unemployed

---

[48] Fideler, *Social welfare*, 134.
[49] There are reviews of this literature in Brundage, *English poor laws*, 27–9 and Kidd, *State, society and the poor*, 13–19.
[50] G. R. Boyer, *An economic history of the English poor law, 1750–1850*, Cambridge 1990, 10–23; F. M. Eden, *The state of the poor: or an history of the labouring classes in England*, London 1797, i. 576–7; M. Neuman, 'A suggestion regarding the origins of the Speenhamland Plan', EHR lxxxiv (1969), 317–22; 'Speenhamland in Berkshire', in E. W. Martin (ed.), *Comparative development in social welfare*, London 1972, 85–127; and *The Speenhamland county: poverty and the poor laws in Berkshire, 1782–1834*, New York 1982.
[51] Kidd, *State, society and the poor*, 15; Boyer, *Economic history*, 14.
[52] Boyer, *Economic history*, 10–23. See also W. A. Armstrong, *Farmworkers: a social and economic history, 1770–1980*, London 1988, 69–70.

relief recipients might be expected to repair the parish roads in return for their parish pay. The final method, the workhouse system, had been in place since the Workhouse Test Act of 1722, but there is little evidence that unemployed men were forced to enter workhouses between 1780 and 1834.[53]

Debate has focused upon whether child allowances, allowances-in-aid-of-wages and unemployment payments immiserated the labouring poor further by lowering productivity and wages.[54] Mark Blaug argued that allowances were widespread in the south and east of England and that they were 'essentially a device for dealing with the problems of structural unemployment and substandard wages in the lagging rural sector of a rapidly growing but still under-developed economy'.[55] Daniel Baugh has examined the payment of allowances in some detail in the three counties of Essex, Kent and Sussex and argues that between 1790 and 1814 poor relief was largely a response to high food prices, due to a mixture of harvest failures and war-time inflation, but that from the 1820s allowances were intended to boost the household incomes of those suffering the effects of chronic unemployment. With the war-time agricultural boom over, farming profits shrank, labour became redundant, wages fell and many found themselves under-employed.[56] More recently, Boyer has revived the old debate on the influence of child allowances on population growth. He argues that couples married young and had a large number of children in a short space of time in order to qualify for child allowances and thereby maximise their income.[57] His conclusions are in stark contrast to those of James Huzel, who turns the argument upon its head and argues instead that child allowances were a necessary response to the pressures of rapidly rising population.[58] Yet even within this literature there is recognition that the prevalence, nature and exact timing of child allowances and allowances-in-aid-of-wages have been seriously under-researched.

Some of the most stimulating research undertaken in the last fifteen years in relation to the poor laws has been on the subject of the 'politics of the parish', which, by its very nature, requires detailed local research. Keith Wrightson introduced the concept, arguing that, 'For the world of the parish was nothing if not a political forum'. Steve Hindle has considerably extended understanding of parish politics; he argues that, 'the politics of the poor rate were arguably the most significant of those at work in early modern

---

[53] Boyer, *Economic history*, 10–23.
[54] For a review of this debate see Kidd, *State, society and the poor*, 13–24.
[55] M. Blaug, 'The myth of the old poor law and the making of the new', *JEcH* xxiii (1963), 151–84 at pp. 176–7, and 'The poor law reexamined', *JEcH* xxiv (1964), 229–45 at p. 229.
[56] D. A. Baugh, 'The cost of poor relief in south-east England, 1790–1834', *EcHR* xxviii (1975), 50–68.
[57] Boyer, *Economic history*, ch. v.
[58] Huzel, 'The labourer and the poor law'.

England'.[59] While power was transmitted and negotiated through the triangle of the labouring poor, parish officers (overseers, churchwardens, the vestry) and the county magistrates, Hindle has located considerable authority in the parish vestry.[60] Research suggests that by the late eighteenth century power might have shifted more decisively towards magistrates through the system of pauper appeals and through magistrates' orders for scaled relief allowances, particularly in the south and east.[61]

Application for relief in small parishes took the form of a face-to-face appeal between the poor and overseers and/or vestries who were familiar with the circumstances of those applying. However, simple need was usually insufficient to secure relief: 'countless value judgements and the nods and winks of personal acquaintance must have affected the way in which relief was administered at a personal level'.[62] L. A. Botelho describes the various ways in which the poor might qualify for relief: they might catch the vestry's attention, elicit sympathy, play on old loyalties, emphasise their good points (such as long years of labour), or, alternatively, promise to mend their bad ways.[63] Even once relief was secured the relationship between the pensioner and the vestry was ongoing and never static; the pension lists were periodically reviewed.[64] Evidence on the proportion of applicants who were successful in their requests for relief is rare, but Steven King has analysed vestry records which do give this information for three north-western town-

---

[59] Whightson, K., 'The politics of the parish in early modern England', in P. Griffiths, A. Fox and S. Hindle (eds), *The experience of authority in early modern England*, London 1996, 10–46; Hindle, S., 'Power, poor relief, and social relations in Holland Fen, c. 1600–1800', *HJ* xli (1998), 67–96, and *On the parish?* See also Fideler, *Social welfare*, 111–12.

[60] Hindle, 'Power, poor relief and social relations', 67. See also idem, '"Without the cry of any neighbours": a Cumbrian family and the poor law authorities, c. 1690–1730', in H. Berry and E. Foyster (eds), *The family in early modern England*, Cambridge 2007, 126–57. Jonathan Healey has recently challenged Hindle on the relative degree of power held by parish vestries and seeks instead to relocate authority with the magistracy: 'Poor relief in Lancashire'.

[61] King, 'Rights of the poor'; P. Dunkley, 'Paternalism, the magistracy and poor relief in England, 1795–1834', *IRSH* xxiv (1979), 371–97, and *The crisis of the old poor law in England, 1795–1834: an interpretative essay*, London 1982, ch. iii. In the latter, Dunkley argues that the New Poor Law circumscribed the authority of magistrates; under the old poor law their role had been one of 'ultimate arbiters in local relief matters' (p. 5). See also the debate on the role of the landed gentry and the magistracy in the making of the New Poor Law: P. Mandler, 'The making of the New Poor Law redivivus', *P&P* cxvii (1987), 131–57; A. Brundage and D. Eastwood, 'The making of the New Poor Law redivivus', *P&P* cxxvii (1990), 183–94; P. Mandler, 'The making of the New Poor Law redivivus: reply', *P&P* cxxvii (1990), 194–201; and Eastwood, *Governing rural England*.

[62] Sharpe, 'The bowels of compation', 87. Other works of relevance here are Sharpe, *Reproducing Colyton*, 211–15, 216–22, and Barker-Read, 'The treatment of the aged poor', 161.

[63] Botelho, *Old age*, 22–3.

[64] Ibid. This was also the case in Shefford: Shefford vestry minutes, BLARS, P70/8/1. See chapter 2 below.

ships in the period 1790–1812. He finds that between one-fifth and one-half of applicants were turned down. Some were rejected because they were not considered sufficiently poor, some because they had relatives who might assist them, and others because they had some moral failing in the opinion of the vestry. They might also come away with relief in kind, such as a bag of potatoes, rather than the pension of 2s. a week that was requested.[65]

It might also be expected that there were further distinctions within parishes between ratepayers and paupers, and certainly the poor laws could embody social distance, but there is evidence to suggest that the boundaries between the two groups could be blurred, as was indeed recognised by contemporaries, thus contributing to a general willingness to support the (settled) poor.[66] Ratepayers, overseers and vestrymen recognised that they too might require poor relief in their old age.[67]

Gender and life-cycle were important features of poverty. Access to regular poor relief was heavily gendered: women alone or widowed accounted for disproportionate numbers of pensioners.[68] Tim Wales found that in seventeenth-century Norfolk women accounted for between 40 and 60 per cent of pensioners, while Susannah Ottaway's analysis of Frederick Eden's data for thirty-two parishes in all regions in the 1790s reveals that elderly women outnumbered men by 284 to 128.[69] It has been argued that this changed with a masculinisation of the relief rolls from the later eighteenth century as parishes increasingly resorted to allowances-in-aid-of-wages, child allowances and unemployment relief.[70] Ottaway believes that up until 1800 the welfare net spread more widely to accommodate couples with young children without squeezing out the elderly, while, on the other hand, Steven King and Richard M. Smith have suggested that, as elderly men became more prominent by the 1820s, aged women might have been displaced from the relief rolls.[71]

There were three points over the course of life when individuals and their

---

[65] King, 'Making the most of opportunity', 232–5.
[66] See chapters 3 and 4 below.
[67] Hindle, 'Power, poor relief and social relations'; P. M. Solar, 'Poor relief and English economic development before the industrial revolution', EcHR xlviii (1995), 1–22 at pp. 7–12; K. D. M. Snell, 'Pauper settlement and the right to poor relief in England and Wales', C&C vi (1991), 375–415 at pp. 400–1; P. King, 'Pauper inventories and the material lives of the poor in the eighteenth and nineteenth centuries', in Hitchcock, King and Sharpe, Chronicling poverty, 155–91 at p. 182.
[68] Fideler, Social welfare, 113–14; A. Tomkins, 'Women and poverty', in H. Barker and E. Chalus (eds), Women's history: Britain, 1700–1850, London 2005, 152–73 at p. 153.
[69] Wales, 'Poverty, poor relief and the life-cycle', 360–4, 366–7; Ottaway, Decline of life, table 5.1 at p. 185. Botelho does not agree with this picture for the seventeenth-century communities of Poslingford and Cratfield, Suffolk, and finds a more complex situation: Old age, 115–17.
[70] King, Poverty and welfare, chs vi–vii; Sharpe, Reproducing Colyton, 223–9, 234–9.
[71] S. R. Ottaway, 'Providing for the elderly in eighteenth-century England', C&C xiii (1998), 391–418; King, Poverty and welfare, ch. vi; Smith, 'Ageing and wellbeing'. Smith

families were far more likely to be poor: in childhood and in middle age, when couples had a number of small children not yet earning, and in old age, when the husband and wife became infirm and had gradually to withdraw from the labour market. These deficit phases were identified by B. Seebohm Rowntree in York in 1899.[72] Poverty was compounded for couples with young children and the aged by the demographic fact that parents entered old age at the point that their children had young families of their own and thus it was frequently difficult for relatives to assist one another.[73] A poor woman called Rachel Shoregh wrote in 1810 that 'my children are all married and got familys which these dear times they have as much as they can do to support and therefore are not able to assist me'.[74] Tim Wales has found that in seventeenth-century Norfolk parish relief was 'especially important for those at certain stages in the life-cycle, notably the orphan and the widow and the aged generally'. Indeed, he found that for most of the aged the only way off regular poor relief was by death.[75] Other historians have explored the impact of life-cycle crises in a variety of urban and rural settings in the seventeenth, eighteenth and nineteenth centuries.[76] That this has revealed a life-cycle of poverty so similar over at least three centuries suggests that there had been no radical shifts in the profile of poverty, at least for those principally dependent on their own labour power for a livelihood.[77] However, the

---

argues that elderly widows might have been displaced from outdoor relief into workhouses, rather than thrown off relief altogether.

[72] B. S. Rowntree, *Poverty: a study of town life*, 2nd edn, London 1902, 137–8.

[73] R. M. Smith, 'Some issues concerning families and their property in rural England, 1250–1800', in Smith, *Land, kinship and life-cycle*, 1–86.

[74] T. Sokoll, 'Old age in poverty: the record of Essex pauper letters, 1780–1834', in Hitchcock, King and Sharpe, *Chronicling poverty*, 127–54 at p. 138.

[75] Wales, 'Poverty, poor relief and the life-cycle', 387, figure 11.1 at pp. 362–4. This was also a finding of Newman-Brown, 'Poor relief and family situation', and B. Stapleton, 'Inherited poverty and life-cycle poverty: Odiham, Hampshire, 1650–1850', *SH* xviii (1993), 339–55. Inherited poverty is discussed more fully in chapter 4 below.

[76] J. Healey, 'Poverty in an industrializing town: deserving hardship in Bolton, 1674–99', *SH* xxxv (2010), 135–6; King, 'Reconstructing lives', and *Poverty and welfare*, 127–34; Sharpe, *Reproducing Colyton*, ch. vii; B. Reay, *Rural Englands: labouring lives in the nineteenth century*, Basingstoke 2004; S. A. Shave, 'The dependent poor? (Re)constructing the lives of individuals "on the parish" in rural Dorset, 1800–32', *Rural History* xx (2009), 67–97. One of the first historians to use life-cycle analysis was Michael Anderson, as early as 1971, in his important study of urban Preston in the mid-nineteenth century: *Family structure in nineteenth-century Lancashire*, Cambridge 1971, 30–2, 48–56, 166–7, 202.

[77] Other studies considering the life-cycle nature of poverty in the old poor law period include M. K. McIntosh, 'Networks of care in Elizabethan English towns: the example of Hadleigh, Suffolk', in P. Horden and R. Smith (eds), *The locus of care: families, communities, institutions, and the provision of welfare since antiquity*, London 1998, 71–89; Newman Brown, 'Poor relief and family situation'; M. E. Fissell, *Patients, power, and the poor in eighteenth-century Bristol*, Cambridge 1991, ch. v; Botelho, *Old age*; P. Thane, *Old age in English history: past experiences, present issues*, Oxford 2000, chs vi, viii; and A. Levene, 'Children, childhood and the workhouse: St Marylebone, 1769–81', *London Journal* xxxiii (2008), 37–55. Steven King disaggregates poor relief lists by sex and age

proportion of the population suffering from life-cycle poverty most probably increased during this period due to the growth of wage-dependency and proletarianisation.[78]

Analyses by Thomas Sokoll of household listings for two Essex communities provide evidence on the depth of poverty at certain life-cycle points as well as the role of gender.[79] In Ardleigh in 1796 the worst deficit phase came when the head of the household was aged about forty and the family income had fallen below even the level to be expected in old age.[80] In Braintree in 1821 the risk of becoming poor increased during the early years of life, reaching its first peak in the age group 10–14. Thereafter it dropped to its lowest point over the entire life-cycle in the age group 25–29. After the age of thirty, the experiences of men and women diverged. For men, the period of relative prosperity in mid-life seems to have lasted some twenty years longer than for women, up to the age of sixty, whereas women would appear to have been subjected to a process of gradual pauperisation. In old age, however, about the same proportion of men and women lived in poverty and after the age of sixty the poverty rate reached its peak for both sexes.[81]

While each of the life-cycle deficit phases has been the subject of detailed research, the elderly have attracted the most attention in terms of the definition of old age in the past, the extent to which the elderly fell into poverty, the relative generosity of their relief, the extent to which kin assisted them, and their residential circumstances.[82] It is clear that there was no concept of 'retirement' in the eighteenth and nineteenth centuries. Instead, poor relief was paid to the aged only when their chronological and functional attributes

---

but dedicates only ten pages to life-cycle poverty: *Poverty and welfare*, 78, 120, 127–34. Steve Hindle only briefly considers life-cycle: *On the parish?*, 274. For the New Poor Law period Lees has found that 65% of those examined were married couples, either with or without children, and single-parent families, and were therefore at the middle stages of the life-cycle: *The solidarities of strangers: the English poor laws and the people, 1700–1948*, Cambridge 1998, 191–5.

[78] Sharpe, *Reproducing Colyton*, 224–5.

[79] T. Sokoll, *Household and family among the poor: the case of two Essex communities in the late eighteenth and early nineteenth centuries*, Bochum 1993, pts II, III.

[80] Idem, 'Large families, wheat prices and the allowance cycle: poverty and poor relief in the agricultural community of Ardleigh, 1794–1801', in R. Wall and O. Saito (eds), *Social and economic aspects of family life-cycle*, forthcoming, passim, with particular reference to Smith, 'Some issues', 68–72.

[81] Sokoll, *Household and family*, 264. See also R. Wall, 'Some implications of the earnings, income and expenditure patterns of married women in populations in the past', in J. Henderson and R. Wall (eds), *Poor women and children in the European past*, London 1994, 321–35 at p. 322.

[82] M. Pelling, 'Old age, poverty, and disability in early modern Norwich: work, remarriage, and other expedients', in M. Pelling and R. M. Smith (eds), *Life, death and the elderly: historical perspectives*, London 1991, 74–101; Botelho, *Old age*; Ottaway, *Decline of life*; R. M. Smith, 'The structured dependence of the elderly as a recent development: some sceptical historical thoughts', *A&S* iv (1984), 409–28; Sokoll, 'Old age in poverty'; J. E. Smith, 'Widowhood and ageing in traditional English society', *A&S* iv (1984), 429–49.

coincided, when they were beyond working and had become infirm, rather than when they had reached a specific age.[83] However, there is considerable debate about the relative generosity of state welfare for the elderly poor, with Pat Thane and Steven King drawing a largely pessimistic picture of the restricted nature of relief, whereas the 'optimists' Richard M. Smith, Tim Wales, Peter Solar, David Thomson and Susannah Ottaway point to substantial levels of assistance and a relatively high proportion of the aged receiving such benefits.[84] There has been further debate between David Thomson and E. H. Hunt concerning pensions to the aged in the early decades of the New Poor Law and the extent to which these were 'old age pensions' or actually 'unemployment benefits'.[85]

Poor children and orphans have been studied primarily in terms of their accommodation in metropolitan workhouses, the role of pauper apprenticeship and the contribution of child labour (and pauper apprenticeship) to industrialisation.[86] Less has been said about the proportion of children relieved by rural parishes.[87] The parents of poor children have been the subject of study in two ways: as couple-headed families in receipt of child allowances and as lone parents – primarily as widows with young children, unmarried mothers and deserted wives – who were also a significant category of poor relief recipients.[88] Snell and Millar were two of the first historians to

---

[83] Ottaway, *Decline of life*, ch. i.
[84] Thane, *Old age*; King, *Poverty and welfare*; Smith, 'Ageing and well-being'; Solar, 'Poor relief and English economic development'; S. King, 'Poor relief and English economic development reappraised', *EcHR* l (1997), 360–8; P. M. Solar, 'Poor relief and English economic development: a renewed plea for comparative history', *EcHR* l (1997), 369–74; D. Thomson, 'The decline of social welfare: falling state support for the elderly since early Victorian times', *A&S* iv (1984), 451–82; Ottaway, *Decline of life*; Wales, 'Poverty, poor relief and the life-cycle'.
[85] Thomson, 'The decline of social welfare'; E. H. Hunt, 'Paupers and pensioners: past and present', *A&S* ix (1989), 407–30.
[86] P. Sharpe, 'Poor children as apprentices in Colyton, 1598–1830', *C&C* vi (1991), 253–70; S. Hindle, '"Waste children?" Pauper apprenticeship under the Elizabethan poor laws, c. 1598–1697', in P. Lane, N. Raven and K. D. M. Snell (eds), *Women, work and wages in England, 1600–1850*, Woodbridge 2004, 15–46; A. Levene, 'Family breakdown and the "welfare child" in nineteenth- and twentieth-century Britain', *History of the Family* xi (2006), 67–79; 'Children, childhood and the workhouse'; and 'Parish apprenticeship and the old poor law in London', *EcHR* lxiii (2010), 915–41; P. Kirby, *Child labour in Britain, 1750–1870*, Basingstoke 2003; K. Honeyman, *Child workers in England, 1780–1820: parish apprentices and the making of the early industrial workforce*, Aldershot 2007; J. Humphries, *Childhood and child labour in the British industrial revolution*, Cambridge 2010.
[87] Exceptions to this point include King, *Poverty and welfare*, 161, 166–9, 205, 212–14, and Newman Brown, 'The receipt of poor relief', table 12.3 at p. 412.
[88] S. Williams, 'Malthus, marriage and poor law allowances revisited: a Bedfordshire case study, 1770–1834', *AgHR* lii (2004), 56–82; K. D. M. Snell and J. Millar, 'Lone-parent families and the welfare state: past and present', *C&C* ii (1987), 387–422; T. Nutt, 'The paradox and problems of illegitimate paternity in old poor law Essex', in A. Levene, T. Nutt and S. Williams (eds), *Illegitimacy in Britain, 1700–1920*, Basingstoke 2005, 102–21, and 'Illegitimacy, paternal financial responsibility, and the 1834 Poor Law

focus upon poor relief to single-parent families. Their analysis of settlement examinations of families with dependent children from south-eastern rural and market-town parishes between 1700 and 1850 revealed that three in ten families with dependent children applying for relief were lone-parent families, and as many as 86 per cent of single parents dependent on poor relief were women. Poor relief represented up to 78 per cent of the average income from employment of their immediate neighbours – a higher proportion than that under the modern welfare state.[89] A particular focus has been unmarried mothers and putative fathers in eighteenth- and early nineteenth-century London. Bastardy examinations, petitions to the London Foundling Hospital and the records of the lying-in hospitals make it possible to comment upon the survival strategies of mothers, the occupations of putative fathers, and the rhetoric used by women when framing their pleas for assistance.[90] However, relatively little is known about levels of outdoor relief to unmarried mothers in London or the frequency with which they were admitted to workhouses. Thomas Nutt has explored the effectiveness of parish officials in enforcing affiliation orders and recovering costs from fathers outside of London.[91]

The growth of social welfare, the crisis of the old poor law c.1780–1834, the wider mixed economy of welfare and the economy of makeshifts, the economic impact of the poor laws, the politics of the poor rate, and the gendered and life-cycle nature of poverty: such are the central themes of this book. Chapter 1 describes the communities of Campton and Shefford, the case studies upon which the findings are based, and the methodology that largely underpins it: the creation of pauper and ratepayer biographies. Chapter 2 makes use of the pauper biographies to present a broad account of trends in poor law expenditure in the two communities. It charts the rapid upward movement in spending on relief and breaks this down by type of

---

Commission Report: the myth of the old poor law and the making of the new', *EcHR* lxiii (2010), 335–61; M. A. Lyle, 'Regionality in the late old poor law: the treatment of chargeable bastards from "Rural queries"', *AgHR* liii (2005), 141–5; P. Crawford, *Parents of poor children in England, 1580–1800*, Oxford 2010.

[89] Snell and Millar, 'Lone-parent families', 395–409.

[90] The historiography on unmarried mothers and putative fathers in the metropolis is now extensive. Studies include T. Hitchcock, '"Unlawfully begotten on her body": illegitimacy and the parish poor in St Luke's Chelsea', in Hitchcock, King and Sharpe, *Chronicling poverty*, 70–86; T. Evans, '*Unfortunate objects*': lone mothers in eighteenth-century London, Basingstoke 2005; J. Black, 'Who were the putative fathers of illegitimate children in London, 1740–1810?', in Levene, Nutt and Williams, *Illegitimacy*, 50–65, and 'Illegitimacy, sexual relations and location in metropolitan London, 1735–85', in T. Hitchcock and H. Shore (eds), *The streets of London from the great fire to the great stink*, London 2003, 101–18; S. Williams, '"A good character for virtue, sobriety, and honesty": unmarried mothers' petitions to the London Foundling Hospital and the rhetoric of need in the early nineteenth century', in Levene, Nutt and Williams, *Illegitimacy*, 86–10; R. Trumbach, *Sex and the gender revolution: heterosexuality and the third gender in enlightenment London*, London 1998; and Crawford, *Parents of poor children*, chs i–ii.

[91] Nutt, 'Paradox and problems', and 'Paternal financial responsibility'.

relief: regular (pensions), occasional cash and relief in kind. The key question is whether social welfare continued to grow or whether it contracted during this 'crisis' period. The relative generosity of the poor law is assessed, both in terms of provision before and after c.1780 and in terms of the value of parish relief. Did relief compare favourably with the incomes of other labouring families? The answer to this question varied according to the family circumstances of the recipient. The proportion of inhabitants a Campton and Shefford receiving relief at particular points in time are also calculated. The turn of the century stands out as a period of particularly harsh economic conditions when large numbers of people required parish assistance. Estimating dependency upon the parish in this way brings with it the methodological problem of accounting for the 'hidden dependants' of paupers listed in overseers' accounts. Pauper biographies allow this problem to be addressed since they include family members. A major focus is the family circumstances of those relieved and how this changed over this period. This issue is approached quantitatively, decade by decade, to reveal the changing characteristics of the pauper host. Paupers are grouped into six family types: the elderly, families, lone parents, lone men and women, young and middle-aged couples and orphans.[92] There was a strong commitment in Campton and Shefford to the elderly and lone parents, but a much weaker one to families headed by married couples. This is in marked contrast to what might be expected from contemporary opinion and a reading of the secondary literature. While it is plausible that the widespread publication of scales in the south and east fostered a sense of entitlement for the labouring poor, overseers in Campton and Shefford only actually resorted to allowances in times of severe economic hardship; it was never the usual method of relieving the poor. Finally the amount of relief available under the old poor laws is compared with that in the first fifteen years of the new. Although it has been argued that there was considerable continuity despite the introduction of the new law in 1834, in Bedfordshire nominal expenditure and relief *per capita* was halved.[93] Relief under the old poor law was certainly more 'generous' than under the new.

How such levels of relief were maintained is the focus of chapter 3. Shefford's ratepayer books and the ratepayer biographies are exploited in order to establish the relative wealth levels of ratepayers and the proportion of inhabitants who were paying the poor rate. The Elizabethan statutes assumed that the majority of inhabitants would be rated, whereas many local studies, including this one, find that this was far from the case. An analysis of the proportion of inhabitants who were rated, the proportion of those in receipt of relief, and those who were in the middle – neither paying into nor receiving from the parish funds – shows that Shefford's parish officers

---

[92] For the construction of these categories see chapter 1 below.
[93] For a review of this literature see Kidd, *State, society and the poor*, 24–45.

were increasingly willing to raise revenue for spiralling relief costs by rating further down the social scale, even into the ranks of the poor, whilst also seeking to protect parish funds by circumscribing eligibility and entitlement to relief. The workings of the 'politics of the poor rate' in Campton and Shefford are explored in detail. Here the work of Peter King, who drew upon the pauper appeals made to Samuel Whitbread, a justice of the peace and member of parliament, who was the magistrate in east Bedfordshire, and thus was responsible for Campton and Shefford, complements other evidence that suggests that magistrates had considerable power in relation to relief policy in Bedfordshire.[94] Moreover, the politics of the parish and the politics of Westminster were not separate; the national and the local were intertwined,[95] and Samuel Whitbread is an example of one who used his local experiences to inform his wider political agenda in Westminster.

Chapter 4 is devoted to a detailed exploration of the life-cycle nature of poverty by means of a qualitative and longtitudinal analysis of the pauper biographies. In Campton and Shefford at least 85 per cent of all regular recipients were elderly individuals or couples, families, lone parents or orphans. In exploring the types of assistance that the parishes provided, a particular focus is on those who received a pension for an extended period, or repeatedly, and who must have experienced particularly pauperised life-courses. The circumstances of ratepayers are also considered, as well as the under-researched issue of the extent to which they too became paupers at some point in the life-cycle, which is measurable for Shefford. There was overlap between the two groups; ratepayers did sometimes receive relief. Furthermore, this was not only during old age but could occur at other points in their lives and a small number of inhabitants both paid into the poor rates and were paid poor relief out of them simultaneously.

Towards the end of the Napoleonic Wars un- and under-employment became a pressing social and economic problem which was dealt with in a number of ways at the local level. The relief policies and make-work schemes adopted in Campton and Shefford are explored in chapter 5. The poor law could play a significant role in structuring local labour markets. The number of male recipients and the cost of such relief are placed within the context of the wider debate concerning the masculinisation of the relief rolls during this period. Although there was a significant lengthening of the recipient lists in the two communities, with large numbers of men and boys in receipt of unemployment payments, in terms of its cost such relief was far less significant. It appears that the welfare safety net was thrown ever wider, to accom-

---

[94] Dunkley, *The crisis of the old poor law*, appendix A at p. 183. Dunkley finds that 64% of Bedfordshire parishes responding to the 1832 'Rural queries' claimed that magistrates were controlling relief (q. 43): *Royal commission of inquiry into administration and practical operation of poor laws*, PP 1834, xxvii.1 C.44, appendix (B.1), 'Answers to rural queries', pt I.
[95] T. Harris (ed.), *The politics of the excluded, c. 1500–1850*, Basingstoke 2001.

modate unemployed males alongside regular pensioners, but the net was showing a significant amount of strain, evident in the contraction of relief in kind. The second half of this chapter moves beyond the poor law to the wider mixed economy of social welfare available at the local level, as well as the multiplicity of activities and resources that the labouring poor used in order to buoy up their family economies. While it is clear that the poor drew upon a wide range of such sources, it is also evident that, in a period of worsening economic conditions and a contracting economy of makeshifts, poor relief became ever more central and essential.

# 1

## People, Place and Poverty

Bedfordshire is a highly appropriate county to study in the context of the crisis of the old poor law: it was one of the counties in which both contemporaries and historians believe parish allowances to have been widespread. The county was labelled by the 1824 *Select committee on labourers' wages* as one of the six most addicted to the allowance system and is one of Mark Blaug's hard core of 'Speenhamland counties'.[1] The *Poor law report* of 1834 cited Bedfordshire, along with Berkshire, Buckinghamshire, Cambridgeshire, Cheshire, Cornwall and Cumberland, as typical of the country as a whole: 'We believe, in short, that a fairer average of the whole country cannot be taken.'[2] That the poverty problem was primarily concentrated in the south and east is reflected in the proportions of county populations on relief in 1831: in Berkshire the figure was 17 per cent; Wiltshire 15 per cent, Essex and Sussex 14 per cent; Dorsetshire and Oxfordshire 13 per cent; Buckinghamshire, Huntingdonshire and Suffolk all over 12 per cent; Cambridgeshire, Kent, Hertfordshire, Norfolk and Northamptonshire 11 per cent or more; and Herefordshire, Leicestershire, Bedfordshire, Shropshire and Hampshire 10 per cent or more.[3]

The economic and social profile of Bedfordshire had a direct impact upon the level and experience of poverty by its inhabitants. Although the county was predominantly agricultural, its economy also rested heavily upon cottage industry. Large numbers of women and children were occupied in spinning, pillow lace-making, straw-plaiting and hat manufacture. While spinning was a largely ubiquitous employment for women until the later eighteenth century, Bedfordshire was part of two larger and overlapping regions dominated by lace-making, straw-plaiting and hat-making. Lace-making occupied substantial numbers of women and children in Buckinghamshire, Bedfordshire, Northamptonshire, Oxfordshire and Huntingdonshire, while the straw trade offered employment to many women and children in Bedfordshire, Hertfordshire, Buckinghamshire, Essex and Suffolk.[4] In 1864 the second

---

[1] For definitions of the Speenhamland system and parish allowances see pp. 9–10 above.
[2] *Poor law report*, 207.
[3] Dunkley, *The crisis of the old poor law*, 46.
[4] There is an extensive literature on the history of lace-making and straw-plaiting. The most recent contributions are N. Goose, 'Working women in industrial England' and 'The straw plait and hat trades in nineteenth-century Hertfordshire', in N. Goose (ed.), *Women's work in industrial England: regional and local perspectives* (LPS Supplement, Hatfield 2007), 1–28, 97–137, and *Population, economy and family structure in Hertfordshire*

report of the Children's Employment Commission noted that where the lace-making areas of Buckinghamshire and Bedfordshire ended, straw-plaiting began, spearheading 'over a great part of Hertfordshire and the western and northern parts of Essex'.[5] Of the 9,800 male and female plaiters recorded in the 1841 census of England and Wales, 84 per cent were in Bedfordshire, Hertfordshire, Essex and eastern Buckinghamshire.[6] In neighbouring Hertfordshire one in six of the occupied population were recorded in the straw and hat trades, accounting for one in three female occupations.[7] The plaiting and hat business offered not just out-work but also work opportunities in some larger scale enterprises in Luton and Dunstable, in south Bedfordshire.[8] In 1830 fifteen straw-hat manufacturers were recorded in Dunstable and seventeen in Luton, as well as makers of straw boxes and straw toys.[9] Nigel Goose argues that these trades never feature prominently in histories of industrialisation despite their importance to the regional economy, the fact that they offered a high level of employment opportunities to women and children, and that they played a significant role in the family economy.[10] This is now being rectified in his detailed work on Hertfordshire, while Leigh Shaw-Taylor and E. A. Wrigley are mapping nineteenth-century female employment more generally.[11]

Straw-plaiting and hat-making were already in evidence in the later seventeenth and eighteenth centuries.[12] The trades benefited considerably from the embargo on imported straw during the Napoleonic Wars, but they remained important in the region into the third quarter of the nineteenth century.[13] Indeed, straw-plaiting enjoyed its heyday in the three decades after 1841, even as mechanisation took hold and despite the reduction in wages following the end of the Napoleonic Wars, and Bedfordshire even remained the strongest of the four straw counties.[14] However, the trade was virtually obliterated by the 1890s in the face of foreign competition from China

---

in 1851, I: *The Berkhamsted region*, Hatfield 1996, 34–46; II: *St Albans and its region*, Hatfield 2000, 47–9, 70–4, 76–7; H. Cunningham, 'The employment and unemployment of children in England, c. 1680–1851', *P&P* cxxvi (1990), 115–50 at pp. 137, 140–2; and N. Verdon, *Rural women workers in nineteenth-century England*, Woodbridge 2002, ch. v. Other works are cited in the bibliographies of these studies.
[5] This is cited in Goose, *Berkhamsted region*, 35.
[6] Idem, *St Albans and its region*, 70.
[7] Ibid. 72.
[8] Ibid, 72–3; Eden, *The state of the poor*, ii. 1–4.
[9] J. Godber, *History of Bedfordshire, 1066–1888*, Bedford 1984, 449.
[10] Goose, 'Straw plait and hat trades', 97.
[11] Idem, 'Working women'; 'Straw plait and hat trades'; *Berkhamsted region*; and *St Albans and its region*; L. Shaw-Taylor, 'Diverse experiences: the geography of adult female employment in England and the 1851 census', in Goose, *Women's work*, 29–50.
[12] Goose, 'Straw plait and hat trades', 99; Cunningham, 'Employment of children', 137.
[13] Goose, 'Straw plait and hat trades', 99.
[14] Idem, *Berkhamsted region*, 35–6; *St Albans and its region*, 48, 70–4, 76–7; and 'Straw plait and hat trades', 99–100. The latter study (table 5.1 at p. 100) gives numbers employed

and Japan.[15] It was predominantly a female trade (89 per cent in 1851, 93 per cent in 1871) but males formed a larger proportion of the labour force in Bedfordshire in the nineteenth century than in other straw counties.[16] Straw-plaiting was seasonal, predominantly occupying the months from January to May, with lower prices being paid in the winter than in spring and summer.[17] Seasonality might in part account for the low proportion of women employed in agriculture, since women's agricultural work was largely confined to spring weeding and straw work offered better remuneration; in Hertfordshire in 1851 1.4 per cent of women were employed as agricultural outdoor labourers and just 0.6 per cent in Buckinghamshire and 0.2 per cent in Bedfordshire.[18] Arthur Young certainly thought this was so when he reported for Hertfordshire that 'The farmers complain of it, as doing mischief, for it makes the poor saucy, and no servants can be procured, or any field-work done, where this manufacture established itself.'[19] However, the relationship might equally have been the other way around since women were increasingly marginalised from agriculture and might have turned to straw work to supplement their husbands' earnings from agricultural labour.[20]

Relatively high numbers of married women were employed in these districts and in Hertfordshire the participation rate even exceeded that of the cotton manufacturing town of Preston, seven Lancashire registration districts, and the Staffordshire potteries.[21] Straw work was essential to the family economy of Lucy Luck, who recorded in her autobiography that she would work almost 'day and night' to support her seven children. In the 'dull season' from July to Christmas she would turn instead to charring, washing and needlework.[22] Both lace-making and straw-plaiting also provided opportunities for children to contribute to the family economy. Hugh Cunningham has shown that Bedfordshire employed the highest proportion of children aged 5–9 in the 1851 census, at 11.9 per cent of boys and 21.5 per cent of girls. Bedfordshire also employed the highest proportion of older girls (aged 10–14) and was only the second county for older boys, with 50.6 per cent of

in the straw plait and hat trades for Bedfordshire, Buckinghamshire, Hertfordshire, Essex and Suffolk for the period 1841–1901.
15  Goose, *St Albans and its region*, 71–2.
16  Idem, 'Straw plait and hat trades', table 5.1 at p. 100, and 'Working women', 27.
17  Idem, *Berkhamsted region*, 34–46.
18  P. Sharpe, 'The women's harvest: straw-plaiting and the representation of labouring women's employment, c. 1793–1885', *Rural History* v (1994), 129–42; Goose, *Berkhamsted region*, 39; M. Berg, *The age of manufacturers, 1700–1920*, London 1985, 24. For the reliability of these figures see Goose, 'Working women', 39; J. Burnette, *Gender, work and wages in industrial revolution Britain*, Cambridge 2008, 18–25; and Shaw-Taylor, 'Diverse experiences', 32–42.
19  This is cited in Goose, *Berkhamsted region*, 39.
20  See Snell, *Annals of the labouring poor*, 58–9.
21  Goose, *Berkhamsted region*, 37, and 'Straw plait and hat trades', 106–10.
22  J. Burnett, *Useful toil: autobiographies of working people from the 1820s to the 1920s*, London 1974, 66–77.

girls employed and 49.6 per cent of boys respectively. Of course, not all children were occupied in lace-making or straw-plaiting, but these trades were the largest employers of girls aged 5–9 and employed substantial numbers of older girls, as well as of younger and older boys.[23] Thomas Batchelor noted in 1808 that in Dunstable in the straw-plaiting industry, 'they begin to pick the straw at four years old; plait at five; and at six earn from 1s. 6d. to 2s. 6d. a week; at seven they use the instrument, and earn 1s. a day; some girls of ten years old earn 12s. a week; and one was named who at eight earned as much'.[24] The Children's Employment Commission of 1843 found children working in plaiting school, 'of all ages from four to fifteen years'.[25]

Arthur Young argued that in Hertfordshire in 1804 the straw-plaiting trade was, 'highly beneficial to the poor … and has a considerable effect in keeping down [poor] rates, which would have been far more burthensome without it'.[26] Frederick Eden had made similar comments about straw work in Dunstable, south Bedfordshire, keeping down poor rates in the mid-1790s; he noted that there was widespread employment 'of every woman, who wishes to work'.[27] At the turn of the century in east Bedfordshire, higher wages encouraged many families to exchange lace-making for straw-plaiting. In 1801 Arthur Young had observed lace-making in Shefford, but by 1808 Thomas Batchelor noted that the plaiting district in Bedfordshire had 'spread rapidly' over the southern, central and eastern districts, 'as far as Woburn, Ampthill, and Shefford'.[28] Earnings for women and children in the lace and straw trades were highest during the Napoleonic Wars: Batchelor reported earnings of between 10s. and 20s. a week in 1808, while in Hertfordshire in 1804 Young noted earnings for female Hertfordshire plaiters of 21s. per week at Redbourn, and at Dunstable, 14s.–18s. per week at Berkhamsted, and up to 5s. a day in St Albans, compared to male agricultural labourers who were earning 10s.–12s. weekly. Rates of pay fell after 1815 and in 1831 earnings at Hatfield were reported at 8s.–10s. per week, while in central Bedfordshire parishes in 1837 earnings were around 5s. per week.[29] However straw work continued to provide a valuable supplement to family incomes.[30] The amount that could be earned from plaiting was also dependent upon location; plaiters in Luton and Dunstable could earn more than those in other districts of Bedfordshire because they could sell plait at the market

---

[23] Cunningham, 'Employment of children', tables 1–4 at pp. 141–5.
[24] T. Batchelor, *General view of the agriculture of the county of Bedford*, London 1808, 594–5.
[25] This is cited in Goose, *Berkhamsted region*, 40.
[26] Ibid.
[27] Eden, *State of the poor*, ii. 1–4.
[28] Batchelor, *General view*, 94.
[29] Goose, *Berkhamsted region*, 43–4, and 'Straw plait and hat trades', 110–14; S. Williams, 'Earnings, poor relief and the economy of makeshifts: Bedfordshire in the early years of the New Poor Law', *Rural History* xvi (2005), 33.
[30] This is cited in Goose, *Berkhamsted region*, 39–40.

themselves rather than through a middleman.³¹ Earnings might also have been higher in Campton and Shefford given that plait could be sold at the market in Shefford. Despite increasing pauperism in the plaiting districts, poverty might have been even worse without its mitigating effects. The precise impact of the trade is difficult to establish however. As Goose argues, although 'the positive impact of the straw plait industry on overall incomes cannot be denied … it remains to be accurately measured'.³²

This is the wider regional and county context within which Campton and Shefford need to be placed. These two communities lie nine miles south-east of Bedford, a corn-growing county in the south Midlands. The settlement of Campton and the town of Shefford were in the same parish, one mile apart, and Shefford was a chapelry of Campton until it became an independent parish in 1903. Baptisms, marriages and burials for the two places were recorded in the same parish registers, but in each place the poor law operated separately. Campton was a small, rural and predominantly agricultural community and Shefford was its neighbouring market town. Shefford thus provides a useful point of contrast to Campton and highlights urban-rural differences in parish administration: John Howlett had observed in 1792 that towns tended to spend less per head on poor relief than country parishes. In the country parishes, he stated, the number of paupers was more than twice as great and the expense of maintaining them almost one-third greater than in manufacturing towns. This meant that in the country parishes around one half of the residents were given either regular or occasional poor relief.³³

Campton had a population of 449 in 1831 and 80 per cent of families were employed in agriculture. Shefford's market was renewed in 1713, it had 763 inhabitants and, as would be expected for a town, a more varied occupational structure, with 40 per cent of families employed in 'trade, manufacture and handicrafts' and 51 per cent in the 'other' category of the 1831 census.³⁴ It was on the Bedford-Hitchin road. Shefford was described in *Pigot's commercial directory* of 1839 as

> clean and well paved, the streets wide, and its general appearance indicative of comfort. The trade is chiefly in corn, timber, coal and iron, transmitted by means of the navigation to and from [King's] Lynn; straw plat, also, in the making of which many women and children are employed, is brought in great quantities to the market.³⁵

---

[31] Eden, *State of the poor*, ii. 1–4.
[32] Goose, *Berkhamsted region*, 43.
[33] J. Howlett, 'On the population and situation of the poor in England', *Annals of Agriculture* xviii (1792), 573–81. It is likely that many rural parishes were subsidising the poor relief costs of nearby towns, through provision of non-residential relief. See, for instance, T. Sokoll, *Essex pauper letters, 1731–1837*, Oxford 2001.
[34] *Abstract of census returns*, 1831. The proportion of families employed in agriculture shrank from 35% in 1811 to less than 10% in 1831.
[35] *Pigot and Co's royal national and commercial directory and topography*, London 1839.

Each week agricultural produce and straw plait were bought and sold at the Friday market, and three times a year cattle fairs were held in the town. Between 1801 and 1841 both parishes experienced population increase, but it was somewhat faster in Shefford than in Campton: Shefford's population increased by 87 per cent, from 474 to 889, while in Campton the number of inhabitants rose by 58 per cent, from 316 to 501. The national increase was of 79 per cent.[36]

Land-owning was more concentrated in Campton than in Shefford.[37] The land tax of 1798 shows that there were just twelve proprietors in Campton, Sir George Osborn being the principal landowner. Only five landowners were owner-occupiers. A further twelve individuals were listed as tenants without any land of their own. A number of landowners let out their land and rented that of others. There were also 'small renters', who were not listed by name. In Shefford there were far more proprietors, at thirty-five, the largest being the duke of Bedford, followed by the Shefford Feoffees. There were seventeen owner-occupiers in the market town, at least a further forty-nine tenants who owned no land, and another group of small occupiers termed 'defferent occupiers' (and, again, not listed by name).

The household listing from 1782 for the parish of Cardington, which is only seven miles away from Campton and Shefford, reveals the characteristic employment patterns of this part of Bedfordshire at the end of the eighteenth century. Most men were employed in agriculture: 11.4 per cent of household heads were farmers, whilst 43.1 per cent were labourers.[38] There were very high levels of women and children working in Cardington: 82 per cent of women aged 20–39 were described as employed, 51 per cent of those aged 40–59, and 60 per cent of those aged 60 and above. The participation of these women in the labour force is much higher than for Corfe Castle, Dorset, in 1790.[39] Most of the women were employed in textiles, with 34.9 per cent in lace-making, 11.9 per cent in spinning linen and 11.1 per cent in spinning jersey.[40] Although spinning collapsed towards the end of the

---

[36] Ibid; Godber, *History of Bedfordshire*, 333; *The merchants miscellany and travellers complete compendium*, Northampton 1785, in *The universal British directory*, London 1792; *Pigot and Co's national commercial directory*, London–Manchester 1830; *Robson's directory*, London 1839; *Post Office directory of Bedfordshire*, London 1847. For the national population totals see Wrigley and Schofield, *Population history*, appendix 6, table A6.7, total (1) at p. 595.

[37] Campton land tax, 1798, and Shefford land tax, 1798, BLARS. Land tax assessments list the owners and occupiers of all the land and the amount of tax that they paid thereon. Ginter advocates 1798 as the most appropriate year to analyse the land tax assessments in terms of wealth: *A measure of wealth: the English land tax in historical analysis*, London 1992, 289.

[38] *The inhabitants of Cardington in 1782*, ed. D. Baker (BHRS lii, 1973), introduction at pp. 1–71.

[39] O. Saito, 'Who worked when: life-time profiles of labour force participation in Cardington and Corfe Castle in the late eighteenth and mid-nineteenth centuries', *LPS* xxii (1979), 14–29 at pp. 22–3.

[40] *Inhabitants of Cardington*, 25.

century, the employment of women remained high in 1851 as women took up lace-making instead.[41] Thomas Batchelor's *General view of the agriculture of the county of Bedford* of 1808 described how lace-making employed three-quarters of the non-domestic servant population, thereby creating a shortage of maidservants. Children as young as four years of age could be involved.[42]

There is more precise occupational information in the 1841 census.[43] In Campton 66.4 per cent of male workers were labourers and 14.5 were recorded in manufacturing occupations. Shefford's highest concentration was in manufacture, at 38.1 per cent (primarily in clothing, carpentry and leather work), but substantial minorities of the male labour force were recorded as agricultural labourers, at 22.2 per cent, and in distribution and trade, at 12.6 per cent. Almost half of the women aged fifteen or over were allocated an occupation and, as in the 1851 census, it is likely that these were only for those women who were regularly employed; many more would have been in irregular employment.[44] The straw-plaiting trade dominated female employment in Campton, with almost 70 per cent of women with recorded occupations so employed, while in Shefford the proportion was smaller, at 36 per cent, followed by 33 per cent employed as domestic servants. A wider range of occupations were available to women in Shefford, but in only small numbers, including a dressmaker, a nurse, a schoolmistress, a charwoman, a milliner and a postmistress. A few women were given as following typically male occupations, such as shoebinders, millers, bakers and proprietors of beer shops. It appears that women's work in agriculture had not disappeared entirely for a small number of women are recorded as agricultural labourers. Only very small numbers of women were occupied in lace-making, despite its prevalence in the north of the county.

The ages recorded in the 1841 census for Campton and Shefford confirm that the age profiles were similar to the country as a whole – and the relative youthfulness of the population at this time – with high proportions of children (37 per cent) and low proportions of the elderly (7 per cent).[45] Households were slightly smaller in Campton, with an average of 4.4 persons, than

---

[41] Saito, 'Who worked when'.
[42] *Inhabitants of Cardington*, 37–42; Goose, *Berkhamsted region*, 40–1.
[43] Manuscript, 1841, census enumerators' books for Campton and Shefford, BLARS.
[44] Shaw-Taylor, 'Diverse experiences'; Goose, *Berkhamsted region*, 38; 'Working women', 21–5; and 'Straw plait and hat trades', 101–3. See also S. Horrell and J. Humphries, 'Women's labour force participation and the transition to the male-breadwinner family, 1790–1865', *EcHR* xlviii (1995), 89–117.
[45] The proportion of children under 15 in the population increased from a low point well under 30% in the 1660s to 40% in the 1820s: Wrigley and Schofield, *Population history*, 215–19, 228–36, table A.3.1 at pp. 528–9. In Hertfordshire figures were also similar in 1851: in the Berkhamsted region 36.8% of the population was aged 0–14 and 7.0% were aged 60 or over, in the St Albans region the figure was 36.0% and 7.9% per respectively, while Mills's Rural Norm was 36.6% and 8.6% respectively: Goose, *St Albans and its region*, table 1 at p. 34.

Table 1
The scale of poverty in Bedfordshire and England and Wales, numbers and proportion of the population, 1803, 1813–15

| Year ending | Total in receipt of poor relief | | Permanently relieved | | | | | | Occasionally receiving relief | |
|---|---|---|---|---|---|---|---|---|---|---|
| | | | Indoors | | Outdoors | | Total | | | |
| | number | % | number | % | number | % | number | % | number | % |
| Bedfordshire | | | | | | | | | | |
| 1803 | 8,037 | 12.7 | 674 | 1.1 | 4,530 | 7.1 | 5,204 | 8.2 | 2,072 | 3.3 |
| 1813 | 7,422 | 10.2 | 923 | 1.3 | 3,040 | 4.2 | 3,963 | 5.5 | 3,459 | 4.7 |
| 1814 | 6,994 | 9.4 | 867 | 1.2 | 3,024 | 4.1 | 3,891 | 5.3 | 3,303 | 4.4 |
| 1815 | 6,677 | 8.8 | 849 | 1.1 | 2,875 | 3.8 | 3,724 | 4.9 | 2,953 | 3.9 |
| England and Wales | | | | | | | | | | |
| 1803 | 1,040,716 | 11.4 | 83,468 | 0.9 | 651,349 | 7.2 | 734,817 | 8.1 | 305,899 | 3.4 |
| 1813 | 971,913 | 9.2 | 97,223 | 0.9 | 434,441 | 4.1 | 531,664 | 5.0 | 440,249 | 4.2 |
| 1814 | 953,995 | 8.9 | 94,085 | 0.9 | 430,140 | 4.0 | 524,225 | 4.9 | 429,770 | 4.0 |
| 1815 | 895,973 | 8.2 | 88,115 | 0.8 | 406,887 | 3.7 | 495,002 | 4.5 | 400,971 | 3.7 |

*Source: Abstract of the poor,* 1803–4, 1–8, 714–15; *Abstract of the poor,* 1818, 1–6, 627–30; *Abstract of census returns,* 1801, 1811, 1821.

in Shefford, with 5.2. Relationships to the household head were not given in the 1841 census and they are difficult to infer. Nevertheless, it would appear that in Shefford it was the hiring of servants that raised the mean household size rather than the presence of children since both places had a similar average number of children per household (1.7 for Campton and 1.9 for Shefford).

Returns to parliament during the early nineteenth century provide information on the nature of poverty and poor relief in the hundreds of Bedfordshire, the county as a whole and England and Wales. This gives a regional and national context within which to set Campton and Shefford. David Eastwood has argued that only official statistics offer a basis for assembling a county-by-county picture about the scale of poverty and the scope of the poor law.[46] In the period before 1834, two detailed enquiries were made: in 1803 parliament ordered a return from all parishes relative to the state of the poor and in 1818 the returns were published relating to the years 1813–15.[47] These cannot be used uncritically because the years 1802–3 and 1812–13 were times of high prices, food shortages and hardship, with the numbers dependent on parish relief larger than usual. Furthermore, the total numbers of the poor are not strictly comparable because the 1818 abstract does not include all children, while the 1803 abstract does. However, it is at least possible to draw comparisons between regions within the county of Bedfordshire and between these and the county and England and Wales as a whole at specific points in time.

Poverty was at its most severe in 1803, falling thereafter, and was higher in Bedfordshire than in England and Wales as a whole (see table 1). The average poor rate in Bedfordshire between 1813 and 1815 was 4s. 4¼d., while the national average was 3s. 2d.: thus Bedfordshire was higher by 35.5 per cent. Bedfordshire was on a par with Essex and Suffolk, and just behind Berkshire, Buckinghamshire and Kent.[48] Within Bedfordshire, by hundred, most paupers were in receipt of permanent relief. Clifton, the hundred containing Campton and Shefford, relieved nearly 80 per cent of paupers permanently and one-fifth occasionally, and was fairly typical in this regard (see table 2). It was atypical, however, in only relieving 7.8 per cent of its population with some of other hundreds relieving proportionately up to twice as many inhabitants. Bedford town is also anomalous, relieving only 5 per cent of its poor. While all other hundreds allocated outdoor relief to

---

[46] Eastwood, *Governing rural England*, 141–2.
[47] *Abstract of answers and returns under act for procuring returns relative to expense and maintenance of poor in England*, PP 1803–4, xiii.1 C.175; *Abridgement of abstract of answers and returns relative to expense and maintenance of poor in England and Wales*, PP 1818, xix.1 C.82.
[48] *Abstract of the poor*, 1818, 627–30; Eastwood, *Governing rural England*, 145.

## Table 2
### Recipients of poor relief in the hundreds of Bedfordshire, 1802-3

| Hundred | Permanently relieved | | Occasionally receiving relief | | Total receiving relief in Beds | |
|---|---|---|---|---|---|---|
| | number | % | number | % | number | % |
| Barford | 421 | 74.1 | 147 | 25.9 | 568 | 14.0 |
| Bedford town | 183 | 89.3 | 24 | 10.7 | 205 | 5.0 |
| Biggleswade | 521 | 80.8 | 124 | 19.2 | 645 | 10.3 |
| Clifton | 225 | 79.2 | 59 | 20.8 | 284 | 7.8 |
| Flitt | 524 | 73.7 | 187 | 26.3 | 711 | 9.2 |
| Manshead | 1,000 | 66.0 | 515 | 34.0 | 1,515 | 10.6 |
| Redbornestoke | 816 | 69.9 | 352 | 30.1 | 1,168 | 12.7 |
| Stodden | 276 | 55.9 | 218 | 44.1 | 494 | 13.2 |
| Willey | 711 | 77.7 | 204 | 22.3 | 915 | 13.3 |
| Wixamtree | 529 | 68.6 | 242 | 31.4 | 771 | 16.1 |

Source: *Abstract of the poor*, 1803–4, 1-8, 714-5; *Abstract of census returns*, 1801, 1811.

most of their poor, Bedford town relieved nearly three-quarters of its poor in the workhouse.[49]

### Pauper and ratepayer biographies

The findings presented in this book are based on the analysis of almost 250 pensioner 'pauper biographies' and more than 1,000 named paupers.[50] All of the extant poor law records for the two communities have been nominally linked to the family reconstitution of Campton and Shefford.[51] Accounts kept by most parish overseers of the poor record how the sums rated for the relief of the poor were spent. For Campton these survive for the years between 1767 and 1834 and for Shefford between 1794 and 1828. In both communities the accounts list by name all those in receipt of a parish payment and frequently the reason for parish assistance. The names appearing in the overseers' accounts were then linked to the family reconstitution. Reconstitution links together the baptisms, marriages and burials recorded in the Anglican

---

[49] All the other Bedfordshire hundreds relieved between 80% and 96% of their paupers outdoors, while Bedford town relieved just 26.8% outdoors and 73.2% indoors: *Abstract of the poor*, 1803–4, 7.

[50] Biographies were created for all poor relief recipients (and their families) named in the overseers' accounts (507 in Campton and 622 in Shefford).

[51] This was completed by J. D. Asteraki. See E. A. Wrigley, R. S. Davies, J. E. Oeppen and R. S. Schofield, *English population history from family reconstitution, 1580–1837*, Cambridge 1997, appendix 1 at pp. 561–2.

parish registers for a parish for each family and across generations. Thus a typical family reconstitution form (FRF) would include information on the marriage date of a couple, their baptism and burial dates, and the dates of the baptisms, marriages and burials of their children (see figure 1).[52] Additional evidence was collected from a wide range of other sources, including all poor law documents, charitable sources, court records, parliamentary papers and Samuel Whitbread's estate papers. Biographies for Shefford's ratepayers were similarly created using ratepayer books, extant for the period 1803–20, and linked to the family reconstitution and to the overseers' accounts.[53]

The example of Lucy Townsend and William Newman illustrates how much more evidence is provided if poor law documents are linked to a family reconstitution (see figure 1). The overseers' accounts alone would simply show that between May 1770 and January 1771 Lucy Townsend was paid by the parish of Campton 1s. a week to care for William Newman, and that would be all that could be known of their lives. Once linked to the reconstitution, however, we find that Lucy Townsend was already pregnant with an illegitimate child when she was employed as a parish carer and that William Newman was a widower with three small children (his previous marriage is recorded on FRF no. 121799). Love blossomed for the couple and on 24 January 1771 William and Lucy were married (FRF no. 201054), after which time the parish authorities no longer paid her to care for him. Between 1792 and 1804, when he progressed from his fifties to sixties, William received considerable assistance from the overseers, including a weekly pension, shoes and fuel, and help with the rent (these details have been written under the 'comments' section on the FRF). The parish paid for his burial in January of 1804. After her husband's death Lucy reappeared in the overseer's accounts, as 'Widow Newman', and received a weekly pension until her own death in 1811, at the age of sixty-five. Without linking the two sources there could have been no reason to connect Lucy Townsend to the 'Widow Newman' who appears on the pension list some thirty-four years

---

[52] Overseers' accounts for Campton and Shefford, BLARS, P18/12/1–2, X514/1–3; P70/12/1–2. The family reconstitution for Campton and Shefford is part of a larger reconstitution that also encompasses the adjoining parish of Southill. The reconstitution is held at the Cambridge Group for the History of Population and Social Structure, University of Cambridge. Overseers' accounts for Southill survive, but do not always give paupers by name, thereby making it impossible to construct the detailed pauper histories assembled for Campton and Shefford. On the technique of family reconstitution see E. A. Wrigley, 'Family reconstitution', in E. A. Wrigley (ed.), *An introduction to English historical demography*, London 1966, 96–159, and Wrigley, Davies, Oeppen and Schofield, *Family reconstitution*, appendix 2 at pp. 563–8.
[53] Campton charity records, BLARS, P18/25/1–15; Shefford bills and vouchers, P70/12/3–4; Shefford settlement papers, P70/13/1–4; Shefford bastardy records, P70/15/1–11; Shefford vestry minutes, P70/8/1; Shefford letters to the overseers, P70/18/4/3–55; Shefford militia documents, P70/17; Shefford pauper inventories, P70/18/6; Shefford charity records, X465. Shefford ratepayer books, P70/11/1–3 (there is a gap in the records between 1817 and 1818).

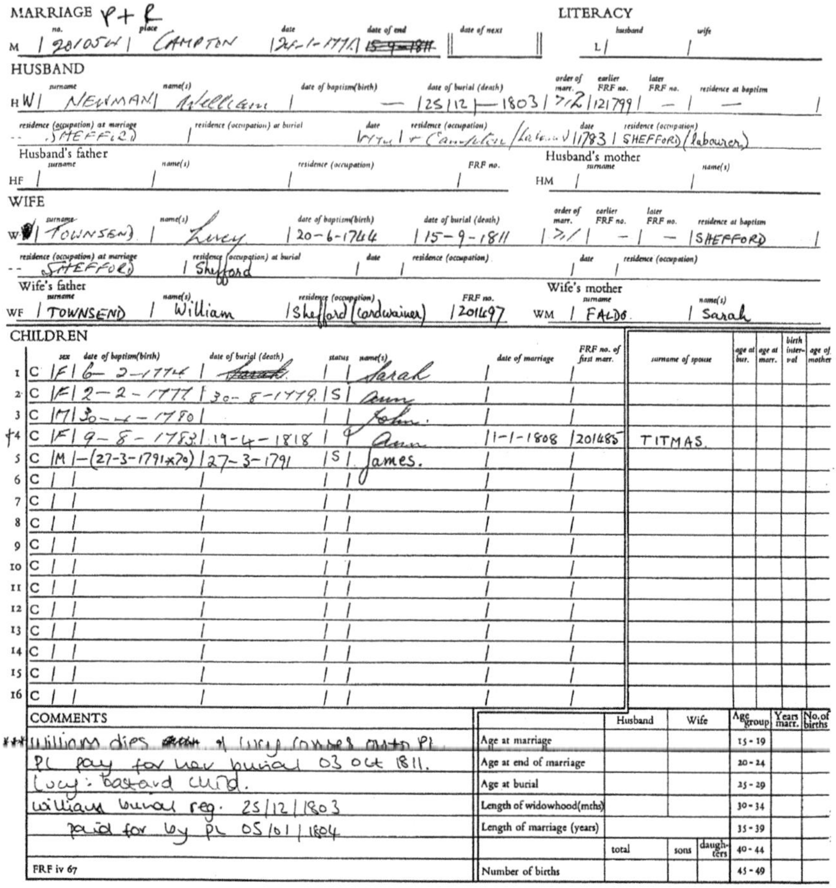

MARRIAGE P + R

| | no. | place | date | date of end | date of next | | LITERACY husband | wife |
|---|---|---|---|---|---|---|---|---|
| M | 20105W | CAMPTON | 24-1-1771 | ~~15-9-1811~~ | | | L | |

HUSBAND

| | surname | name(s) | date of baptism(birth) | date of burial (death) | order of marr. | earlier FRF no. | later FRF no. | residence at baptism |
|---|---|---|---|---|---|---|---|---|
| H W | NEWMAN | William | — | 25/12 — 1803 | 2/2 | 121799 | — | — |

residence (occupation) at marriage: SHEFFORD | residence (occupation) at burial: | date: 1771 | residence (occupation): Campton (labourer) | date: 1783 | residence (occupation): SHEFFORD (labourer)

Husband's father — surname: | name(s): | residence (occupation): | FRF no.:
Husband's mother — surname: | name(s):

WIFE

| | surname | name(s) | date of baptism(birth) | date of burial (death) | order of marr. | earlier FRF no. | later FRF no. | residence at baptism |
|---|---|---|---|---|---|---|---|---|
| W | TOWNSEND | Lucy | 20-6-1744 | 15-9-1811 | 1/1 | — | — | SHEFFORD |

residence (occupation) at marriage: SHEFFORD | residence (occupation) at burial: Shefford | date: | residence (occupation): | date: | residence (occupation):

Wife's father — surname: TOWNSEND | name(s): William | residence (occupation): Shefford (cordwainer) | FRF no.: 201497
Wife's mother — surname: FALDO | name(s): Sarah

CHILDREN

| | | sex | date of baptism(birth) | date of burial (death) | status | name(s) | date of marriage | FRF no. of first marr. | surname of spouse | age at bur. | age at marr. | birth interval | age of mother |
|---|---|---|---|---|---|---|---|---|---|---|---|---|---|
| 1 | C | F | 6-2-1774 | ~~Sarah~~ | | Sarah | | | | | | | |
| 2 | C | F | 2-2-1777 | 30-8-1779 | S | Ann | | | | | | | |
| 3 | C | M | 30-4-1780 | | | John | | | | | | | |
| †4 | C | F | 9-8-1783 | 19-4-1818 | | Ann | 1-1-1808 | 201485 | TITMAS | | | | |
| 5 | C | M | –(27-3-1791×70) | 27-3-1791 | S | James | | | | | | | |
| 6 | C | | | | | | | | | | | | |
| 7 | C | | | | | | | | | | | | |
| 8 | C | | | | | | | | | | | | |
| 9 | C | | | | | | | | | | | | |
| 10 | C | | | | | | | | | | | | |
| 11 | C | | | | | | | | | | | | |
| 12 | C | | | | | | | | | | | | |
| 13 | C | | | | | | | | | | | | |
| 14 | C | | | | | | | | | | | | |
| 15 | C | | | | | | | | | | | | |
| 16 | C | | | | | | | | | | | | |

COMMENTS

***William dies & Lucy comes onto PL
PL pay for her burial 03 Oct 1811.
Lucy: bastard child.
William burial reg. 25/12/1803
paid for by PL 05/01/1804

FRF iv 67

| | Husband | Wife | | Age group | Years marr. | No. of births |
|---|---|---|---|---|---|---|
| Age at marriage | | | | 15-19 | | |
| Age at end of marriage | | | | 20-24 | | |
| Age at burial | | | | 25-29 | | |
| Length of widowhood(mths) | | | | 30-34 | | |
| Length of marriage (years) | | | | 35-39 | | |
| | total | sons | daughters | 40-44 | | |
| Number of births | | | | 45-49 | | |

**Figure 1. A typical family reconstitution form: William Newman and Lucy Townsend, married 1771**

later (*see* their pauper careers in figure 12). Further linkage to Shefford's ratepayer books reveals that in 1803 William was assessed for the poor rates in Shefford and after his death his assessments were transferred to Widow Newman until her own death. Campton's overseers paid the rates assessed between 1803 and 1807, but after 1807 the overseers ceased paying Widow Newman's rates. Presumably she had to find them (between 1*s.* 6*d.* and 2*s.* 6*d.*) from her weekly pension.

The case of Esther Merryweathers likewise illustrates the quality of the pauper biographies and the ebb and flow of poor relief over the life-course (*see* figure 14). Esther is one example of the many widows with young children who came onto parish relief at their husbands' deaths but who continued to receive parish assistance long after their children had grown up and flown the nest; many of these pensions continued into old age. Esther married Thomas in 1757 and between then and 1782 they received odd payments and occasional cash, and a doctor's bill was paid on their behalf. In February 1782 Thomas was allocated a large weekly allowance in the months preceding his death and the parish then paid for his funeral. Thomas left Esther with their five live children (four dead), and one on the way. Esther was immediately allocated a widow's pension and she continued to receive a parish pension until her own death, some thirty-seven years later, in 1819. The parish paid for the christening of the new baby girl, Phoebe, when she arrived and Esther also received fuel and clothing. In her last illness her allowance increased and her daughter Rhode was paid to nurse her. She was buried in June 1819 at a cost of £1 18s. 4d. to the parish. Another daughter, Hannah, also became a regular recipient after coming onto poor relief for illness in July 1807. The parish tried to find a cure for her by sending her, twice, to the Bedford Infirmary and her sister Rhode was also paid to look after her too. In the 1841 census Rhode and Hannah were living together.

The creation of pauper and ratepayer biographies generated some 90,000 individual records on more than 1,000 individuals and their families,[54]

---

[54] In Campton 68% of named pension recipients can be linked to the reconstitution, a further 11% can be linked to the parish registers (but not an FRF), leaving 21% who cannot be linked to either the reconstitution or the parish registers. In Shefford 51% can be linked to the reconstitution, 34% to the parish registers, and 15% remained unlinked. 65% of Shefford's ratepayers could be linked to the family reconstitution. It is not surprising that linkage was more successful in the small rural community of Campton, where more people would have lived long enough to appear in the demographic records, than in the neighbouring market town of Shefford, where there would have been a higher turnover of population. Recent research has shown that Bedfordshire burial registration might have been deficient by between 21% and 27%, largely due to clerical negligence and partly due to religious nonconformity. This would explain why the burials of some paupers were recorded in the overseers' accounts (and paid for by the authorities) but were not recorded in the Anglican burial register: P. Razzell, C. Spence and M. Woollard, 'The evaluation of Bedfordshire burial registration, 1538–1851', *LPS* lxxxiv (Spring 2010), 31–54. The methodology of assembling pauper biographies has been outlined by S. R. Ottaway and Samantha Williams and has also been used to good effect by other historians in their research into the lives of the poor: 'Reconstructing the life-cycle experience of poverty in the time of the old poor law', *Archives* xxiii (1998), 19–29; S. Williams, 'Poor relief, welfare and medical provision in Bedfordshire: the social, economic and demographic context, c. 1770–1834', unpubl. PhD diss. Cambridge 1998, ch. iii. Other historians have assembled pauper biographies using a variety of methods. Sharpe has employed the 'total reconstitution' method, linking all available sources to the family reconstitution for Colyton for the years 1538–1837: *Reproducing Colyton*, 11–18, appendix at pp. 318–25. Botelho collected 337 biographies for the elderly poor in seventeenth-century Suffolk: *Old age*, 14. M. Williams did not have overseers' accounts and instead assembled pauper biographies for 92 people and their families (totalling 400 people) for Earls Colne, Essex, from wills, court records and other sources in the Earls Colne on-line archive, available at http://www–earlecolne.socanth.cam.ac.uk/: '"Our poor people in tumults arose": living in poverty in Earls Colne, Essex, 1560–1640', *Rural History* xiii (2002), 123–43. Shave

providing a rich data set of the circumstances of recipients as well as ratepayers. The great advantage of the data is that it is longitudinal; for paupers the data covers all types of beneficiary weekly for the seven decades between the 1770s and the 1830s for Campton and the four decades between the 1790s and the 1820s for Shefford, and for all ratepayers between 1803 and 1820. This rich seam of evidence is first exploited by analysing the biographies quantitatively decade by decade in order to reveal the changing familial characteristics of recipients.

has assembled detailed pauper biographies: 'The dependent poor?', and King used the methodology of community reconstruction: 'Reconstructing lives', 321.

# 2

# *Policy and Paupers*

Social welfare expanded considerably in the south and east in the seventeenth and eighteenth centuries, but started to contract during the early nineteenth. This chapter explores the extent to which Campton and Shefford conformed to this picture by means of an in-depth analysis of all aspects of parish expenditure: the policy of the parish vestry, trends in expenditure, numbers relieved and the categories of spending. The pauper biographies are analysed quantitatively in order to put together a picture of the changing nature of the pauper host: who exactly was relieved and how generously, what were their family circumstances, and how did this change over the seven decades of this study? In this context the effect of the Poor Law Amendment Act of 1834 is crucial. Did it mark a radical departure in terms of levels of 'generosity', policy and attitudes towards the poor?

## Parish policy and payments

Despite rapid growth in provision in both Campton and Shefford, there is little direct evidence of parish officials trying one method to relieve the poor and then another, such as switching between direct outdoor relief and workhouses contracted to a workhouse master, as happened in some other parishes within Bedfordshire and elsewhere.[1] Almost all parish assistance in Campton and Shefford was outdoor relief given as cash pensions (weekly), occasional cash sums and payments in kind.[2] Only a handful of the poor was housed in poor houses in both communities, but these were more like modern council houses than workhouses, and those accommodated were usually the transient and the expenditure on them small, never exceeding

---

[1] An example is the Bedfordshire parish of Eaton Socon, which used a mixture of direct relief, contracts, the workhouse, the roundsman and allowance systems (for definitions see chapter 1 above): F. G. Emmison, *The relief of the poor at Eaton Socon* (BHRS xv, 1933). Potton had a workhouse and master in 1783: Godber, *History of Bedfordshire*, 333. See also Broad, 'Parish economies of welfare', 985–1006.

[2] Within the account books for Campton and Shefford weekly outdoor relief payments were not easily differentiated into 'pensions' and 'occasional' relief, and so in the present study 'pensions' were deemed payments to the same individual or family for a minimum of six months and any other payments in cash or in kind of shorter duration were 'occasional' payments.

6 per cent of total spending.³ Nevertheless, there is evidence that periodically the vestry chose to cut relief to those regularly relieved, and that they offered accommodation in a poor house or on occasion expected pensioners to live with their relatives as a condition for receipt of regular relief. The two communities were also similar to others in the south and east after the 1790s in the adoption of various new policies in response to harvest failures, rapid inflation and widespread unemployment. In the high price years of 1795–1801 and 1815–22 both parishes relieved families with short-term child allowances. During the post-war period, unemployed men and boys had their wages topped up (allowances-in-aid-of-wages), were paid poor relief for periods without work, and were employed either as 'roundsmen' or on parish work, such as mending the roads. In addition, a variety of new policies were adopted in relation to medical relief, such as contracts with practitioners and hospital subscriptions.

Expenditure rose rapidly in the south and east during the later eighteenth and early nineteenth centuries, and spending in Campton and Shefford reflected this trend.⁴ The expansion of provision in both communities was indicated by a steep increase in nominal expenditure and a rising number receiving poor relief, all paid for by an increasing number of ratepayers.⁵ Campton's spending increased ten-fold over the period from an average of £26 in the 1770s to a high-point of £312 in 1829; there was a peak in spending around 1801 of £310, followed by a fall, and then expenditure climbed once more with the post-war depression. In Shefford spending lagged somewhat behind that of Campton until Waterloo, when it raced ahead, and costs peaked in the 1820s at just over £300 in 1820 and again in 1827 (see figure 2).⁶ There were similar rises in other Bedfordshire parishes.⁷ The rise in spending in the 1770s and 1780s occurred despite a static cost of living, but rapid inflation from the 1790s meant that spending rose steeply, particularly in Campton. With the end of the French wars, and the resulting agricultural depression, parish overseers were unable to take better advantage of the reduction in the cost of living. Rather, depression hit these communities hard and relief pushed up poor law expenditure once more. The post-war depression affected Shefford more severely than Campton, but Campton's

---

³ On parish housing see J. Broad, 'Housing the rural poor in southern England, 1650–1850', *AgHR* xlviii (2000), 151–70.
⁴ Eastwood, *Governing rural England*, table 6.1 at p. 135; King, *Poverty and welfare in England*, ch. vi.
⁵ See chapter 3 below.
⁶ These figures encompass all poor law expenditure, including spending not just on regular and occasional relief to paupers, but also on county and church rates, legal advice and disputes, militia, constables, overseers' journeys and meetings. These forms of administrative spending have been omitted from the other figures.
⁷ Godber, *History of Bedfordshire*, 416.

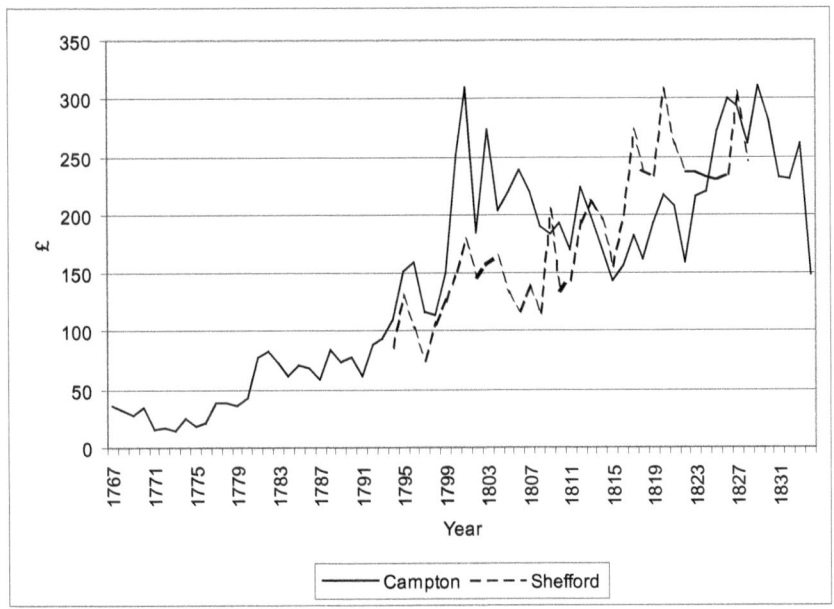

Figure 2. Annual expenditure on the poor in Campton (1767–1834) and Shefford (1794–1828)

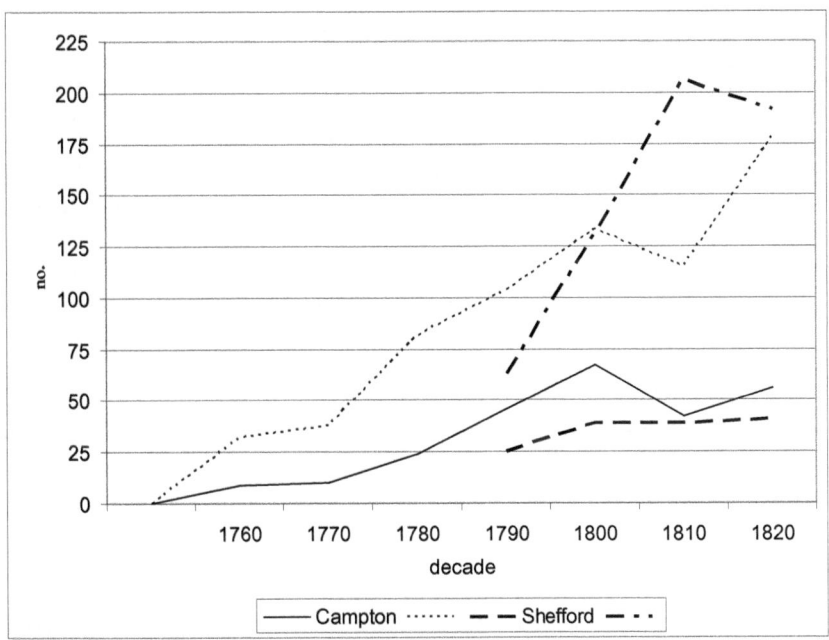

Figure 3. Growth in the number of pensioners and all paupers, Campton and Shefford, 1760s–1830s

### Table 3
### Spending on the poor *per capita* and *per pauper*, Campton and Shefford, 1801–31

| | Population | All paupers | Spending on the poor | Spending per head of population (shillings) | Spending per pauper (£) |
|---|---|---|---|---|---|
| **CAMPTON** | | | | | |
| 1801 | 316 | 48 | £310 | 19.6 | 6.5 |
| 1811 | 324 | 23 | £170 | 10.5 | 7.4 |
| 1821 | 410 | 33 | £208 | 10.1 | 6.3 |
| 1831 | 449 | 50 | £232 | 10.3 | 4.6 |
| **SHEFFORD** | | | | | |
| 1801 | 474 | 35 | £179 | 7.6 | 5.1 |
| 1811 | 536 | 34 | £144 | 5.4 | 4.2 |
| 1821 | 618 | 48 | £260 | 8.4 | 5.4 |
| 1828/31* | 763 | 48 | £247 | 6.5 | 5.1 |

Source: *Abstract of census returns*, 1801, 1811, 1821, 1831; Campton overseers' accounts, BLARS, P18/12/1–2, X514/1–3; Shefford overseers' accounts, P70/12/1–2.

\* = 1828 overseers' accounts; 1831 census figures.

spending surged once more in the 1820s.[8] Accompanying these increases in expenditure was a substantial rise in the total number of people receiving some form of poor relief, with those relieved occasionally outstripping the rise in the number of pensioners, particularly in Shefford (*see* figure 3).[9] The end of the period is in sharp contrast with the beginning: on a weekly basis in the 1760s and 1770s Campton's overseers were relieving only a handful of regular pensioners; by the 1820s and 1830s the weekly relief lists were very long and the nature and 'problem' of poverty had altered substantially.

There were further differences between the two communities. John Howlett commented on the propensity for towns to spend less per head on poor relief than country parishes.[10] This was indeed the case in Shefford, which spent roughly half the amount per head of population on their

---

[8] C. H. Feinstein, 'Pessimism perpetuated: real wages and the standard of living in Britain during and after the industrial revolution', *JEcH* lviii (1998), 625–58.

[9] The numbers in the 1760s and 1830s are lower partly because the data is not for a whole decade and only covers the financial years 1767–9 and 1830–4 respectively.

[10] J. Howlett, 'On the population and situation of the poor in England', *Annals of Agriculture* xviii (1792), 573–81. It is likely that many rural parishes were subsidising the poor relief costs of nearby towns, through provision of non-residential relief. See pp. 82–91 below and Sokoll, *Essex pauper letters*.

poor when compared with Campton (*see* table 3). In 1801 Campton spent almost three times as much, but in the 1820s the difference was far less (10.1s. *per capita* in Campton, 8.4s. in Shefford). However, the difference between the two communities is far less if the amount *per pauper* is calculated. Thus Shefford relieved a smaller proportion of its population, but, of those relieved, relief was not necessarily markedly less generous (*see* table 5).

It is possible to test Howlett's arguments further by analysing returns to parliament in the early nineteenth century for the whole of Bedfordshire.[11] Such an exercise reveals that poor law expenditure per head of population in 1802–3 was at an average of 9.5s. in the ten market towns and 13.2s. in the rural parishes. To some extent these averages disguise the fact that *per capita* spending varied widely from place to place, between market towns and between rural parishes. While Campton spent 9.8s. per head and Shefford 5.6s., Shefford in fact spent the least of all the market towns. Three market towns spent more than Campton: Potton (12s.), Toddington (12.3s.) and Biggleswade (16.9s.). But in general rural parishes spent more and all the really high spending parishes were rural.

Despite the burgeoning list of occasional recipients, commitment to regular weekly pensions remained high in both Campton and Shefford over the period, with at least 70 per cent spent on this type of relief. Increasing numbers of casual beneficiaries did have an impact upon the proportion of expenditure allocated to occasional cash payments, however, which increased from the 1810s, squeezing payments in kind and, although to a much smaller extent, regular weekly pension payments, but not to the extent found in other studies.[12] In Campton, pensions fell from around 85 per cent of spending between the 1790s and the 1810s to 78 per cent in the 1820s and 1830s, while in Shefford regular weekly relief declined from 84 per cent in the 1790s and 1800s to 71 per cent in the 1820s.[13] The decline in relief in kind was far more severe in Campton than in Shefford: from 31 per cent in the 1760s to 17 per cent in the 1770s, and steadily thereafter to 7 per cent in the 1830s, while in Shefford such payments declined from 10 per cent to 8 per cent between the 1790s and the 1820s. In contrast, the market town spent far more on casual cash payments: cash accounted for more than one-fifth of spending by the 1820s – twice that of Campton. However, although the number of casual recipients rose sharply, spending on them did not run in parallel and most relief continued to be spent upon regular weekly pensioners. In addition, pensioners also received occasional

---

[11] *Abstract of the poor*, 1803–4, 2–6; *Abstract of census returns*, 1801.

[12] In King's south-eastern parishes spending on pensions fell from almost two-thirds to around 40% between the 1770s and the 1820s, while spending on kind remained fairly static: *Poverty and welfare*, 155–9.

[13] Calculations were based on the amount spent on regular weekly pension payments, occasional cash and relief in kind to named recipients, and all other payments (for administration) were excluded.

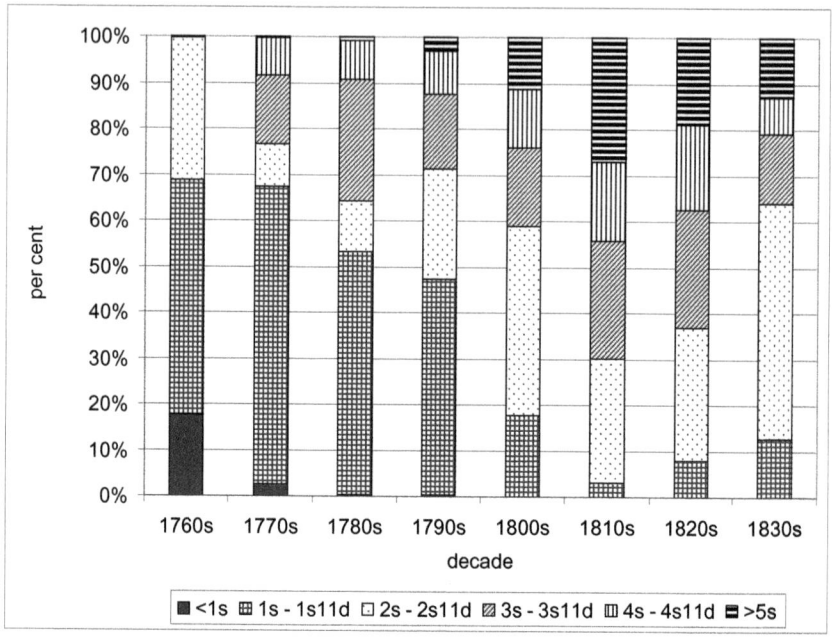

Figure 4. Distribution of weekly pensions, Campton, 1760s–1830s

cash and kind handouts, and these were worth an additional 8 per cent of their pension values.[14]

There was a general trend to larger nominal pension sums over the period in both communities although Shefford allocated fewer high payments (*see* figures 4 and 5). There was some reversal in this upward trend by the 1820s, but pension amounts remained higher than they had been before 1800 and they did not fall to the extent of the cost of living.[15] Despite deflation after 1815 the poverty problem persisted: total expenditure remained high, there was an increase in the number of those given occasional relief, the amount of relief in kind declined, and relatively high nominal pension sums continued.

The two communities provided a wide variety of relief in kind but with varying levels of generosity. In general, Campton and Shefford conform to Keith Snell's picture of the widely encompassing nature of relief. At the beginning of life, overseers paid for childbirth and christenings, in the middle of life they might meet the costs of weddings, and they also provided

---

[14] The proportion could be higher, as in Campton in the 1760s at 16% and in the 1790s at 13%.

[15] A more detailed analysis of parish spending for Campton and Shefford appears in S. Williams, 'Poor relief, labourers' households and living standards in rural England, c. 1770–1834: a Bedfordshire case-study', *EcHR* lviii (2005), 485–519.

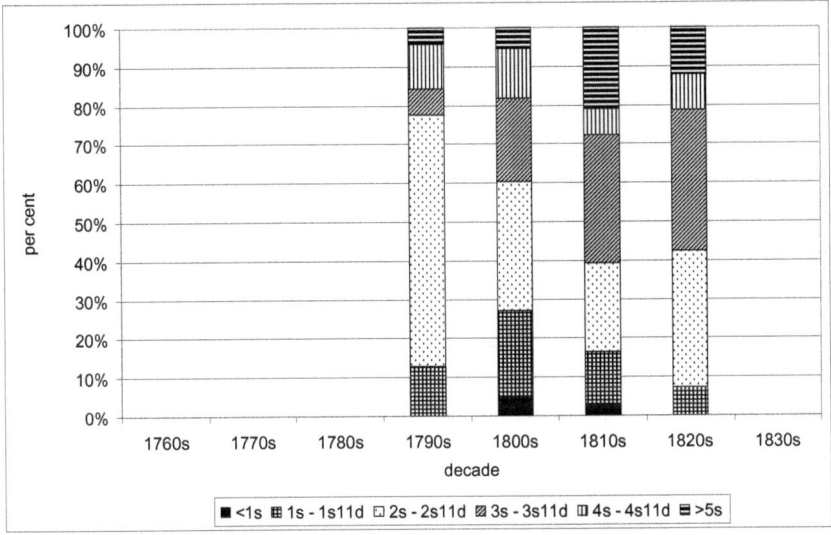

Figure 5. Distribution of weekly pensions, Shefford, 1790s–1820s

care in the last months of a person's life and paid for their funeral. Help with the costs of childbirth feature in the overseers' accounts, but was by no means common. In twenty cases the costs of lying-in were paid and payments could be substantial, amounting to between £1 and £3, with one payment in October 1814 of £5 for the delivery of Clark Herbert's illegitimate son, James Hayes. Other payments were for less than 10s. (usually for nourishment, called 'caudle'). In October 1767 3s. was allocated for 'eateing and drinken at John Wallers wifes cry out' (her labour). Just three christenings are listed in the overseers' accounts, such as the one in July 1782 for 'Churching, Crisoning Ester Meniwethers Child', Phoebe. Campton and Shefford paid for the weddings of twelve couples, usually because there was a baby already on the way. In contrast, parish overseers were prepared to meet the costs of many more funerals. Campton paid for the burials of eighty-two people, with Shefford paying for those of fify-one individuals. Expenses paid were comprehensive: for laying out of the corpse, the coffin, the cap, muffler and wool the body was wrapped in, the affidavit and church fees, and the bread, cheese and beer for the mourners. The cost of a burial increased over time, from an average in Campton of 14s. 4d. in the 1760s to £1 16s. 8d. in the 1810s, falling back a little in the wake of deflation to £1 7s. 3d. in the 1820s. Similar figures were spent in Shefford. These would have been substantial sums for labouring households to find for themselves:

they would have represented between two and five weeks' earnings for an agricultural labourer.[16]

Up to half of all burials in the two communities that were paid for by the poor law were of pensioners (50 per cent in Campton, 39 per cent in Shefford), which means that up to half of all pauper burials were to those only ever occasionally relieved. This perhaps underscores the point that even relatively independent households could not meet these costs without assistance. On the other hand, not all pensioners received a pauper burial and one-third of those who died whilst pensioners did not have their funerals paid for by the parish. These individuals relied upon the parish for a weekly dole for years up to their deaths and yet someone else had managed to pay for the funeral – relatives, perhaps, or possibly the pensioner had saved for their funeral costs through a friendly society.[17] This suggests that some of the most pauperised pensioners managed to set aside a penny or so a week for insurance against the costs of burial. It is difficult to ascertain whether the shame attached to a pauper burial under the New Poor Law also applied to those provided under the old poor law, and could explain the rise in saving for funerals. The fact that so many people were buried at the parish's expense might indicate that pauper burials carried little shame, or simply that many could not afford to pay for their funerals or even for weekly friendly society subscriptions. It is not surprising to find that many who received a pauper burial were elderly. Forty per cent of all those buried at the parishs' expense were aged over sixty. Just 4 per cent were young adults (15–24), and only 0 per cent were infants (0–4). Rather more were children at 12 per cent (5–14) and the remaining 37 per cent were adults (25–59). Adult women were slightly more likely to be buried at the parish's expense than men, as were elderly women in Campton (twice that of men), but not in Shefford, which buried more elderly men than women.

Clothing was another expense that many labouring families could not meet without assistance from the parish. John Styles, Steven King and Peter Jones have all analysed the types and costs of clothing provided under the old poor law.[18] In Campton and Shefford shoes, and their mending, were

---

[16] The sums for burials were compared with weekly male wages in agriculture in Bedfordshire: ibid. table 5 at p. 507.
[17] The role of friendly societies in Campton and Shefford is discussed in chapter 5 below.
[18] J. Styles, *The dress of the people: everyday fashion in eighteenth-century England*, London 2007, ch. xvi; S. King and C. Payne (eds), 'The dress of the poor, 1700–1900', *Textile History* (special edition) xxxiii (2002), 1–127; S. King, 'The clothing of the poor: a matter of pride or a matter of shame?', in Gestrich, King and Raphael, *Being poor in modern Europe*, 365–87, and, '"I fear you will think me too presumtuous in my demands but necessity has no law": clothing in English pauper letters, 1800–1834', *IRSH* liv (2009), 207–36; P. Jones, 'Clothing the poor in early-nineteenth-century England', *Textile History* xxxvii (2006), 17–37, and '"I cannot keep my place without being deascent": pauper letters, parish clothing and pragmatism in the south of England, 1750–1830', *Rural History* xx (2009), 31–49.

## Table 4
### Clothing and footwear items provided by Campton's overseers (1767–1834) and Shefford's overseers (1794–1828)

| Item | Shefford Number | Cost | Campton Number | Cost |
|---|---|---|---|---|
| Shoes | 78 | 1s. 8d.–12s. 6d. | 141 | 3s.– 13s. |
| Shoes mended | 33 | 3d.–3s. 1d. | 27 | 3d.–3s. 4d. |
| Shirts | 56 | 2s. 8d.–7s. 6d. | 99 | 1s. 6d.–8s. 6d. |
| Stockings & hose | 16 | 8d.–7s. | 69 | 1s.–5s. 2d. |
| 'Clothes' | 15 | 2s.–£4 5s. | 54 | 5s. 4d.–£4 13s. 3d. |
| Clothes mended | 2 | 4d.–9s. 1d. | 17 | 3d.–3s. |
| Breeches | 14 | 2s. 4d.–12s. | 24 | 1s. 6d.–16s. 6d. |
| Cloth | 14 | 5½d.–9s. | 39 | 6d.–£1 5s. 6d. |
| Shifts | 14 | 3s. 2½d.–6s. 5d. | 69 | 2s.–5s. 6d. |
| Waistcoats | 11 | 3s.–5s. | 9 | 2s.–10s. |
| Gowns & bed gowns | 8 | 6s. 4d. | 20 | 1s. 10½d.–9s. 4d. |
| Coats | 5 | 10s. 6d.–£1 7s. 7d. | 18 | 4s. 1d.–11s. |
| Great coats | | not given | | £1 |
| Round frock | | not given | | 5s. 6d.–10s. |
| Smock frock | | not given | | 4s. 6d.–6s. 6d. |
| Handkerchiefs | 5 | not given | 21 | 1s.–2s. 4d. |
| Petticoats | 5 | 3s. 8d. | 14 | 2s. 6d.–4s. 2½d. |
| Aprons & strings | 4 | 2s. ½d. | 15 | 11d.–1s. 6d. |
| Hats, bonnets, hoods | 2 | 2s.–2s. 6d. | 12 | 1s. 3d.–2s. 9d. |
| Caps | 5 | 6d.–1s. | 9 | 1s. 4d.–2s. 6d. |
| Cloak | 1 | 2s. | 1 | not given |
| Jacket | 1 | 2s. 6d. | 8 | 8s. 6d.–19s. 3d. |
| Patterns | 1 | 1s. | 3 | 1s. |
| Girdles | 0 | | 7 | 1s. 10d.–2s. |
| Buckles | 0 | | 1 | not given |
| Buttons | 0 | | 1 | 2s. 11d. |
| Stays | 0 | | 6 | 2s. 10d.–7s. 3d. |
| Making clothing | | 4d.–7s. 4d. | | 6d. – 5s. |

*Source*: Campton overseers' accounts, BLARS, P18/12/1-2, X514/1-3; Shefford overseers' accounts, P70/12/1-2.

the most frequently provided items (38 per cent in Shefford, 25 per cent in Campton), followed by shirts (19 per cent, 14.5 per cent respectively), then stockings (5.5 per cent, 10 per cent), shifts (5 per cent, 10 per cent) and breeches (5 per cent, 3.5 per cent) (see table 4). Not all the clothes were ordinary, day-to-day wear. In one case, for instance, the parish paid for 'Making Sunday Things for Smiths Children'. In some cases ready-made items were provided, but in many others the cloth (flannel, calico, dowlas, lace) was bought and the item made up especially, or, occasionally, cash was given towards the buying of clothing by paupers themselves. The provision of ready-made clothing and the making up of clothes implies that recipients had little choice over the types or quality of the clothes that were provided, despite a burgeoning consumer market (largely second-hand) for those who could afford to buy clothing themselves.[19]

In Campton in the provision of clothing and footwear pensioners were favoured over occasional recipients: in 64 per cent of cases the beneficiaries of clothing and footwear were the regularly-paid pensioners, while 36 per cent were occasional recipients.[20] Pensioners were given far more individual items, with some 80 per cent of all items going to them. Thus clothing was given in addition to pensions and pensioners were not necessarily expected to find the money from their weekly doles to pay for re-clothing themselves. Nevertheless, clothing and footwear was also available as discrete items to those in occasional need but not requiring regular maintenance. Jones has shown how access to sufficient and appropriate clothing could be contested between applicants and overseers. Indeed, paupers within the jurisdiction of the JP Samuel Whitbread complained to him regarding the provision of clothing and he frequently ordered overseers to provide clothing and bedding, and to have shoes mended.[21]

Many of those allocated parish clothing were elderly pensioners (33 per cent) or lone parents (30 per cent) – the groups already favoured as pensioners. Within families (with families accounting for just 6 per cent of payments) around half of the clothing/footwear was intended for children and the other half their parents, while in lone-parent households all payments to widower-headed families were for their children and three-quarters of payments to female-headed families were for their children. While far less is known about occasional recipients it is clear that around one-third of payments for clothing/footwear were given to children. Age information is scarce for all the children discussed here, but where it is available it appears that children over the age of ten were prioritised, possibly because they were being fitted out for service or apprenticeship. In 1827, for example, £1 0s. 6d. was spent on '2 shirts, stockings' for Robert Jude upon his apprenticeship. Clothing was also provided for other occasions, such as that for Stevens 'to Equip him for the infirmary'.

The sharp decline in the provision of relief in kind in Campton (from 31 per cent to 7 per cent) lends support to Keith Snell's contention that there was a marked tightening up on relief in kind after 1780; he finds that there were cuts in particular in the provision of clothes, fuel, nursing, burials and shoes.[22] The detailed payment data makes possible a more nuanced picture

---

[19] Styles, *The dress of the people*, ch. xv.
[20] 55% in Shefford and 59% in Campton.
[21] *Samuel Whitbread's notebooks, 1810–11, 1813–14*, ed. A. F. Cirket (BHRS 1, 1971).
[22] Snell, *Annals of the labouring poor*, 104–7.

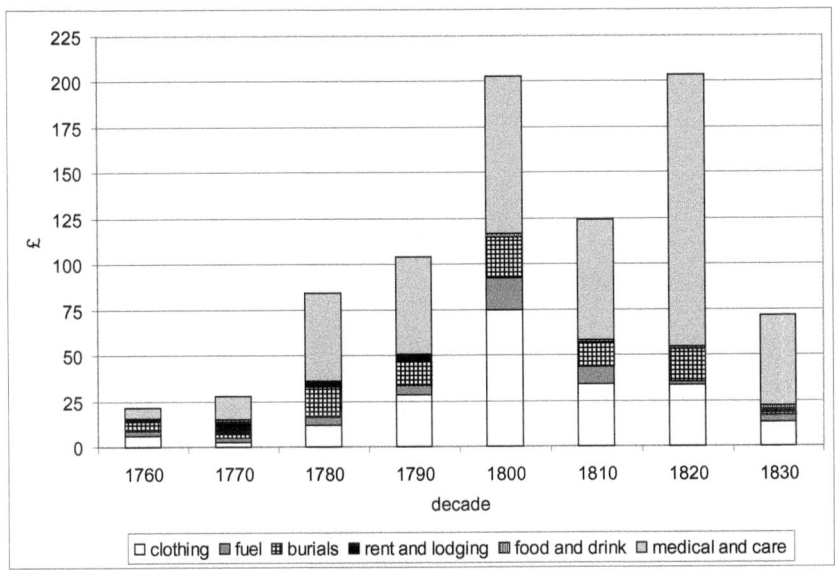

Figure 6. Payments in kind in Campton, 1760s–1830s

of this decline for Campton and Shefford (*see* figures 6 and 7). Campton's overseers did not reduce their spending on clothing until the 1810s, while spending on this in Shefford remained largely static. There was some squeezing of the amount spent on burials in Campton, particularly in the 1830s, but again spending was static in Shefford. Spending on fuel increased in both communities and then fell again from the 1810s. More was spent on food and drink by Shefford's overseers and this too declined over time. Rent and lodging payments were also reduced, but, perhaps surprisingly, only remarkably small nominal sums were ever spent on these.[23] It is evident that in Campton and Shefford the reduction in spending in kind came decades later than that found by Snell, from the 1810s.

What is extraordinary is the increase in spending on medical care. The poor law was one of the most important sources of medical assistance for the poorest part of society. In many cases, sickness and associated unemployment was a distinctive reason for seeking support, usually in the short-term, while for others chronic illness or long-term infirmity necessitated an extended period of dependency upon the parish.[24] These two communities offered a

---

[23] Rent was paid and housing provided for the elderly in five parishes in Kent: Barker-Read, 'The treatment of the aged poor', 76–84.
[24] M. E. Fissell, 'The "sick and drooping poor" in eighteenth-century Bristol and its region', *Society for the Social History of Medicine* ii (1989), 35–58, and *Patients, power and the poor*; E. G. Thomas, 'The old poor law and medicine', *Medical History* xxiv (1980), 1–19; Healey, 'Poverty in an industrializing town'; Sharpe, *Reproducing Colyton*, 235–6.

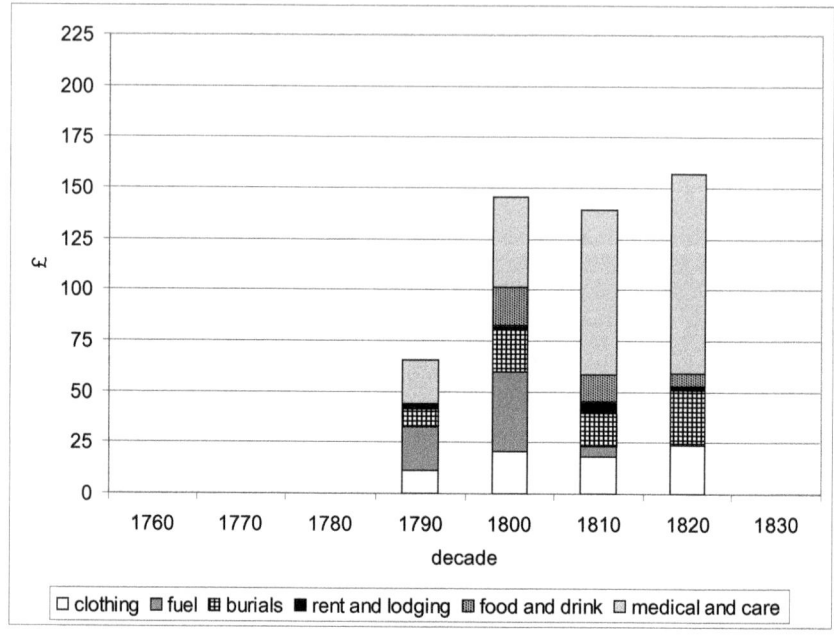

Figure 7. Payments in kind in Shefford, 1790s–1820s

wide variety of medical support, including outdoor assistance in the form of cash payments to those who were ill, to offset the shortfall in earnings, and extra food and fuel. The poor were also inoculated against smallpox and offered institutional care in infirmaries and lunatic asylums. The parish employed a variety of medical practitioners and attendants, ranging from surgeon-apothecaries, midwives and occasionally physicians, together with fringe practitioners, including bonesetters, inoculators and nurses. Finally, the parish also provided domiciliary care: when they were too sick or infirm, paupers were helped with their laundry and household tasks and were nursed, either back to health or in their final days, by parish carers and nurses.[25]

Campton and Shefford and other Bedfordshire parishes sought to contain medical costs in a variety of ways. By the first decade of the nineteenth century almost three-quarters of parishes in east Bedfordshire had replaced billing by contractual agreements with a surgeon-apothecary.[26] Medical contracting was an attempt to place medical care on a more regular footing,

---

[25] S. Williams, 'Practitioners' income and provision for the poor: parish doctors in the late eighteenth and early nineteenth centuries', *Social History of Medicine* xviii (2005), 1–28, and 'Caring for the sick poor: poor law nurses in Bedfordshire, c. 1770–1834', in P. Lane, N. Raven and K. D. M. Snell (eds), *Women, work and wages, c. 1650–1900*, Woodbridge 2004, 141–69. See also Sharpe, *Reproducing Colyton*, 236, 244–5, and Barker-Read, 'The treatment of the aged poor', 100–19.

[26] Williams, 'Practitioners' income'.

contain costs and predict future expenditure. It is likely that many parishes only went over to this system once they found their finances under extraordinary pressure in the latter half of the eighteenth century and were forced to seek ways of reducing parish spending.[27] Campton employed George Hicks for five years starting in 1785, then Obadiah Rose for the next seven years. After that date, James Layman was contracted to the parish until his death in 1826, when his son, also James Layman, took over the contract until the end of the old poor law period in 1834 (at least thirty-eight years). Such long-term contractual arrangements suggest that surgeon-apothecaries took on and maintained these contracts to keep out potential competitors and/or that some parishes preferred long-term arrangements with one doctor over any others. Shefford also employed George Hicks, Charles Gay and James Layman on rotation after 1796 (and, likewise, James Layman, Jr, took over his father's contract). These doctors were also involved in long-term contractual agreements with other parishes as sole practitioner, which suggests that a specific medical man had not managed to monopolise the post of Shefford doctor, although he might have managed to do so in a neighbouring parish. The exact services covered by the contacts were negotiated between parish and practitioner and parish doctors increasingly inserted exemptions – so that the contracted sum did not include midwifery or the treatment of venereal disease, which incurred additional costs – in an attempt to increase their value.[28]

Another instance where a certain type of medical provision was sought in order to contain costs was hospital treatment. Parishes, commercial firms and friendly societies were all increasingly subscribing to their local infirmaries.[29] The Bedford Infirmary was founded in 1803. The following year there were just ten parish subscribers, but by 1811 almost two-thirds of county parishes had taken out subscriptions.[30] It took three decades for parishes surrounding the Salop infirmary, Shropshire, to start subscribing in any numbers, while 30 per cent of parishes in Oxfordshire and 20 per cent of Berkshire parishes subscribed to the John Radcliffe hospital in Oxford.[31]

Before the founding of the hospital at Bedford, the sick poor could be sent to hospitals in Northampton and Cambridge.[32] Both Campton and Shef-

[27] G. W. Oxley, *Poor relief in England and Wales, 1601–1834*, Newton Abbot 1974, 65–73.
[28] Williams, 'Practitioners' income'.
[29] A. Berry, 'Community sponsorship and the hospital patient in late eighteenth-century England', in Horden and Smith, *The locus of care*, 126–50; Thomas, 'Poor law and medicine'.
[30] Bedford Infirmary annual reports, BLARS, HO:B/A1.
[31] E. G. Thomas, 'The treatment of poverty in Berkshire, Essex and Oxfordshire, 1723–1834', unpubl. PhD diss. London 1971; A. Tomkins, 'Paupers and the infirmary in mid-eighteenth-century Shrewsbury', *Medical History* xliii (1999), 208–27.
[32] In 1794 Campton sent Ann Newman to Cambridge Infirmary. See also Emmison, *Eaton Socon*, 77–8.

ford made use of the new hospital at Bedford, but there is no evidence of Campton subscribing, and Shefford only subscribed from the late 1820s.[33] Campton sent ten of its paupers, two of whom were admitted twice; Shefford sent six. These patients were sent under the recommendations of local subscribers, who included three clergymen and two major landowners.[34] This saved the parish the cost of subscription, such that the infirmary was, in terms of cost, a minor element of medical relief in kind (at most 6 per cent). However, per individual, parish costs were not insubstantial. The average cost of £1 10s. included caution money of 1 guinea, travel expenses, washing at the infirmary and clothing and linen.

In many instances it would seem to have made economic sense for parishes to send their more intractable cases to hospital.[35] The case of Hannah Merryweathers of Campton illustrates the value of using a hospital. In receipt of occasional poor relief from 1807 and of a parish pension, of 3s.–5s. a week, from 1813, the parish sent Hannah to the infirmary in September 1814 where she stayed for five months.[36] The parish saved around £5 in pension payments, as well as the cost of her medicines, nursing and fuel. The expenses of attending hospital could soon mount up, however, and it cost Campton a further £2 4s. for Hannah's travel expenses and for new clothing. Yet despite these additional costs, the parish had still saved money in sending her to the infirmary, especially in light of the fact that Sir George Osborn Bart sponsored her, rather than the parish.[37] The family circumstances of Joseph Stevens make his case somewhat different, however. Joseph was sent to the infirmary twice. The parish saved the money that they had been giving him for periods out of work and for illness, but on each occasion the parish had to support his wife and family while he was away, on a pension of between 4s. and 7s. a week. In Joseph Stevens's case it is unlikely that

---

[33] Shefford's vestry minutes record subscribing to the Bedford Infirmary long before they appeared on the hospital's subscription lists: Bedford Infirmary annual reports, BLARS, HO:B/A1, HO:B/V18–19, and Shefford's vestry minutes, BLARS, P70/8/1. Long delays in sending subscriptions are noted by A. Berry: 'Patronage, funding and the hospital patient, c. 1750–1815: three English regional case studies' unpubl. PhD diss. Oxford 1995.
[34] Campton and Shefford never appeared as subscribers on the annual reports: Bedford Infirmary annual reports, BLARS, HO:B/A1, HO:B/M3–5. Names of the paupers sent to the infirmary were linked with the lists of admissions to the hospital, which gave the sponsor's name. Sponsors were the Revd Edward Williamson (Campton), the Revd Edmund Williamson (Campton), Sir George Osborn Bart, (Chickands Priory), Sir John Osborn Bart (Chicksands Priory), and the Revd Daniel Oliver (Clifton).
[35] Berry, 'Community sponsorship'.
[36] Hannah Merryweathers appears in the 'foul minutes' for Bedford Infirmary. The minutes do not tell us a great deal, only the dates of admission and discharge and that she was admitted under the patronage of Colonel Osborn and was discharged 'cured': Bedford Infirmary foul minutes, BLARS, HO:B/M4.
[37] Ibid.

the parish made a saving from sending him to hospital. Thus, only in some cases did the parish actually save money by sending paupers to the infirmary.

Those with mental illness could be cared for in the local asylum. There is mention of only two paupers being admitted to the county asylum after it was opened in 1812.[38] It was not cheap: it cost Campton nearly £20 to send William Jordan for twenty-two weeks (1830), and considerably more to send John Leonard, who was admitted for over three years. Leonard's stay cost £50, and pension payments to his family cost the parish a further £25 18s. 6d. In Shefford, in October 1833, Mrs Bloomfield, who was of 'infirm mind as to require another person to watch her conduct, and prevent her from doing mischief to herself or others', was kept in the parish.

Smallpox epidemics could be expensive but were thankfully infrequent; there were epidemics in Campton in 1781–2, 1787, 1809 and 1832, and in Shefford in 1796, 1799 and 1824. The costs for the parish were as high as one-quarter of expenditure in kind in Campton in the 1780s and 8 per cent in Shefford in the 1790s. The outbreak in Campton in 1781–2 cost the parish just over £9 for 'candels, oatmeal, milk, Goods, mutton, food, & John Hare for waiting' and the epidemic in 1787 cost almost £5 for firewood, twelve gallons of milk, nursing and attendance. The medical contract of that year was far less at two guineas. Smallpox nurses could earn good money: one nurse earned 2 guineas for three weeks' attendance. Inoculating parishioners against smallpox (somewhat sporadically) was also costly and boosted the pay of contracted surgeons by around two to three guineas for a few individuals, and James Layman earned almost £22 for inoculation and the setting of broken bones in 1809. In the epidemic of 1809 Samuel Ebden lost almost all of his family in December, when his wife Martha (who was in her forties) and three children (William, aged fifteen, Charles, seven and Joseph Lamson, four) all died at the same time. He was left a widower with a toddler, Patience (aged two) and baby Levi (aged just five months). In November and December the parish paid the family 11s. in cash and also paid 14s. for care and £3 7s. 7d. for wine and food. The funerals of the three children and Martha cost the parish £5 13s. 6d. Samuel was then given £1 8s. 0d. over the following six months, but thereafter largely managed without any further parish assistance. Eight months after he was widowed he remarried, Frances, with whom he had a further two children.

Both parishes had poor houses. An inventory of Shefford's main poor house in 1812 reveals that it had five rooms – a pantry, the best chamber, second chamber, first and second garrets.[39] The best chamber included two bedsteads and flock beds and one straw bed, while the second chamber contained the same with an additional straw bed; the first garret had one bedstead with feather bed and one straw bed, while the second garret was

---

[38] Godber, *History of Bedfordshire*, 426
[39] Shefford's overseers' accounts, BLARS, P70/8/1–2, entry for 4 Apr. 1812.

empty. Bedding and blankets, bed-cords, rugs and boxes were paid for by the overseer. The pantry contained pots, pans, boilers and kettles for cooking, plus six to twelve plates, bowls and cutlery. The house also contained two tables, five chairs, a coal grate, pot hook, candlesticks, pails, a mop and a brush, and a bell.[40] The overseers kept a keen eye on the contents of the house, taking inventories frequently. The house was owned by the charity feoffees and a rent was paid by the overseers, increasing from £3 10s. in 1794, to £6 10s. in 1805, to £12 in 1822, but it was not rated. Fuel, food, gin and beer, clothing, soap, washing and medical care were also provided to those living or staying there.

Campton's poor house was also provided by a charity.[41] It was whitewashed and thatched and had a new privy and a barn. For a brief period, September 1783 to April 1784, the parish paid a housekeeper, C. Clarks, 2s.3d. a week. The parish provided all the fuel and sometimes milk porridge. The majority of the costs for the poor house were for its rent and upkeep. Campton spent an incredible £116 on repairs in 1803. Annual rent was around £4, but it appears that rent was waived by the charity from 1803.[42] The inhabitants grew their own potatoes. The poor house provided work opportunities for other paupers – such as washing sheets, hoeing the potatoes and other small jobs, plus opportunities to local suppliers and builders.

Unfortunately, there is little specific information on the people accommodated in these houses. Campton declared no inmates in the workhouse in 1813, 1814 and 1815, but Shefford claimed that there were nine, eight and six respectively.[43] In Campton's overseers' accounts just three inmates are mentioned – two lived in the house in the last few months of their lives, while Ann Herbert was a very long-term pensioner who lived in the poor house for many years. Those accommodated in Shefford were usually the transient, described as 'man' or 'woman'. In December 1871, for instance, 5s. 7½d. was spent on a man for tea, butter, oatmeal, salt, loaf, milk and meat before he proceeded on his journey. A pregnant woman was given tobacco, bread, cheese and beer during her brief stay. John Newman stayed there in the months while he awaited removal to Shillington and was given over £4 in cash plus oatmeal, candles, bread and mutton, and he was paid for a day's work at the house. There was at least one longer-term inmate. When John Bowers petitioned Samuel Whitbread for relief in November 1811, it was settled with the overseer that he (and presumably his wife, Ann) were to

---

[40] The records do not make it clear whether this furniture and these goods were the property of the parish or of the paupers living in the poorhouse.
[41] *Commission of inquiry into charities in England and Wales: eighth report*, PP 1823, viii.1 C.13, appendix, 7; *List of counties reported on, and not reported on, by commissions of inquiry into charities in England and Wales*, 1819–28, PP 1828, xxi.31 C.389, 6.
[42] No rent is paid after 1803 and the parliamentary paper of 1831–2 records that no rent was charged on the poor's cottage: *Analytical digest of coms.' reports on public charities*, PP 1831–2 xxix.1 C.63, 6.
[43] *Abstract of the poor*, 1818, 13–18.

live in the workhouse and to be given 4s. a week.[44] Five months after Bowers entered the poor house an inventory was taken of his goods. He was given a weekly pension of between 4s. and 6s. until his death in May 1815, as well as sitters up, food and drink, soap, candles and fuel in his final illness; he presumably continued to live in the poor house throughout. It would appear that Ann left the poor house some time after her husband's death, since in 1818 and 1824 the parish paid her poor rates, although she continued to receive a weekly pension.

In Bedfordshire there were 291 parish houses in 1834.[45] There are instances of both types of house – workhouses and poor houses – in the county with wide variations in practice. Some bigger parishes made contracts with workhouse masters.[46] The workhouse or poor house was the main alternative for the pauper who could not, even with parish relief, earn enough to live, although there was limited provision in almshouses for those deemed sufficiently 'deserving'.[47] Samuel Whitbread ordered the Dunton overseer to take a pauper to Southill by cart when it was decided that 'The man to go into the workhouse if not contented with his allowance. The woman [his wife] to provide for herself if she will not follow him.' In a similar case, Mary Bosworth of Clophill had a bastard child and an allowance from the parish of 1s. 6d. per week and she earned 4s. a week straw-plaiting. When she asked the overseers for a bed and a blanket they offered her the poor house and Whitbread dismissed her complaint.[48] The offer of accommodation in the poor house, which would usually be rent-free, was taken into account when assessing relief.

In the neighbouring parish of Southill in 1811 there were twenty-one men and ten women in the workhouse, while in Cardington workhouse in 1782 thirty-two individuals (one-third of all recipients) were inmates, all of whom were the 'impotent': single orphans, unmarried mothers and single individuals.[49] In 1808 the number living inside had fallen slightly to twenty-nine, looked after by a matron. The men were all elderly, whereas some of the women were middle-aged as well as old. There were fourteen children under the age of twelve while those who had been put out to service (another nine children) were provided with clothing which was washed and mended in the workhouse.[50] Perhaps under the direction of Whitbread, a set of rules and regulations was set out for the workhouse in 1810 at the Session

---

[44] *Whitbread's notebooks*, entries 381, 384. Ann is not mentioned in Whitbread's notebooks, but she is in the overseers' accounts.
[45] Broad, 'Housing the rural poor', table 1 at p.168.
[46] Godber, *History of Bedfordshire*, 333, 367–8.
[47] *Whitbread's notebooks*, entries 410, 535, 592, 808, 809, 1020, 1021, 1082. Campton and Shefford did not record any almshouses in 1823, but the nearby parish of Woburn had twelve: *Coms. of inquiry into charities*, appendix, 7–9, 38.
[48] *Whitbread's notebooks*, entries 401, 410.
[49] *Inhabitants of Cardington*, 47.
[50] Whitbread collection, BLARS, W1/767.

of the Peace. These are fascinating and set out the responsibilities expected of the governor and the behaviour expected of the inmates. The governor was expected to ensure the attendance of the poor at divine worship; attend the sick properly and employ sitters-up; ensure that inmates were 'neat clean and wholesome'; provide decent apparel, including clean cloth stockings on every Sunday morning and clean sheets for their beds once a month; provide three meals a day, including three-quarters of a pound of beef, mutton or pork two days a week for those aged over twelve; employ the most able and fit, either inside or outside the house; teach the children to read and the girls knitting and plain needlework. The inmates were to behave respectfully and obediently in the house and when set to work; they were not to fight, quarrel or swear; they should keep clean; they were only to leave the house when permitted; if they broke these rules punishments included confinement for up to forty-eight hours, bread and water, or even imprisonment for up to two months and hard labour. Complaints by inmates were to be heard by the visiting justices.[51] In Ampthill workhouse in 1814 misbehaving inmates were indeed refused their Sunday dinners.[52]

Conditions in local workhouses varied enormously and the neighbourhood's JP, Samuel Whitbread, took a keen interest in his area of jurisdiction and further afield as a visiting justice.[53] The state of the poor houses in Campton and Shefford must have been perceived as at least adequate since neither feature in Whitbread's reports on workhouses in poor condition.[54] Whitbread brought accounts of the deficiencies of local workhouses to quarter sessions and got orders made for improvements, such as paving the floors and providing a minimum of furniture and proper bedding for all inmates. He was ruthless in his pursuit of a particular overseer who escorted a sick man from the workhouse and then left him lying in a field which was just within the boundary of a neighbouring parish.[55] There were complaints by paupers about these miserable conditions. In 1808 the seventy-two-year-old Samuel Binyon of Cranfield petitioned quarter sessions for an increase in his weekly pension of 3s.; it is recorded that 'he has real objection to be put in the workhouse, which is in a very filthy and uncomfortable state, as he has always been till lately in a clean and comfortable situation as a tradesman'.[56] Three years later a letter records that William Silley was 'in such distress' and that he 'was formally a considerable Farmer in Ashwell; But never considered of bright Abilities ... (after having spent his whole Estate) he

---

[51] Ibid. W1/768.
[52] Ibid. W1/771, 772.
[53] 'Letter from Edward Law, Lincoln's Inn, 26 Dec 1801', ibid. W1/764.
[54] Ibid. W1/762–772, 808: Haynes, Houghton Conquest, Riseley, Cardington, Milton, Amphill, Clophill; *Whitbread's notebooks*, entries 592, 535.
[55] Whitbread collection, BLARS, W1/762–72; R. Fulford, *Samuel Whitbread, 1764–1815: a study in opposition*, London 1967, 77–8; Godber, *History of Bedfordshire*, 427–9.
[56] Godber, *History of Bedfordshire*, 428.

became in a manner disconsolate ... choosing the Life of a Vagrant strolling about the Country, than submit to the Fare of a workhouse'.[57] It is possible that Campton and Shefford were committed to outdoor relief rather than workhouse provision due to the cost; Whitbread noted in his 1807 Bill that 'it hath been found by Experience, that the Expence of maintaining poor Persons in Workhouses is much greater than the Expence of maintaining such poor Persons at their own Habitations'. Based on his local experience, Whitbread suggested within his bill of 1807 the setting of strict rules for the better regulation of workhouses.[58]

Parish overseers had to meet the costs of administration of the poor laws from the poor rates. It was costly: in Shefford administration accounted for up to two-fifths of total expenditure. Overseers had to find the money for a wide variety of items, including (in order of importance) a range of taxes, the poor house, various bills, the militia, constables, collecting the poor rate and keeping the overseers' accounts (and having them audited), travel, vestry meetings, legal costs and postage. The county tax, land tax and vagrancy tax accounted for up to 46 per cent of administrative spending. The other categories of expenditure each accounted for 15 per cent or less.

The parish was also responsible for meeting some of the costs of the militia. Samuel Whitbread heard cases relating to serving men's families, whether in the regular militia or in the volunteer forces, the Bedfordshire Local Militia, of which Whitbread was Colonel. A number of men asked him to sign papers certifying that they were in the militia so that their wives and families could draw an allowance while they were serving. When Mary Barnard, a soldier's wife, appealed to Whitbread for an allowance for her seven-month-old child, he referred her to Shefford's overseers.[59] In Campton and Shefford costs relating to the militia – such as for warrants, lists, substitutes, swearing and other administration – were small, never exceeding £23 and they were paid from 1775. Until 1802 payments were infrequent, but more regular thereafter. Substitute costs were up to £12 10s.[60] There were twelve families who received an allowance in Campton. Ann Croft, for instance, received an allowance of 1s.–2s. in 1782–3 and Mary Brinkly received amounts varying from 1s. to 4s. between 1793 and 1799. Nine families were relieved between 1809 and 1813 for shorter time periods. Shefford relieved twenty–five militia men's families. In May 1795 Shefford's overseers paid just over £23, 'Towards Raisin the Sailors'. Shefford's overseers also recorded the reimbursement of money relating to the army of defence and the treasurer of the county.

---

[57] Whitbread collection, BLARS, W1/325.
[58] *Bill for promoting and encouraging industry among labouring classes of community, and for relief of necessitous poor*, PP 1807 i.81 C.32, 3, 8–9.
[59] *Whitbread's notebooks*, entries 307, 311, 23–4.
[60] Substitutes were found in Campton for Newman, John Merryweathers, Thomas Lincoln, Thomas Odell and Thomas Day, and in Shefford for Edward Whitbread and Mr Inskip.

## Table 5
### Proportion of the population benefiting from poor relief in Campton and Shefford, 1801–31

| Census date and population | Named pensioners (number) | Named occasional recipients (number) | All paupers (i plus ii) as a proportion of population (%) | Pensioners plus dependants (number) | Pensioners plus dependants (% of population) | Pensioner families (% of families) | Occasional recipients plus (estimated) dependants (number) | All paupers and their dependants (% of population) |
|---|---|---|---|---|---|---|---|---|
| | (i) | (ii) | (iii) | (iv) | (v) | (vi) | (vii) | (viii) |
| **CAMPTON** | | | | | | | | |
| 1801  316 | 32 | 16 | 15.2 | 98 | 31.0 | 63.8 | 48 | 46.2 |
| 1811  324 | 18 | 5 | 7.1 | 40 | 12.3 | 28.6 | 11 | 15.7 |
| 1821  410 | 20 | 13 | 8.0 | 44 | 10.7 | 25.0 | 29 | 17.8 |
| 1831  449 | 25 | 25 | 11.1 | 33 | 7.3 | 26.7 | 33 | 14.7 |
| **SHEFFORD** | | | | | | | | |
| 1801  474 | 26 | 9 | 7.4 | 61 | 12.9 | 22.4 | 21 | 17.3 |
| 1811  536 | 15 | 19 | 6.3 | 30 | 5.6 | 12.0 | 38 | 12.7 |
| 1821  618 | 20 | 28 | 7.8 | 43 | 7.0 | 15.0 | 62 | 17.0 |
| 1828/31* 763 | 23 | 25 | 6.3 | 38 | 5.0 | 16.2 | 43 | 10.6 |

Source: *Abstract of census returns*, 1801, 1811, 1821, 1831; Campton overseers' accounts, BLARS, P18/12/1–2; Shefford overseers' accounts, X514/1–3, P70/12/1–2; Campton and Shefford family reconstitution.

\* = 1828 overseers' accounts; 1831 census figures.

## The poor and their families

The study of all poor individuals and families in Campton and Shefford poses considerable methodological problems. Overseers' accounts usually list the name of the recipient of relief and their payment only, and thus little is known of the size and composition of the recipient's family (which might have influenced the nature and size of any poor relief payment). Any calculation of the proportion of the population who were poor that relies upon the number of names listed in overseers' account books thus fails to include the 'hidden dependants'. However, the pauper biographies allow an estimate to be made that incorporates these additional beneficiaries.[61] If dependants are not taken into account, then the proportion of the populations of Campton and Shefford on relief is, at most, 15 per cent (*see* table 5, columns i–iii), whereas the pauper biographies reveal that roughly twice as many people might have benefited from pension payments (column iv). This figure corroborates the multiplier proposed by Paul Slack, and, moreover, is supported by the number of named paupers to their dependants calculated from the household listing for Cardington, east Bedfordshire, in 1782.[62] In fact the multiplier could vary over time: in Campton, in the crisis year of 1801, some three times as many people benefited from a pension; in 1811 and 1821 twice as many individuals benefited; and in 1831 the multiplier was 1.3. In Shefford, however, the multiplier was always around two. A further calculation of the proportion of families (also given in the census), rather than individuals, in receipt of parish pensions (column vi) reveals that in Campton just over one quarter of families were in receipt of pension funds between 1811 and 1831, and that in 1801 this figure was as high as

---

[61] The number of dependants could be calculated from the FRFs. In many cases it is also possible to infer the number of dependants for those recipients who could not be linked to the reconstitution. If a man's wife and children are mentioned, for instance, a minimum figure of four will be inferred (man, wife and two children). The number of potential dependants will therefore be under-estimated (since, for example, 'children' could mean more children than just two). Since parish payments did not necessarily support all members of a family, the number of beneficiaries in families linked to the reconstitution might present an upper bound, but for those not linked to the reconstitution the number of potential dependants will have been under-estimated, since figures were inferred. A number of rules were adopted: (1.) 'dependant' children were defined as those aged 14 and under; (2.) where there were two or more people listed in the accounts books separately as pensioners but from the same family the household members were counted only once. The fact that a significant minority could not be linked to the reconstitution or the parish registers suggests that pensioners did not have to have been long-term residents in order to receive relief. For age at leaving home see Armstrong, *Farmworkers*, 21–3, and R. Wall, 'Leaving home and the process of household formation in pre-industrial England', *C&C* ii (1987), 77–101. In 1782, in the parish of Cardington, near Campton and Shefford, the chances of a son having left home were 4 to 1 at ages 15–19: Armstrong, *Farmworkers*, 22.

[62] Slack, *Poverty and policy*, 173–87; *Inhabitants of Cardington*, introduction at pp. 44–52.

almost two-thirds of families. In Shefford the proportion was always much lower, at between 10 and 15 per cent of families, but was as high as 20 per cent in 1801.

If the same multiplier is applied to occasional recipients, then the total number/proportion of all paupers and their dependants can be calculated (columns vii and viii). The results suggest that potential beneficiaries could account for around 15 per cent of residents, except, once again, in Campton in 1801, when all paupers made up almost half the population. These figures amount to compelling evidence that, in the south and east, a very sizeable proportion of the labouring poor were in receipt of poor relief during the late eighteenth and early nineteenth centuries. These data also show that, in Campton and Shefford at least, the proportion of dependants fell more sharply between 1801 and 1831 than the proportion of families, which indicates that the size of those households being relieved declined over time.

From reading the *Poor law report* of 1834, which was obsessed with relief afforded to able-bodied men as young single men or heads of couple-headed families, one would have been forgiven for thinking that men made up a large section of the poor, particularly after 1795. The report stated that 'The great source of abuse is the Out-door Relief afforded to the Able-bodied on their own account, or that of their families.'[63] Men might qualify for weekly relief as fathers of large families (child allowances), or for allowances-in-aid-of-wages, or for unemployment relief. Many historians have simply assumed that these allowances were widespread and prevalent after 1795.

That the population was relatively youthful during the later eighteenth and early nineteenth centuries, with a much higher dependency ratio, increased the likelihood of family poverty.[64] The figures from 1801 (*see* table 5) suggest that many couple-headed families were indeed relieved in the two Bedfordshire communities. However, in Campton and Shefford most of those receiving regular weekly long-term pensions over the entire period, the most valuable form of relief, were not couple-headed families, but the elderly and lone parents (primarily widows with young children).[65] The

---

[63] *Poor law report*, 8.
[64] Wrigley and Schofield, *Population history*; E. A. Wrigley, 'British population during the "long" eighteenth century, 1680–1840', in R. Floud and P. Johnson, *The Cambridge economic history of modern Britain*, I: *Industrialisation, 1700–1860*, 57–95 at p. 69.
[65] Pensioners were allocated to the following groups: (1.) 'The elderly': those aged 60 or over; (2.) 'Families': married couples with children aged 14 and under; (3.) 'Lone parents': male- and female-headed households with children (such as widows and widowers, deserted wives and unmarried mothers), the vast majority of whom were headed by women; (4.) 'Lone men and women': those recipients who were single at any point in the life-cycle under the age of 60; (5.) 'Couples' who were not elderly; and (6.) 'Orphans'. In order to place individuals and families into one of these six categories, the dating of pension payments to named recipients was linked to the family structure of those recipients on their FRFs at exactly the same point in time. Pensioners were reallocated to different groups when their situations changed. Numbers in each category were (predominant category only, no double counting): Campton: 'elderly', 53; families, 24; lone parents,

### Table 6
### Number of pensioners in each family category by decade in Campton and Shefford, 1760s–1830s

| | Elderly | Families | Lone parents | Lone men and women | Couples | Orphans | Total |
|---|---|---|---|---|---|---|---|
| Campton | | | | | | | |
| 1760s | 1 | 1 | 5 | 2 | 0 | 0 | 9 |
| 1770s | 4 | 1 | 1 | 3 | 0 | 0 | 9 |
| 1780s | 9 | 0 | 7 | 6 | 0 | 1 | 23 |
| 1790s | 9 | 12 | 13 | 3 | 0 | 4 | 41 |
| 1800s | 15 | 12 | 13 | 3 | 0 | 3 | 46 |
| 1810s | 19 | 9 | 6 | 3 | 1 | 1 | 39 |
| 1820s | 19 | 7 | 8 | 10 | 0 | 2 | 46 |
| 1830s | 14 | 2 | 4 | 7 | 0 | 2 | 29 |
| Shefford | | | | | | | |
| 1790s | 8 | 4 | 5 | 5 | 0 | 1 | 23 |
| 1800s | 12 | 11 | 6 | 6 | 0 | 0 | 35 |
| 1810s | 14 | 5 | 7 | 6 | 0 | 2 | 34 |
| 1820s | 17 | 9 | 9 | 3 | 0 | 4 | 42 |

*Source*: Campton overseers' accounts, BLARS, P18/12/1–2; Shefford overseers' accounts, X514/1–3, P70/12/1–2; Campton and Shefford family reconstitution.

pauper biographies reveal that both the elderly and lone parents received relatively generous weekly pensions, that they were long-term recipients and that they were over-represented in the relief rolls. There was indeed a rise in the number of couple-headed families receiving weekly relief in the 1790s and 1800s and after 1815; however, relief was targeted, restricted to specific years and was less 'generous' than that given to the aged and to lone mothers. The decadal figures of numbers of families (*see* table 6) make families appear more prominent than they were; in fact relief was limited in duration and was largely restricted to the years 1799–1802 and 1815–22. In terms of regular weekly pensions, couple-headed families received only half the proportions of total resources that their numbers warranted.[66] Over the

---

49; lone men and women, 23; couples, 1; orphans, 7 (total 157); Shefford: 'elderly', 33; families, 21; lone parents, 18; lone men and women, 13; couples, 0; orphans, 6 (total 91). For more on the methodology see Williams, 'Poor relief', 499–500.
[66] Ibid. A more detailed version of this analysis appears in idem, 'Malthus'.

entire period there were only twenty-four clear cases of pensions to families in Campton (1767–1834) and twenty-one in Shefford (1794–1828).[67] The vast majority of families received relief only after 1790; in the final three decades of the eighteenth century, before the crisis years of the turn of the century, only four families received a pension. Relief was usually for only specific and limited periods, such as the harvest crises of the period 1799–1802 and the post-war years; although in Shefford, there was more of a steady trickle of family-pensioners after 1811.

The crisis at the turn of the century was particularly severe. Scarcity was such that at the Bedfordshire quarter sessions in 1795 a general order was published to the effect that 'The Justices having taken into their consideration the present scarcity of bread-corn do ... prohibit every baker ... from making [or] selling ... any sort of bread of a superior quality to the standard wheaten bread.'[68] In January 1800 the magistrates for both the county and the borough of Bedford reissued that prohibition. In September of the same year, magistrates made three resolutions: that the free supply of markets was the best way to relieve distress, that overseers should give extraordinary relief to all their labouring poor in proportion to the size of their families (scaled relief similar to the Speenhamland system), and that the overseers should provide substitutes for bread corn to be retailed to the poor at modest prices.[69] The hundreds of Manshead and Redbournestoke, Flitt and Clifton (containing Campton and Shefford), Biggleswade and Wixamtree reported in 1801 that substitutes were generally given. The three remaining hundreds in the north of the county replied that relief was partly in kind and beef, potatoes and rice were commonly given.[70]

Between December 1799 and March 1802 Campton paid pensions which conform to 'classic' child allowances in that they were paid on a scale according to the number of children in a family and were adjusted every few months in line with volatile prices. They began at the second child, with 6d. per child per family per week. Payments were flexible and did not follow the scale slavishly, and allowances were tailor-made for each family (running for limited periods between seven and twenty-eight months). Pensions were restricted to very large families only.[71] At the same time, the crisis period brought many others on to the relief rolls, not just families, and this was the period when the largest proportion of the population was relieved.[72] The 1790s were years of great hardship as shown by the deficits recorded in the budgets of labouring households collected by both David Davies and

---

[67] Idem, 'Malthus', tables 1 and 2 at pp. 69–70.
[68] This is quoted in Emmison, *Eaton Socon*, 56.
[69] Ibid. 57–8.
[70] Ibid. 58–9.
[71] Williams, 'Malthus', tables 1–5 at pp. 69–73.
[72] Idem, 'Poor relief', table 1 at pp. 496, 498.

Frederick Eden.[73] Although all the payments were made for a set number of children, in fact most of these couples had more children than the number specified in the overseers' accounts, for whom they were not receiving an allowance. In addition, many of these families went on to have further children but did not require additional parish assistance (only six required further relief in Campton). After 1802 the parish ceased paying scaled allowances.

After 1802 only 10–20 per cent of families in Campton required pensions and the figure was half that in Shefford. During 1824 and 1832 – the years of the parliamentary questionnaires – just three families and two families respectively were receiving relief. Furthermore, the real value of pensions was only ever supplementary, and worth far more in 1795, at 29 per cent on average of their neighbours' earnings, than in 1832, at just 17 per cent.[74] Only a handful of families ever received payments so high that the parish must have been their main source of income. In addition, there were important urban–rural differences between Campton and Shefford: Shefford relieved fewer families, less generously. Such detail can only be established from the careful construction of pauper biographies.

This is powerful evidence to counter Malthus's argument that poor relief could be responsible for encouraging early and improvident marriages amongst the poor who could least afford large families. The question of the poor laws and their operation was central to Malthus's writings on the interrelationship between population and resources. His preferred option was the gradual abolition of the poor laws, although his view was tempered in different editions of his *Essay on population*. Malthus argued that relief by a scale which increased in monetary value upon marriage and with the addition of each child was, 'a direct, constant, and systemical encouragement to marriage before removing from each individual that heavy responsibility which he would incur by the laws of nature for bringing human beings into the world which he could not support'.[75] Such a mechanism would lead to a situation in which poor relief would, paradoxically, create more of the poor it was seeking to maintain. Malthus's influence on contemporary debates was profound; it has been argued that he formulated the terms of discourse on the subject of poverty for half a century and his views pervade the *Poor law report* of 1834.[76] His influence is evident in the material presented by Mr Okeden, Assistant Commissioner for Oxfordshire, in his own report. He argued that, 'a series of early marriages has ensued, for the avowed purpose

---

[73] T. Sokoll, 'Early attempts at accounting the unaccountable: Davies, and Eden's budgets of agricultural labouring families in late eighteenth–century England', in T. Pierenkemper (ed.), *Zur Ökonomik des privaten Houshalts, Haushaltsnechnungen als quellen historicher wirtschaftsund Sozialforschung*, Frankfurt–New York 1991, 34–58; Armstrong, *Farmworkers*, 41–3.
[74] Williams, 'Poor relief', 506, 510, and 'Malthus', 76–8.
[75] T. R. Malthus, *Essay on population*, London 1798, 83; 9th edn, London 1888, 415.
[76] E. A. Wrigley and D. Souden, 'Introduction', to *The works of Thomas Robert Malthus, IV: Essays on population*, ed. E. A. Wrigley and D. Souden, London 1986, 7–9 at p. 7.

of increasing income, until a generation of superfluous labourers has risen up, all demanding work, or pay from the scale. If this system continues, in ten years more another generation will be hastening on'.[77] Samuel Whitbread was one of very few critics of Malthus.

Historians have debated the validity of Malthus's views using data from contemporary parliamentary papers and birth rates. The most recent contributor, George Boyer, is adamant that 'Malthus was right'.[78] Analyses of the *Select committee on labourers' wages* of 1824 and the 'Rural queries' collected in 1832 suggest that in 1824 at least three-quarters of parishes were giving child allowances, while in 1832 the figure had fallen to 50 per cent. Boyer's calculations reveal that child allowances were particularly widespread in the grain-producing south-east, where more than 90 per cent of parishes used child allowances in 1824, declining to 80 per cent in 1832. Boyer claims to have established a strong correlation between parishes which allocated child allowances at the third child and higher birth rates, calculating that parishes that began allowances at three children experienced birth rates 25 per cent greater than those parishes without allowances.[79]

There are substantial problems with these sources, however, which apply not only to any attempt to establish the prevalence of child allowances but also to the extent of the adoption of allowances-in-aid-of-wages. Mark Blaug used the 1824 data to draw his map of 'Speenhamland counties' and compared this with the data from 1832.[80] The 1824 *Return* failed to indicate the proportion of parishes per county responding to the questionnaire and their relative populations and it is therefore impossible to establish whether the replies constitute anything like a representative sample and makes any assessment of the extent of the allowance system and child allowances difficult.[81] Answers to the questionnaire were published under broad headings, usually 'hundreds' and 'districts', without stating which parishes within these localities had returned their answers. Some hundreds and districts were made up of many parishes and it is extremely unlikely that all parishes within them responded. In Bedfordshire, for instance, just six replies were returned. One was from 'Bedford Town', which incorporated five parishes, but whether the response represented the situation in all five parishes was not specified. Another reply came from the 'Northern District', but again it is not at all clear how many parishes this 'district' included, but it could have been up to three hundreds and anywhere between fourteen and forty parishes. Other responses came from Biggleswade (one parish), Eversholt (one parish), Luton (one parish) and St Neots (one parish). This list might seem representative,

---

[77] *Poor law report*, 73.
[78] Boyer, *Economic history*, 150 and ch. v.
[79] Ibid. ch. v.
[80] Blaug, 'Myth of the old poor law', 158, and 'Poor law reexamined'.
[81] Idem, 'Myth of the old poor law', 235.

since the parishes were drawn from north, east, south, and central Bedfordshire, but in fact they were all towns except for Eversholt, which was the only small rural parish. Indeed, these parishes only accounted for between one-fifth and one-third of the county's population.[82] Furthermore, even for these six places the answers are contradictory and confusing. The wording of the 1824 and 1832 questionnaires is problematic and encouraged respondents to answer positively.[83] The 1824 select committee asked the question: 'Do any labourers in your District employed by the Farmers receive either the whole or any part of the Wages of their Labour out of the Poor Rates?' The use of the word 'any' would allow an area to answer positively while perhaps making only negligible or sporadic use of these supplements. Indeed, Bedfordshire is one of Blaug's second most heavily shaded counties, but there were only six replies to the questionnaire and only three of these were, in fact, positive, with another reply of 'Very few instances'.

The relevant question posed in the 'Rural queries' of 1832 asked 'Have you any, and how many, able-bodied Labourers in the Employment of Individuals receiving Allowance or regular Relief from your Parish on their own Account, or on that of their families; and if on account of their Families, at what Number of Children does it begin?'[84] This question confused subsidising wages with the provision of child allowances and some parishes also included the unemployed in their responses. For instance, one parish in Bedfordshire answered, 'Allowance often made out of the Poor Book when the number of children exceeds three. Sometimes idle able-bodied men are let at a low rate of wages to the farmers, and the deficiency paid out of the Poor Book.'[85] By confusing so many parish schemes, the Commissioners made positive responses almost inevitable. The 'Rural queries' suffer from similar problems of representativeness, since replies were returned for only 10 per cent of the 15,000 parishes in England and Wales, accounting for just twenty per cent of the population.[86] In the case of Bedfordshire, just sixteen parishes responded out of 141, which represents 12 per cent of rural parishes and 12 per cent of the population.[87]

---

[82] *Abstract return on practice of paying wages of labour out of poor rates*, PP 1825, xix.363 C.299, 2–3; *Abstract of census returns*, 1821.

[83] This could perhaps account for the extremely high level of parishes reporting the allocation of child allowances.

[84] 'Answers to rural queries', q. 24.

[85] Blaug, 'Poor law reexamined', 234.

[86] Ibid. 234–5. For an assessment of the usefulness of the 'Rural queries' as a source on other questions in the questionnaire see also N. Verdon, 'The rural labour market in the early nineteenth century: women's and children's employment, family income, and the 1834 poor law report', *EcHR* lv (2002), 299–323, and A. Howkins and N. Verdon, 'Adaptable and sustainable? Male farm service and the agricultural labour force in midland and southern England, *c.* 1850–1925', *EcHR* lxi (2008), 467–95.

[87] Blaug, 'Poor law reexamined', table 1 at p. 236; Dunkley, *Crisis of the old poor law*, appendix A at p. 183.

Neither Blaug nor Boyer assess whether the parishes giving answers in 1824 and 1832 were the same parishes or even the same types of parish. In Bedfordshire only four parishes *might* have responded to both questionnaires (four parishes responding in 1832 fell within the 'Northern District' of 1824, but they did not necessarily respond in 1824). For Bedfordshire at least, most of the parishes responding to the 'Rural queries' were rural, while those responding in 1824 were urban.

Yet more crucial is the fact that analysis of this evidence has limited much of the discussion to the decades immediately preceding the Poor Law Amendment Act of 1834 and relatively little is known about their prevalence between the 1790s and 1824. There is an assumption in much of the literature that allowances were widespread from the Speenhamland decision of 1795. Peter Dunkley has argued that 1795 'marked a permanent alteration in the pattern of poor relief' and James Huzel argued that, 'By any criteria, the 1790s must be viewed as a turning point, for it was in the critical middle years of this decade that poor relief underwent a major and, in some cases, radical transformation.'[88] Contemporaries, however, were vague on the origins and prevalence of allowances and contemporary comments largely date after 1815.[89] Poynter has drawn attention to the lack of empirical research by historians, stating that 'a great deal more research into local practice, and into what might be called the ecology of the allowance system, is needed before we can be certain how widely such scales and allowances were adopted, and above all how far their use continued after the immediate period of stress'.[90] The evidence for Campton and Shefford reveals that payments to able-bodied heads of families in any form were not continuous between the 1790s and the 1830s. Although magistrates issued orders for scaled relief in the county these scales were abandoned after the crises had passed. Child allowances or allowances-in-aid-of-wages were never a normal method of maintaining labourers. Other local evidence supports the conclusion that allowances were short-term. Mark Neuman's study of sixteen Berkshire parishes found that allowances were sporadic and locally diverse.[91] A number of other local studies also show that allowance schemes were largely temporary expedients in response to high prices, extremely localised at the parish level, and were abandoned after the crisis had passed.[92]

---

[88] Dunkley, *Crisis of the old poor law*, 47; Huzel, 'The labourer and the poor law', 773.
[89] J. R. Poynter, *Society and pauperism: English ideas on poor relief, 1795–1834*, London 1969, 76–85.
[90] Ibid, 47.
[91] Neuman, 'Speenhamland in Berkshire', 99, 101–9.
[92] E. M. Hampson, *The treatment of poverty in Cambridgeshire, 1597–1834*, Cambridge 1934; Neuman, 'Speenhamland in Berkshire', and *The Speenhamland county*; Sokoll, *Household and family*. A review of the Speenhamland decision can be found in Aspinall and Smith, *English historical documents*, 414–15.

Furthermore, age at marriage had been falling for a century before 1795. Child allowances were only given to very large families and, as Rowntree identified, it was largeness of family that made one so vulnerable to the second deficit phase of the poverty life-cycle. Families could not have relied upon such allowances. Moreover, it is far more likely that allowances were a necessary response to increases in population which had begun early in the eighteenth century, long before 1795. Average age at first marriage had been falling for men and women in Campton and Shefford since at least 1700.[93]

The increase in pauperism in Campton and Shefford had begun before 1795. Dunkley has argued that, 'prior to this crisis, the parish pension lists were brief and made up chiefly of females, mostly widows, with a smattering of children, invalids, and old men. Then quite suddenly the lists lengthened, and the bulk of the new names were male, a situation that remained common right up to 1834'.[94] This was not true in Campton and Shefford. Expenditure on the poor in Campton had started its upward trend during the late 1770s and 1780s and numbers of both pensioners and occasional recipients had also started to rise in the 1780s. Furthermore, the bulk of the new names added in the overseers' accounts between 1795 and 1834 were not overwhelmingly male, particularly of high-cost pensioners. The 1790s and early 1800s were undoubtedly a very expensive decade with large numbers of poor people requiring relief, but after this particular crisis passed both costs and numbers of paupers declined again before another upward surge after 1815. The situation was far more complex than Dunkley's broad brush picture would suggest.

Parish overseers in Campton and Shefford were far more prepared to support 'broken' families than complete families, primarily those of widows and unmarried mothers, but there were instances of widower-headed families. Broken families were also the most numerous households in receipt of relief in Bolton, Lancashire, in the late seventeenth century.[95] Although lone parents were frequently given slightly lower average pensions in Campton and Shefford than couple-headed families, they were allocated pensions for much longer average durations (4.1 years in Campton, 7.3 years in Shefford), and the pensions of one-third in Campton and 14 per cent in Shefford continued into their old age. Of the unmarried mothers who had their illegitimate children baptised in Campton and Shefford, 44 per cent received poor relief. Snell and Millar have also charted a strong commitment

---

[93] Williams, 'Malthus', table 9 and figure 1 at p. 80; J. P. Huzel, 'Malthus, the poor law, and population in early nineteenth-century England', *EcHR* xxii (1969), 430–52; 'The demographic impact of the old poor law: more reflections on Malthus', *EcHR* xxxiii (1980), 367–81; and 'Parson Malthus and the Pelican Inn protocol: a reply to Professor Levine', *Historical Methods* xvii (1984), 25–7. See p. 109 n. 30 below.
[94] Dunkley, *Crisis of the old poor law*, 47.
[95] Healey, 'Poverty in an industrializing town'.

to lone-parent families under the old poor law in south-eastern rural and market-town parishes. They found that three in ten families with dependent children applying for relief were lone-parent families, and as many as 86 per cent of single parents dependent on poor relief were women.[96]

The elderly were one of the most prominent family categories in Campton and Shefford and it is important to note that they are probably under-recorded since ages could not be ascertained for all pensioners; there is no evidence of age for many of those allocated to the 'lone men and women' categories, but, given Campton and Shefford's commitment to the elderly, it is likely that some of these individuals were elderly. Many other studies have highlighted the prominence of the elderly as recipients under the old poor law.[97] It is in the case of the elderly that changes in 'generosity' can most probably be seen, since many of the elderly poor largely lived off the parish pension. Between the 1760s and the 1820s average pension sums given to Campton's aged poor increased more than three-fold, over and above inflation, and, although there was a slight downturn in the 1830s, these sums remained relatively high compared to falling prices. In Shefford, average pensions also increased over time, but were given in amounts that on average were 6d. less than in Campton. Elderly couples always received higher mean pensions than single elderly men and women.[98] Although a useful tool for comparing relief generosity between groups, average pension sums can disguise the highly tailored nature of relief to individuals and their dependants. This is easiest to see in relation to individuals without dependants. Mary Bricket, for instance, was given 1s. a week between 1768 and her burial in 1781 with some extra cash on odd occasions. In contrast, Elizabeth Bryant's relief rose over time. Her pensions started at 1s. per week in 1776 and continued until 1780 when, for five weeks, she was given 2s., the regular weekly sum falling back again to 1s. 6d. In 1787 her regular pensions sum increased to 2s., then 3s. She was given sugar, ale, butter, gin, oatmeal, ginger, spice and candles in July 1781 and care after a fall in 1787.

Many of the elderly were in receipt of parish pensions for considerable lengths of time. In Campton, 35 per cent of pensions paid in excess of ten years were given to the elderly and the figure was 47 per cent in Shefford. For many, death was the only way off relief.[99] The elderly were over-represented in the relief lists.[100] In 1841 8 per cent of Campton's and 7 per cent of

---

[96] Snell and Millar, 'Lone-parent families', 404–9.
[97] See chapter 4 below.
[98] In Campton elderly couple's pensions were 1.5 to 2.8 times higher than those given to lone elderly pensioners, while in Shefford they were 0.8 to 1.8 higher.
[99] See also Wales, 'Poverty, poor relief and the life-cycle', and Ottaway, 'Providing for the elderly'.
[100] This was also the case in Aldenham, Hertfordshire, where the elderly accounted for around 20% of household heads but almost 60% of pensioners in the seventeenth century: Newman Brown, 'The receipt of poor relief', 412.

Shefford's populations were aged sixty or over, while the elderly made up 48 per cent of pensioners in the rural community (1830–4) and 40 per cent in the market town (1820s). Eden had found in the 1790s that the proportion of the elderly on relief was higher in agricultural areas. In the Bedfordshire parish of Humbershoe the figure was 45.6 per cent.[101] The data provides compelling evidence of a strong commitment by the parish overseers of Campton and Shefford to the aged poor. As has been observed by Susannah Ottaway, 'There was a long tradition from late Medieval through early modern times, of considering the aged poor as among those "impotent" poor most deserving of charity or poor relief.' It also appears that Campton and Shefford continued to relieve the elderly and threw the welfare safety net more widely in order to encompass other needy groups.[102]

In assessing the efficacy of relief it is important to estimate the value of poor relief to recipients and their families in their local context. The best comparison is of pension sums to the household budgets of labouring families in nearby Bedfordshire parishes, which record the earnings of all members of the household.[103] Such calculations reveal that pensions accounted for 10–20 per cent of the household incomes of neighbouring labouring families in Campton in 1795 and 15–30 per cent in Shefford in the same year, varying by family type. In 1830s Campton pensions were worth 12–23 per cent of labouring incomes. These calculations do not take into account the age structure and gender composition of families, and, if the proportion pensions accounted for in terms of adult equivalents is estimated, then pensions appear more generous. The results indicate that the elderly (lone and couples) received the highest value pensions at between 46 and 62 per cent of the adult-equivalent income of labouring households. Lone men and women received less than the aged poor, at between 28 and 45 per cent; it is likely that many of these pensioners were not yet infirm and were possibly still earning something. Pensions to families were only ever supplementary, and worth far more in 1795 (29 per cent) than in 1832 (17 per cent). As might be expected pensions to families with children headed by a widow, deserted wife or widower (26–37 per cent) were more valuable than those paid to couple-headed families, but it is likely that sums were supplementary because children were earning. This suggests that there had been a degree of continuity in the relief of families since the seventeenth century.[104]

---

[101] This is cited in Ottaway, *Decline of life*, 183–9.
[102] Ibid. 176–7.
[103] On sources and methodology see further Williams, 'Poor relief', 506–13.
[104] Hindle, *On the parish?*, 274; Wales, 'Poverty, poor relief and the life-cycle', 364–5; Slack, *English poor law*, 12, and *Poverty and policy*, 27–8; Newman Brown, 'Receipt of poor relief', 411; Hampson, *Poverty in Cambridgeshire*, 178–9.

## The New Poor Law

A relatively generous system of poor relief was operating in Campton and Shefford in the later eighteenth and early nineteenth centuries, in line with much of the south and east of England, although there are indications of a tightening up on relief after the 1810s. It is important to recognise and analyse these changes over time, but such fluctuations in the value of relief up to 1834 are less significant when compared with what happened afterwards. Poor relief expenditure in Bedfordshire was cut drastically within just two years, both in absolute terms and *per capita* sums, halving between the late 1820s and the late 1830s (*see* figures 8 and 9). Among English counties Bedfordshire dropped from fourth to eleventh place (and to nineteenth by 1847) in *per capita* spending and lower levels of spending were maintained than in many other counties.[105] William Apfel and Peter Dunkley argue that the new law was implemented in the county with 'speed and relative thoroughness'.[106] This sparked serious outbreaks of violence and intimidation in the county in the 1830s and 1840s, the most serious rioting occurring at Ampthill in 1835 when the union workhouse was attacked by labourers from the neighbouring parishes. When James Turner investigated conditions in the county on behalf of the Anti-Poor Law campaign, he commented that, 'the ill feeling between the labouring people and those above them is very bad ... more than is generally imagined, much more than I have witnessed in the north on any occasion'.[107]

The extent to which the reduction was at the expense of able-bodied men is a matter of debate between Apfel and Dunkley and Anne Digby.[108] It is clear that payments for 'insufficiency of earnings' and for 'want of work' did decline, but Digby has argued that New Poor Law Guardians managed to continue to give unemployed labourers outdoor allowances-in-aid-of-wages in the eastern counties by exploiting the loop–hole which allowed for medical relief in cases of sickness or accident.[109] The six counties she analysed included Bedfordshire, along with Essex, Suffolk, Norfolk, Cambridgeshire and Hertfordshire. In the period 1842–6 two out of every three adult able-bodied paupers were receiving outdoor allowances for sickness or accident compared with fewer than one out of two in England and Wales. Apfel and Dunkley concede that the cost of medical relief was relatively high in Bedfordshire, but, they argue, this was not because expenditure on medical relief rose after 1834, but rather that severe cuts in other types of relief to

---

[105] W. Apfel and P. Dunkley, 'English rural society and the New Poor Law: Bedfordshire, 1834–47', *SH* x (1985), 37–68 at pp. 39–40, and n. 7 at p. 40.
[106] Ibid. 48.
[107] Ibid. 53–5; Williams, 'Economy of makeshifts', 21–52; *The Times*, 19 May 1835.
[108] Apfel and Dunkley, 'English rural society', 41–5.
[109] Ibid. 41–8; A. Digby, 'The labour market and the continuity of social policy after 1834', *EcHR* xxviii (1975), 69–83 at pp. 72–3.

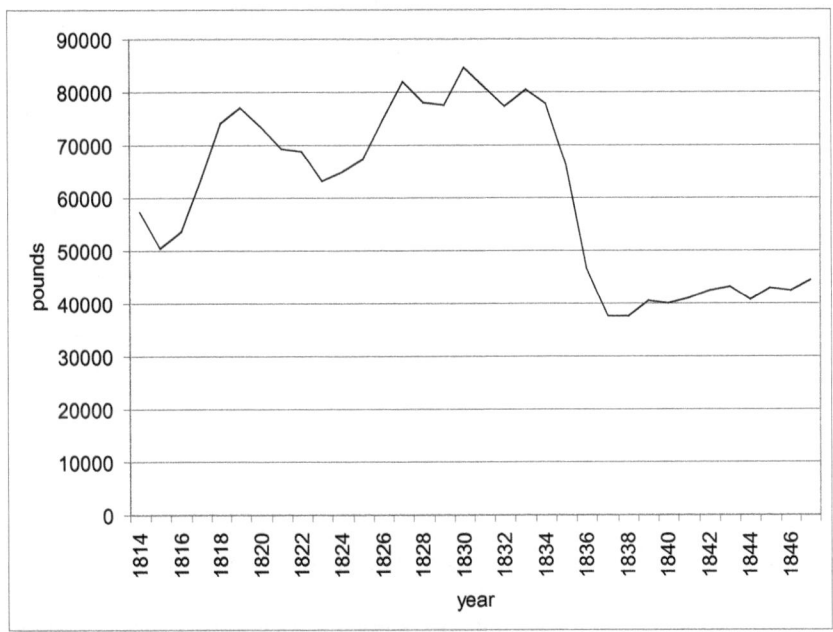

**Figure 8. Poor relief expenditure in Bedfordshire, 1814–47**
Source: Apfel and Dunkley, 'English rural society', 40.

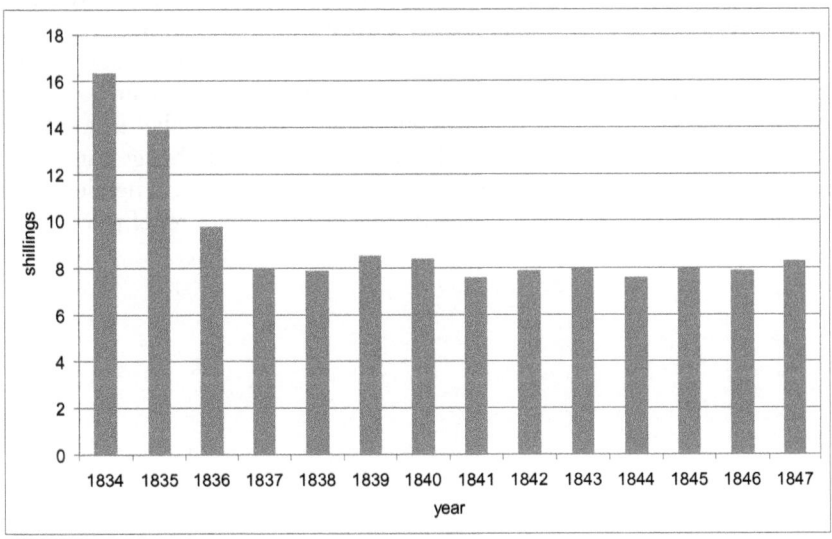

**Figure 9. *Per capita* poor relief spending in Bedfordshire, 1834–47**
Source: Apfel and Dunkley, 'English rural society', 40.

the able-bodied meant that medical relief accounted for a rising proportion of relief, despite remaining steady or perhaps even declining in absolute terms.[110] The numbers of the aged or infirm who were relieved were similar in 1833 and 1836, suggesting that this group – in terms of access to relief – was relatively unaffected.[111] However, in Campton and Shefford allowances to able-bodied men accounted for a relatively small share of total poor law spending and so it is highly probable that the cuts in poor law expenditure after 1834 not only affected able-bodied men but also the pensions given to the aged or infirm. What is beyond dispute is that the situation under the New Poor Law contrasted sharply with that prevailing under the old.

The wide-scale growth of social welfare under the old poor law, particularly in the south and east, was reflected at the local level in Campton and Shefford. The relief lists grew markedly, as did payment sums, and by 1800 provision was extensive. There was a rapid expansion in the numbers of occasional recipients, but the costs of their relief did not rise by the same degree and parish commitment to pensioners remained high in both communities. This was the most valuable form of relief and was frequently topped up further with relief in kind. The elderly benefited the most from this system, followed by lone parents, and, while couple-headed families were relieved in larger numbers than earlier in the eighteenth century, overseers largely restricted relief to periods of economic crisis and such relief was supplementary. Over time the characteristics of the pension pauper host were changing, as the household size of recipients shrank, with fewer families and lone parents relieved as increasing numbers of the elderly, and elderly men in particular, took their place. The whole poor law system was clearly under strain after the end of the Napoleonic Wars, at the local and national level, and the post-war deflation did not result in lower poor law expenditure. Instead, un- and under-employment was widespread in the south and east and was a persistent problem in Campton and Shefford. Relief in kind was a particular casualty of rising costs. However, the greatest change came with the change in the law in 1834, with a halving of relief costs. The New Poor Law must surely be seen as a radical discontinuity in poor relief provision.

---

[110] Apfel and Dunkley, 'English rural society', 47.
[111] Ibid. table 2 at p. 42. Campton and Shefford were in Biggleswade Union. The total number of 'aged and infirm' was 640 in 1833 and 584 in 1836.

# 3

# Paying for Poverty

The relief of poverty at the parish level had to be paid for locally. The Elizabethan statutes of 1598–1601 made provision for the raising of poor rates by overseers of 'every inhabitant and occupier of lands' in the parish and they could distrain the goods of those refusing to pay.[1] Overseers were responsible for estimating local need, the making of the rates and their collection, the distribution of poor relief, and the drawing up of the accounts, which were to be audited by the local magistrate.[2] Overseers had to use their discretion in levying the rates and in the disbursement of poor relief. The acts imply that only a small proportion of parish inhabitants would need relieving and that the rest of the population could be rated, although, in practice, this is not what happened and far fewer inhabitants were actually assessed.[3] The implementation of rating came earlier in towns and was much patchier in rural communities, but may well have been widespread even before the Civil War.[4] There were disputes about who was liable to be rated and about whether liability should be based upon ability to pay, as judges suggested, or the value of land or houses owned or occupied, as came to be the general practice.[5] As Steve Hindle has shown, the setting of the poor rate could be subject to disorder.[6] The operation of the poor law was thus a constant process of negotiation between overseers and inhabitants as ratepayers, as well as between overseers and the parish poor. Indeed, overseers were encouraged to 'endeavour to proportion the rates by the necessities of the poore, and not the poore by the direction of your rates'.[7] Over the seventeenth century there had been a shift from rating parishioners by the yardland to making assessments on the basis of the rental value of the lands and tenements occupied ('pound rates').[8] Such a base for assessment

---

[1] Slack, *English poor law*, 61, and *Poverty and policy*, 174.
[2] Hindle, *On the parish?*, 251; King, *Poverty and welfare*, 20.
[3] Sokoll, *Household and family*, 126.
[4] Slack, *Poverty and policy*, 127–8; Hindle, *On the parish?*, 229–53. See also chapter 1 above.
[5] Slack, *Poverty and policy*, 127.
[6] S. Hindle, 'Exhortation and entitlement: negotiating inequality in English rural communities, 1550–1650', in M. J. Braddick and J. Walter (eds), *Negotiating power in early modern society: order, hierarchy and subordination in early modern Britain and Ireland*, Cambridge 2001, 102–22.
[7] Botelho, *Old age*, 20–1.
[8] Hindle, *On the parish?*, 372; Slack, *Poverty and policy*, 174; E. Cannan, *The history of local rates in England*, 2nd edn, London 1912, 80. The rental value of each property was

## Table 7
### Trends in rate-paying in Shefford, 1803–20

| Financial year | Rate in the £ | Number of assessments per year | Total rate in the £ each year | Number of ratepayers | % of population * | Number of ratepayers exempted or defaulting on one or more assessments |
|---|---|---|---|---|---|---|
| 1803 | 1s. | 3 | 3s. | 73 | 15.4 | – |
| 1804 | 9d. | 6 | 4s. 6d. | 77 | | – |
| 1805 | 6d.–1s. | 4 | 3s. 6d. | 94 | | 17 |
| 1806 | 1s. | 3 | 3s. | 90 | | – |
| 1807 | 6d.–1s. | 3 | 2s. 6d. | 91 | | – |
| 1808 | 6d.–1s. | 3 | 2s. 6d. | 87 | | – |
| 1809 | 1s. | 5 | 5s. | 93 | | 3 |
| 1810 | 1s. | 4 | 4s. | 96 | | 3 |
| 1811 | 1s. | 3 | 3s. | 95 | 17.7 | 1 |
| 1812 | 1s. | 6 | 6s. | 100 | | 2 |
| 1813 | 1s. 6d. | 5 | 4s. 6d. | 106 | | 3 |
| 1814 | 1s. | 5 | 5s. | 114 | | 3 |
| 1815 | 1s. | 4 | 4s. | 117 | | 3 |
| 1816 | 1s. | 4 | 4s. | 118 | | 2 |
| 1817 | – | – | – | – | | – |
| 1818 | – | – | – | – | | – |
| 1819 | 1s. | 4 | 4s. | 115 | | 1 |
| 1820 | 1s. | 4 | 4s. | 128 | 20.7 | 8 |

*Source*: Shefford ratepayers' books, BLARS, P70/11/1–2; *Abstract of census returns*, 1801, 1811, 1821.

\* = Census figures from 1801, 1811 and 1821. There is a gap in the ratepayer books in 1817 and 1818.

did not include profits from the occupation of land, nor rent, salary or profits from moveable property; nevertheless, 'rental value of the property occupied was ... generally adopted as a basis for estimating the relative ability of the ratepayers'.[9] Paul Slack suggests that there was an increase in the number of ratepayers over the second half of the seventeenth century.[10]

## Rating and ratepayers

Variations in the pattern of settlement, the structure of property-holding and wealth led to considerable variations in the social spread of the liability for rates. There were substantial local variations in the scale of pauperism and the ability to pay poor rates.[11] Historians still know very little about ratepaying, the proportion of the parish paying the rate, the wealth distribution of ratepayers and their familial characteristics. The ratepayer books, which survive for Shefford for the period 1803–20 and have been analysed and linked to the family reconstitution in order to produce ratepayer biographies,[12] can be used to comment upon all of these issues.

The national average for poor rates in England in the period 1813–15 was 3s. 2d. Bedfordshire, at 4s. 4¼d., was 35.5 per cent greater than the national average, but was on a par with counties with similar characteristics, such as Essex and Suffolk, and just behind Berkshire, Buckinghamshire and Kent.[13] It appears that Shefford's relative lack of generosity in relief giving was in large part due to less wealth in the town and a small rate base. In 1803 Shefford's rate (5s.) was more than twice that of Campton's (2s. 3d.) and higher than the county average of 3s. 9¼d. Of the ten parishes/townships in Clifton Hundred, only two were paying (slightly) higher rates and only one-fifth of all Bedfordshire parishes were paying the same rate or higher.[14] In 1815 the estimate of the annual value of real property in Shefford was £868; very low in comparison with other Bedfordshire parishes and just over half that of Campton at £1,526.[15] Each assessment in Shefford was between 6d. and 1s., but the number of assessments made varied from year to year from three to six (see table 7). Six rates were collected in 1804 and 1812 and five in 1809 and 1814; these were either relatively high spending years or followed a higher spending year. However, after 1815, despite poor relief expenditure continuing to climb, only four rates a year were collected.

---

used in Ardleigh in 1796 and Braintree in 1821 in Essex: Sokoll, *Household and family*, 124–30, 216–20.
[9] Cannan, *History of local rates*, 80–1.
[10] Slack, *Poverty and policy*, 178.
[11] Hindle, *On the parish?*, 285, 376.
[12] There is a short gap in the ratepayer books between 1817 and 1819.
[13] *Abstract of the poor*, 1818, 627–30; Eastwood, *Governing rural England*, 145.
[14] *Abstract of the poor*, 1803–4, 4–11.
[15] *Abstract of the poor*, 1818, 2.

### Table 8
### Proportion of ratepayers, non-ratepayers and paupers in Shefford, 1803–20

| Census date and population | | Named ratepayers (number) | % population | All ratepayers and their dependants (% of population) | All paupers and their dependants (% of population) | Remaining population = non-ratepayers |
|---|---|---|---|---|---|---|
| 1801/3* | 474 | 73 | 15.4 | 29.3 | 17.3 | 53.4 |
| 1811 | 536 | 95 | 17.7 | 33.7 | 12.7 | 53.6 |
| 1820/1* | 618 | 128 | 20.6 | 39.0 | 17.0 | 44.0 |

*Source: Abstract of census returns*, 1801, 1811, 1821; Shefford ratepayers' books, BLARS, P70/11/1–2; Campton and Shefford family reconstitution.

\* = 1801 census figures, 1803 ratepayer books; 1821 census figures, 1820 ratepayer books. To account for hidden dependants a multiplier of 1.9 was used for the families of ratepayers and paupers.

In Shefford, as in many other places, the poor rate was levied on immovable property within the parish, which in the market town comprised lands, cottages, gardens, shops and other buildings, and included a bowling green, a brew-house and malting, a school, the George Inn, the parish houses, and the feoffment cottages, garden and shop. Rates were levied on tenants as well as owners. The rental value of each property was used as the rateable value and many ratepayers paid the rate on more than one property. Assessments were sensitive to the changing value of land and property and the vestry reviewed individual assessments. New buildings were also allocated a value.[16] The rates were presented each year to Samuel Whitbread, as justice of the peace.[17] Paying poor rates conferred settlement.[18]

The number of ratepayers in the market town increased over time, over and above the rate of population growth: in 1803 around 15 per cent of Shefford inhabitants were assessed for the rates, the figure was 18 per cent by 1811 and by 1820 nearly 21 per cent of inhabitants were rated (*see* tables 8 and 9). Vestry policy was to rate an increasing proportion of people as relief expenditure continued to rocket, rather than routinely to increase the

---

[16] Shefford vestry minutes, BLARS, P70/8/1, entries for 27 Sept. 1809, and 29 Mar. 1821.
[17] *Whitbread's notebooks*, entries 54, 393, 549, 924.
[18] Ibid. entries 419, 1032. See also N. Landau, 'The eighteenth-century context of the laws of settlement', *C&C* vi (1991), 417–39 at p. 432 n. 8. She argues that there was no need for overseers to rate someone if they did not want to confer settlement. After 1795 ratepaying did not confer settlement unless attached to £10 tenement rental: Snell, 'Pauper settlement', 411 n.104.

rate. Of course these figures are a proportion of the total population and are not of households. If the figures are multiplied by 1.9 to take account of dependants, then between 30 and 40 per cent of Shefford's residents might have been in ratepayers' families (see table 8). A comparison can then be drawn with the proportion of paupers' families, who always accounted for a far smaller percentage at 12–17 per cent.[19] What is most noteworthy from these figures is the remaining proportion of the population who were neither ratepayers nor paupers – the 'middling ground' – who could account for more than half of the population. This indicates that a significant proportion of the population was too 'poor' to pay the poor rates, but was not poor enough (or recognised as such) to be in receipt of poor relief. The actual number of ratepayers was a long way from the majority envisaged in the Elizabethan statutes.[20] What these figures also reveal is an increase in the ratepayer base over time.

Comparative figures exist primarily for the seventeenth century, with a few studies for the later eighteenth and early nineteenth centuries. For the seventeenth century Paul Slack estimates that between one-third and two-thirds of householders were paying the rates in different places. In some towns around half of all householders were being rated by 1700 which, he suggests, indicates that effective ceilings were reached quite early.[21] In urban Boroughside, London, up to one-third of inhabitants were rated, while in twelve rural north Norfolk parishes an average of 38.3 per cent of adults contributed to the parish rates, varying widely from 12.9 per cent to 60 per cent. In two Warwickshire parishes the proportion of households contributing was 31 per cent and 38 per cent and in Aldenham, Hertfordshire, 45 per cent of households were ratepayers.[22] Estimates of those who were neither assessed nor relieved fall between 16.9 per cent and 39.1 per cent in Aldenham during the seventeenth century and 30 per cent in Bristol.[23] Other studies from the late sixteenth and early seventeenth century reveal that between 60 per cent and 80 per cent of households were able to pay the rate; 20–30 per cent were unable to pay the rate but were self-supporting; 6–6.5 per cent were 'poor' but not given aid; and 2–14 per cent were give

---

[19] The figures for ratepayers needs to be handled with caution since a small number of ratepayers might have held land in the parish or rented property conferring rate responsibilities and yet lived outside the town (and they are not identifiable from the ratepayer books). Sokoll is in the fortunate position of being able to identify such 'outsettlers'. He calculates that they accounted for 11% of the rateable value of Ardleigh in 1796: Household and family, 126 n. 5. See also Slack, Poverty and policy, 174, and Snell 'Pauper settlement', 400.
[20] This is also observed by Sokoll for Ardleigh: Household and family, 126.
[21] Slack, English poor law, 34, 178.
[22] Idem, Poverty and policy, 178; J. Boulton, Neighbourhood and society: a London suburb in the seventeenth century, Cambridge 1987, 106–19; Hindle, On the parish?, 286–7, 376.
[23] Newman Brown, 'The receipt of poor relief', table 12.2 at p. 410; Boulton, Neighbourhood and society, 106–19; Slack, Poverty and policy, 178.

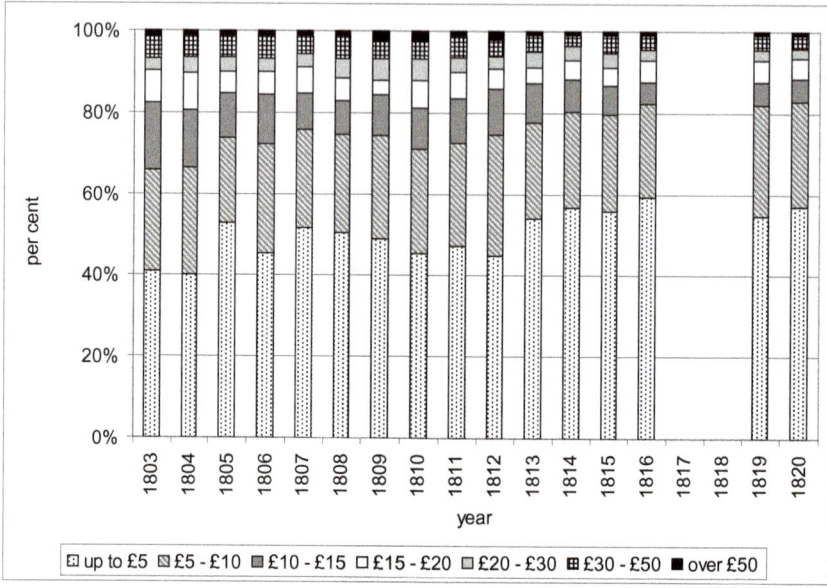

Figure 10. Rental values of ratepayers in Shefford, 1803–20

poor relief.[24] These figures underline that there was a substantial 'middling' group of householders who did not contribute to local taxation but who were earning enough to maintain their households without parish assistance.[25] In York after 1652 rising expenditure was met by extending the tax base rather than by increasing the average rate.[26] Some towns were better able to cope with growing relief expenditure than others: in parts of London and Exeter it was possible to rate many more householders than could be assessed in York, Bristol or Norwich.[27]

For the later eighteenth and early nineteenth century the research of Thomas Sokoll and Anthea Newman provides the most appropriate comparisons. Sokoll found that in Ardleigh, Essex, in 1796, only a quarter of households paid poor rates and that they supported the bottom 40 per cent of the population. Those in the middle, neither contributing nor drawing from parish funds, comprised the remaining third of households.[28] In east Kent Newman found that in 1801 more than half of all households was not rated: the exact figures are 58 per cent in Chislet, 56 per cent in Eastry and 56 per cent in Ash-next-Sandwich.[29]

[24] Fideler, *Social welfare*, 113.
[25] Boulton, *Neighbourhood and society*, 106–19.
[26] Slack, *Poverty and policy*, 176.
[27] Ibid. 181.
[28] Sokoll, *Household and family*, 126.
[29] This is cited in Landau, 'Laws of settlement', 418.

Not only did Shefford's parochial officials rate greater numbers of people, but they also increasingly rated lower down the social scale (*see* figure 10). The proportion assessed at between 5s. and £5 rose from 40 per cent to just under 60 per cent. The social distance between paupers and ratepayers was narrowing. Those in the next tax bracket in Shefford – paying £5 to £10 – kept steady at 20–30 per cent of ratepayers, but those in the tax bracket £10–£15 paid proportionately less over the period: falling from over 16 per cent to 6 per cent. However, those assessed at the top end – £20–£50 – fell less substantially, from 10–12 per cent to 7 per cent. Thus, there was both a core elite group at the top paying a large section of the rate, while at the same time there was a longer tail of poorer ratepayers at the other end of the spectrum. The ratepaying base extended to meet the doubling of poor relief expenditure between 1803 and 1820, from £156 to £308. The number of pensioners whom ratepayers were supporting grew only slowly but the number of occasional recipients increased faster. In 1803 seventy-three ratepayers supported fifteen pensioners and eleven occasional beneficiaries; in 1810 ninety-six ratepayers supported twenty pensioners and twenty-one occasionals; and in 1820 127 ratepayers supported twenty-four pensioners and thirty-three occasionals.

According to Boyer, in general the annual rateable value usually exceeded a minimum level, usually of £1 or £5.[30] In this particular market town rating began at £1 10s. in 1803 and 1804, but from 1805 the tax threshold fell to just 5s., to incorporate just one ratepayer – Richard Thompson, assessed for his garden (*see* figure 11). The fastest growing group valued at under £5 were those in the £2–£2 10s. band. Although all the respondents in the Bedfordshire replies to the 1832 'Rural queries' (not including Shefford) stated that cottagers were exempt from paying the poor rate, in Shefford clearly they were not.[31] However, after 1795 these ratepayers did not gain settlement in Shefford from paying the rates, since they had to rent a £10 tenement in order to qualify.[32] The wealth spectrum of ratepaying in the market town can be compared with those of larger urban centres, such as Shrewsbury, Oxford and York in the slightly earlier period 1740–80.[33] Ratepayers assessed at between £1 and £5 accounted for widely varying proportions: almost 70 per cent in St Mary, Shrewsbury, around 16 per cent in St Martin, Oxford. Few were valued at over £21. In Shefford between 7 per cent and 10 per cent were valued at this higher level, but only the two parishes in the urban sample of Holy Cross, Shrewsbury and St Martin, Oxford were so valued.

---

[30] Boyer, *Economic history*, 95. Tomkins's figures start at £1: *Experience of urban poverty*, 26. Newman Brown has a category of 'less than £2' rateable value: 'Poor relief and family situation', table 12.1 at p. 409.
[31] 'Rural queries', pt I.
[32] Snell, 'Pauper settlement', 411 n. 104.
[33] Tomkins, *Experience of urban poverty*, 24–8.

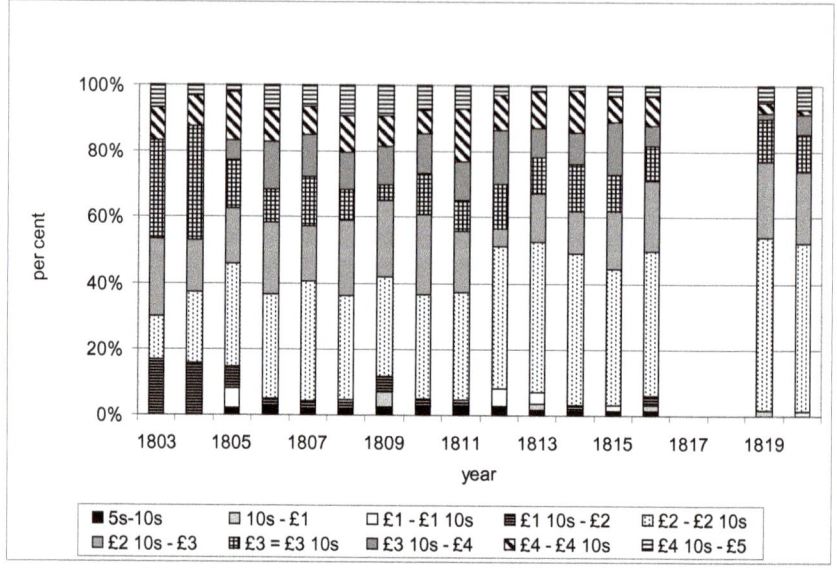

Figure 11. Rental values under £5 of ratepayers in Shefford, 1803–20

As the parish rated further down the social scale, some poorer ratepayers began to default or were exempted from paying the rates, for odd payments if not altogether. From 1809 there were ratepayers in every year whose names appeared in the rate books but who actually paid nothing and they accounted for up to 7.8 per cent of ratepayers (*see* table 7).[34] In Essex there are thirty-one pauper letters relating to the inability to pay arrears in poor rates and requesting assistance from the home parish.[35] The opinion of the parliamentary committee reporting in 1812–13 was that such a system was open to abuse and that decisions on individuals' ability to pay the poor rate should be made by justices.[36] Shefford ratepayers also questioned the fairness of rate assessments. An appeal was lodged at quarter sessions by Joseph Ibbs,

---

[34] Regarding those exempted figure 10 and table 7 are not comparable. The figures in the figure are average payments per ratepayer per year, while the table shows the numbers of those exempted or defaulting on one or more assessments. Thus the figure shows only the proportion in each year listed as a ratepayer but actually paying nothing on average in that year. The table, since it gives the number of those exempted or defaulting from one or more payments, includes all those who missed at least one payment but who might have paid later in the year.

[35] For a discussion of pauper letters see pp. 86–91 below. See Sokoll, *Essex pauper letters*, letters 161, 269, 296, 317, 391, 440, 442, 449, 459, 463, 466, 467, 468, 473, 474, 492, 518, 521, 525, 531, 536, 544, 545, 549, 551, 557, 558, 571, 572, 582, 585. They all date after 1824.

[36] *Select committee on local acts for building houses for poor, or for better collection of poor rates*, PP 1812–13, iii. 463 C.113, 5–6.

Stephen Whitbread and Henry Stonebridge on 4 July 1805 against their poor rate assessments: 'Because the said Levy Rate or Assessment is not a fair and equal levy Rate or Assessment upon all and every the Inhabitants and Occupiers of Messuages Lands Tenements tythes and Hereditaments in the Hamlet Township or parish of Shefford'. They claimed that they were overrated while others – John Godfrey, William Walker and Joseph Weston – were underrated and still others were not rated at all: 'Samuel Hebden and William Seymour are not rated and not divers other occupiers of Messuages Lands Tenements or Hereditaments ... are not rated or assessed.'[37] However, quarter sessions did not find in their favour and ordered that 'the said Rate be confirmed' and they continued to be levied.[38] Other Bedfordshire ratepayers appealed to petty or quarter sessions.[39] William King, a Clophill schoolmaster, considered that he had been wrongly assessed for the poor rate and complained to the justice Samuel Whitbread, who told him that 'if he thinks himself aggrieved he must refuse to pay, and the overseers will summon & bring the matter to issue'.[40]

Contemporaries commented negatively upon the increasing propensity to rate the poor. Arthur Young wrote in 1801 that the practice was 'abominable'.[41] At the national level, as MP for Bedford Borough, Samuel Whitbread sought in his abortive bill of 1806 to exempt cottagers whose annual value was less than £5. However, he also sought to increase the power of the largest property-owners by giving them between two and four votes at vestry meetings, depending upon the amount at which they were assessed. He complained that vestry meetings tended to be 'disorderly and tumultuous' affairs where the poorest ratepayers decided how to spend the money raised by the wealthiest proprietors. William Cobbett defended small ratepayers, arguing that the real burden actually fell on them.[42] The 1818 select committee discussed the rating of lower value property and noted that even labourers sometimes had to pay poor rates, many of them worse off than those receiving relief. John Clare in 'The parish: a satire' waxed lyrical on the parish overseer, '[C]arrying the parish book from door to door, Claiming fresh taxes from the needy poor.'[43] While the rating of poorer ratepayers might be expected to have had an impact on the politics of the parish – Whitbread's 'disorderly and tumultuous' affairs – the power of small ratepayers was circumscribed by the Sturges Bourne Act of 1818, which gave

---

[37] Quarter sessions records, BLARS, QSR/19/1805/13, entry for 4 July 1805; quarter sessions minutes, QSM 22/1805, 85.
[38] Quarter session minutes, ibid. QSM 22/1805, 85; Shefford ratepayer books, P70/11/1–2.
[39] Quarter sessions minutes, QSM 19/1792–6, 24, 47, 59, and other appeals alongside Ibbs, Whitbread and Stonebridge in QSR/19/1805.
[40] *Whitbread's notebooks*, entry 300.
[41] Eastwood, *Governing rural England*, 125–6.
[42] Ibid.
[43] This is cited in Snell, *Annals of the labouring poor*, 109–10.

the more substantial ratepayers additional votes in the vestry for every £25 of rateable value up to a maximum of six votes.[44]

For some, ratepaying must have continued throughout their adult lives, and the ratepayer books do reflect this, but for many others ratepayers in Shefford the period for which they were assessed was fairly short. Of Shefford's ratepayers 39 per cent were assessed for just one or two years, with a further 32 per cent assessed for between three and nine years. Only 10 per cent were assessed for the whole period for which the rates are extant (1803–20): this was the core of long-term ratepayers. The period for which the rates survive is problematic in the calculation of ratepaying durations, because ratepayers already paying in 1803 and paying during 1820 might also have had longer ratepaying careers either side of these dates (and hence the records truncate their ratepaying careers), and knowledge of their ratepaying might have increased the proportion of long-term, core ratepayers. Nevertheless, that so many ratepayers were assessed for relatively short periods of time is significant and points towards a high rate of mobility into and out of the parish and/or a high turnover of the ownership or tenancy of land, shops or houses. In the market town a number of residents were both ratepayers and paupers during their lifetimes. Such findings suggest that status distinctions between ratepayers and relief recipients could be blurred, or that, at least for some, status could change considerably over the life-course.

As might be expected, most ratepayers for whom there is occupational information were from the 'middling sort' (*see* table 9). James Haddow, for instance, a tailor, was assessed up to £5 10s. on his house and shop. Of the professions, there were six apothecaries/surgeons, including the parish medical attendants Dr Gay and Dr Layman (who thus both paid into the poor rate and received their medical contract stipend out of the rates). Just 3.3 per cent of ratepayers were farmers; perhaps this is not so surprising for a market town dominated by 'trade, manufacture and handicrafts' and with a shrinking agricultural sector. Significantly, 34.7 per cent of ratepayers were labourers or servants, reflecting the vestry policy of rating lower down the social scale and confirming the views of the 1818 select committee. In contrast, in Ardleigh, Essex, an agricultural community, ratepayers were largely farmers, followed by a smaller group of tradesmen and craftsmen.[45] It is likely that Campton's ratepayers were far more similar to those in Ardleigh than in Shefford.

In the market town, not all ratepayers were male: 16 per cent (43) of ratepayers were women, described either as 'Widow', 'Mrs', or 'Miss'. Widow Elizabeth Hilliard, for instance, was a ratepayer throughout the period (1803–20) and was assessed on her rented house at a value of £2. The largest

---

[44] Eastwood, *Governing rural England*, 34–5.
[45] Sokoll, *Household and family*, 126–9.

### Table 9
### Occupations of male ratepayers in Shefford, 1803–20

| Occupation | % |
|---|---|
| **Primary** | |
| Farmers | 3.3 |
| Labourers and servants | 34.7 |
| Stewards | 1.7 |
| **Secondary** | |
| Building and construction | 9.9 |
| Clothing and footwear manufacture | 10.7 |
| Manufacture | 2.5 |
| Manufacture of food, drink, meat, fish and poultry | 5.0 |
| Manufacture of iron and steel | 2.5 |
| **Tertiary** | |
| Armed services | 0.8 |
| Dealers | 0.8 |
| Independent | 0.8 |
| Inn-holders | 1.7 |
| Professions | 7.4 |
| Public and government | 1.7 |
| Sellers of food, drink and tobacco | 6.6 |
| Services | 2.5 |
| Small trades | 6.6 |
| Transport | 0.8 |

*Source*: Shefford ratepayers' books, BLARS, P70/11/1–2; Campton and Shefford family reconstitution.

*Notes*: Occupations were given for 121 of the 191 ratepayers who could be linked to the family reconstitution, which gave male occupations at the baptism of children.

ratepayer was a woman – Mrs Endersby – who was valued in 1803 at £88 for her land and malting, almost twice that of the next largest ratepayer, Mr Walker, who was valued at £45. A number of women took on ratepaying responsibilities at their husbands' deaths.

Parish overseers and vestries faced a constant balancing act between the level of need in their communities and the tax burden on local ratepayers. Judgements had to be made on the level of the rate, the number of assessments in any one year, and who to rate, alongside the level and scope of poor relief to recipients. As John Walter has highlighted, parish officers attempted to preclude a vicious spiral by which the burden of poor rates might itself push households from independence into dependency, although the fact that some households in Shefford did default suggests that some might have been on the margins.⁴⁶ The size of the three groups – ratepayers, those neither paying nor receiving, and paupers – all had to be carefully managed. One way to limit parish spending was to circumscribe eligibility to parish assistance through the settlement laws; ratepayers only wished to relieve their own settled poor.

It is not possible to undertake the same detailed analysis for Campton since the ratepayer books no longer survive, but it is likely that ratepaying practices differed in the rural parish. Analysis of the land tax of 1798 reveals that land-owning was far more concentrated in Campton than in Shefford, with twelve proprietors in the former community and thirty-five in the latter, and there were many more tenants in Shefford.⁴⁷ Shefford had a far larger proportion of its inhabitants employed in the secondary sector and it is likely that a larger proportion of rates was imposed upon property other than land. As well as land, cottages, gardens, shops, a bowling green, a brew-house, a malting, a school and a pub were all rated. There was, therefore, a larger pool of potential ratepayers to draw upon in the market town. The concentration of land-ownership (and, to a lesser extent, tenancy) in Campton also suggests tighter control of parish policy by fewer 'principal inhabitants' and substantial tenant farmers than in its neighbouring market town. Shefford was likely to be more representative of other urban centres in the south-east than of all parishes.

## Eligibility and entitlement

Under the old poor law relief was generally restricted to those who had a settlement in the parish. In theory everyone had a place of settlement if born within England and Wales, but not Scotland, but since there were routes to gaining a new place of settlement, the process of establishing where a person's settlement might be at any one time was complicated. A whole legal process had developed following the Settlement Act of 1662, with examination before a magistrate to ascertain the last place of settlement, the procedure of removal, and the issuing of indemnity certificates. Certificates were issued to migrants by their parish of settlement, promising to pay their poor relief if they fell on hard times. According to Keith Snell, the vast majority of certificates were given to men (not women) and he argues that the system of certification was in steep decline after the 1750s.⁴⁸ New places of settlement could be obtained through service, apprenticeship, marriage or ratepaying.⁴⁹ Parishes used the settlement laws to limit the number of

---

⁴⁶ This is cited in Hindle, *On the parish?*, 377.
⁴⁷ Campton land tax, 1798; Shefford land tax, 1798, BLARS. See chapter 1 above.
⁴⁸ Snell, *Parish and belonging*, 98–102.
⁴⁹ For the settlement process see ibid. 85–6, and Fideler, *Social welfare*, 143–6.

chargeable poor. The law was changed in 1795 so that those potentially chargeable could not be removed until they actually were.[50] The documents that this legal process generated means that it is possible to examine the law as it was applied at the local level. The removal process and legal disputes between parishes could prove costly and were paid for from the poor rates. The motivating factor behind removal was that, whatever the legal costs, removal of a chargeable pauper and his/her family could still prove cheaper than relieving them. However, establishing legal settlement could be a contested and protracted process.

Shefford's overseers sought to remove a variety of potentially or actually chargeable paupers – around half were families and a further quarter were female-headed lone parent families – categories of pauper who might prove expensive, particularly the latter.[51] None the less, Shefford had to receive its own paupers from elsewhere if their settlements were proved to be in the parish; one-third of those with removal orders into Shefford were women with children and almost one-fifth were families.[52] Like many parishes, officials in Shefford would go to some lengths in order to establish that a potentially chargeable pauper's settlement was elsewhere: there were disputes with the Bedfordshire parishes of Islington and Shillington and, in another case, the marriage certificate of Frances Woodward was obtained in order to prove that Frances's settlement was at Hitchin, Hertfordshire. In addition, when Frances Elms died while awaiting removal to Southwark, her body was still removed, presumably to be buried at Southwark's expense.[53] There was also a case of disputed settlement between Campton and Shefford. Campton sought to remove Ann Blundell, widow of Henry, and their six children, to which Shefford appealed due to 'nonchargeability'. The legal bill came to £49 1s. 4d. The case reads: 'Mr King being examined it then appeared by his evidence that the relief had been given to Blundell's Wife in her husbands life time and not since his death & that the order was therefore made on wrong Premises and the court quashed it.' Campton took out another order of removal, the overseers 'acting upon it, by conveying away the paupers in pursuance of such order', but Shefford appealed once more.[54] Many settlement disputes came before Samuel Whitbread. His attitude to the non-settled poor in his own parish was to remove them; his recommendation for a man settled in Warden was that 'they should be got rid of out

---

[50] Snell, *Parish and belonging*, 99; Fideler, *Social welfare*, 178.
[51] Shefford settlement papers, BLARS, P70/13/2. Of removals back to Colyton, Devon, between 1762 and 1853 66% were family groups, including female-headed households: Sharpe, *Reproducing Colyton*, 247. Levene also explores the removal of children, some within, and some outside of, families in London: 'Poor families, removals and "nurture" in late old poor law London', *C&C* xxv (2010), 233–62.
[52] Shefford settlement papers, BLARS, P70/13/3.
[53] Ibid. P70/13/2 /5, 16, 19, 17–18.
[54] Settlement papers, solicitor's bill for a removal appeal, Henry and Ann Blundell, 1833, ibid. P18/16/1.

of the parish if possible'.⁵⁵ Such cases illustrate just how important it was to overseers to impose boundaries of entitlement upon 'their' poor and also how blurred such boundaries could be, since a person could gain more than one settlement over their life times, with each dissolving the last. Such cases have implications that go far beyond the economic and the right to relief, since a sense of belonging was tied to the parish and settlement disputes imposed migration upon the poor.⁵⁶

Migration horizons were localised. Most of the settlement cases were within Bedfordshire, with only a small number between Shefford and parishes in Cambridgeshire, Hertfordshire, Buckinghamshire, Middlesex, Huntingdonshire, Northamptonshire, and Surrey.⁵⁷ Indemnity certificates reveal that single men, couples and families all decided to move to Shefford and were indemnified by their parishes of settlement and, again, these are all largely from within the county.⁵⁸ It was usually men who were issued with certificates in Shefford, with the exception of a handful of widows with children, such as Sarah Hillyard and her five children who received a certificate from Meppershall to travel to Shefford in October 1790. In Shefford certification lasted until at least 1790.⁵⁹

However, a substantial number of people did not live in their parish of settlement and they had not acquired a new settlement in their place of residence. A system developed whereby parishes provided relief to the 'non-resident poor' with legal settlements in their parish. Thus, it was possible for paupers living in a parish other than that of their settlement to receive poor relief. The paupers concerned were relieved in the parish in which they resided, on the basis of an informal agreement between the two parishes concerned. The overseers of the 'residence' parish advanced the necessary payments which were then reimbursed by the 'settlement' parish. Under this arrangement, the legal requirements under the settlement laws, according to which a pauper who had become chargeable in another parish was supposed to be 'removed' to his or her place of settlement and then to be relieved there, were in practical terms circumvented.⁶⁰ E. Dawson, vicar of Alford, Lincolnshire, referred to the non-resident poor as 'outeners' or 'absent paupers'.⁶¹ In the industrial parishes in the northern counties support was forthcoming from rural parishes to unemployed labourers during periods of trade depression and it has been described as a 'system of parochially funded labour migration that promoted a work force for the expanding industries',

---

⁵⁵ *Whitbread's notebooks*, entries 232, 237.
⁵⁶ Snell, *Parish and belonging*, ch. i. See also chapter 1 above.
⁵⁷ Shefford settlement papers, BLARS, P70/13/1–3.
⁵⁸ Ibid. P70/13/1.
⁵⁹ Snell, *Parish and belonging*, 98–102.
⁶⁰ Sokoll, *Essex pauper letters*, 10–18; S. King, '"It is impossible for our Vestry to judge his case into perfection from here": managing the distance dimensions of poor relief, 1800–40', *Rural History* xvi (2005), 161–89.
⁶¹ *Poor law report*, 500.

while at the same time it also benefited the rural parishes, who preferred such limited relief payments to the constant burden which returning out-migrants would have imposed in their settlement parish. This meant that poor relief could be kept to a minimum, as a supplement to whatever the pauper might be able to earn, and, moreover, the pauper sojourner might earn a new settlement elsewhere. The system in the north involved regular weekly pensions and other regular benefits.[62]

The extent of the system in the south is less clear. In Devon 'nonresident relief was common but not pervasive', while by the 1820s overseers in all of the large Essex towns were operating non-resident relief schemes, in the belief that by paying for periods of unemployment, paupers who lived elsewhere would stay away and were more likely to find work.[63] No less than a fifth of the paupers chargeable to Braintree, Essex, in 1821 lived elsewhere, not only in the closer vicinity, but also in places like London, Norwich, Leeds and York.[64] The hope of parish officers was that the work opportunities in the new parish would allow them to gain a settlement, so that they would no longer be their responsibility. It was also generally cheaper to relieve someone elsewhere, where they might find work, and avoided the costs of removal and relocation.[65]

Analysis of the overseers' accounts for Campton and Shefford can throw further light on this aspect of poor law provision. Firstly, for the period when both parishes were spending the most on non-resident poor relief, the 1810s, the proportion of paupers who lived outside of the parish can be calculated: 17 per cent in Campton and 19 per cent in Shefford – similar figures to Braintree. It would appear that the *Abstract of the poor* of 1803–4 underestimates the number of non-resident poor. In the 141 parishes in Bedfordshire, there were 761 non-resident recipients. This works out at 5.4 non-resident paupers per parish, although many parishes stated that they had no non-resident poor, while others had very large numbers, such as Potton with 96, Leighton Buzzard with 114, and Hockliffe with 250.[66] Campton and Shefford, however, replied that they had no non-resident poor, although from the overseers' account it is clear that there were a number of non-resident paupers receiving poor relief out of Campton and Shefford's poor rate in 1803–4.

Table 10 shows minimum and maximum figures for the proportion of expenditure allocated to the non-resident poor. The minimum figures cover

---

[62] J. S. Taylor, 'A different kind of Speenhamland: nonresident relief in the industrial revolution', JBS xxx (1991), 183–208 at p. 184, and *Poverty, migration, and settlement in the industrial revolution: sojourners' narratives*, Palo Alto, CA 1989.
[63] Taylor, 'A different kind of Speenhamland', 188; Sharpe, 'The bowels of compation', 88.
[64] Sokoll, *Essex pauper letters*, 140.
[65] See also Boyer, *Economic history*, 258.
[66] *Abstract of the poor*, 1803–4, q. 14 at pp. 4–7.

## Table 10
### Minimum and maximum proportions of annual expenditure to the non-resident poor in Campton and Shefford, 1760s–1830s

|       | Campton % | | Shefford % | |
|-------|------|------|------|------|
|       | min. | max. | min. | max. |
| 1760s | 0.0  | 1.2  |      |      |
| 1770s | 1.8  | 1.9  |      |      |
| 1780s | 1.7  | 1.4  |      |      |
| 1790s | 0.1  | 1.1  | 10.8 | 29.1 |
| 1800s | 13.7 | 16.1 | 6.6  | 23.8 |
| 1810s | 7.6  | 28.6 | 9.6  | 25.4 |
| 1820s | 2.1  | 12.3 | 6.9  | 20.2 |
| 1830s | 4.8  | 20.9 |      |      |

*Source*: Campton overseers' accounts, BLARS, P18/12/1–2, X514/1–3; Shefford overseers' accounts, P70/12/1–2.

only those payments made explicitly to paupers living out of the parish. In 1795, for instance, Shefford's overseer paid £1 2s. 2d. to 'The Overseer of the Parish of Biddenham For James Chapman Wife'. Maximum figures also include payments which are to those probably living outside the parish. Between 1798 and 1805, for instance, Charles Bland's wife was relieved every few months, and it is highly likely that such regular and large lump payments were paid to the overseers of other parishes in which Campton and Shefford's non-resident poor lived.

The maximum figures in table 10 reveal striking differences between the two parishes, and, for Campton, there is startling change over time. In Campton, non-resident relief cost the parish less than 2 per cent of annual expenditure between 1760 and 1799, but after the turn of the century, it accounted for up to 29 per cent, with payments peaking in the 1810s. In Shefford, non-resident relief consistently cost between 20 and 30 per cent. These sums can be compared with those in James Taylor's study of non-resident relief in the industrial north: Lancaster's expenses for its poor living elsewhere were about half the cost of its weekly pension list of paupers living in the city, while in Wakefield, Yorkshire, the proportion of non-resident relief was twice that of pensions.[67] In Campton, the non-resident poor cost less than 5 per cent of the expenses on pensioners between the 1760s and the 1790s; from 1800 the figures were much higher, at 26 per cent in the 1800s, 43 per cent in the 1810s, 19 per cent in the 1820s and 35 per cent in the 1830s. In Shefford, the amount spent on the non-resident poor was always a larger proportion of pension expenses, at 65 per cent in the 1790s,

---

[67] Taylor, 'A different kind of Speenhamland', 194.

### Table 11
### Non-resident pensions as a proportion of total non-resident expenditure in Campton and Shefford, 1760s–1830s

|       | Campton % | Shefford % |
|-------|-----------|------------|
| 1760s |           |            |
| 1770s |           |            |
| 1780s | 11.8      |            |
| 1790s | 40.0      | 37.6       |
| 1800s | 25.3      | 55.3       |
| 1810s | 21.6      | 63.0       |
| 1820s | 2.5       | 47.0       |
| 1830s | 2.3       |            |

*Source*: Campton overseers' accounts, BLARS, P18/12/1–2, X514/1–3; Shefford overseers' accounts, P70/12/1–2.

49 per cent in the 1800s, 46 per cent in the 1810s, and 41 per cent in the 1820s. Thus, in some periods, the amount spent on the non-resident poor in Campton and Shefford was comparable with the high rates of spending on the out-poor in Lancaster, but it was never as high as in Wakefield. It is also possible to compare the Bedfordshire parishes with the north with regard to the proportion the non-resident regular poor made up of pensioners. In Manchester the figure ranged from 8 per cent to 27 per cent.[68] In Campton, the regular non-resident poor represented between just 2 and 16 per cent of pensioners, while in Shefford the proportions were much higher, even higher than Manchester, at between 12.5 and 37.5 per cent.

There is yet another striking disparity between the two parishes: in Campton, most non-resident relief was occasional, except for the 1790s when 40 per cent of such relief took the form of regular pensions, whereas in Shefford pensions were always a much higher proportion of non-resident relief, and reached 63 per cent in the 1810s (*see* table 11). Perhaps the most unexpected finding is that on the whole at least half of non-resident poor relief was occasional. This suggests that it was difficult to secure a regular weekly pension if one was living away from one's settlement parish. This was certainly the case in St Botolph's, Colchester: Pamela Sharpe's examination of the Hall family's correspondence with the overseers reveals that even when a pension had been granted, non-resident pensioners had difficulty in obtaining their regular pay.[69] This surely has implications for Snell's discus-

---

[68] Ibid. 200.
[69] Sharpe, 'The bowels of compation', 91–103.

sion of 'home' and 'belonging'.[70] Although pauper correspondents expressed such sentiments about their parish of settlement, it seems that it could be easier to ignore and put off those who were absent. This was surely yet another way for parish officials to limit the number of high-cost pension recipients and it emphasises the importance of the face-to-face connection between overseer and pauper in establishing a right to relief.

Non-resident relief generated correspondence, not just between overseers but from paupers resident elsewhere back to their parishes of settlement ('pauper letters').[71] This source can shed considerable light on issues of eligibility and entitlement. Correspondence supplements what can be unearthed from overseers' accounts on the amount spent on non-resident relief with claimants' appeals for relief. It is a rich source from which to explore claimants' and overseers' reasons for assistance and has been mined by historians in order to explore the process of negotiation between overseer and claimant, as well as the rhetorical devices employed by the poor in their quest for relief.[72] There was a language of 'home' and 'belonging', linked to the parish of settlement, in pauper correspondence, a language that was shared by paupers and overseers.[73]

In Shefford old age, widowhood, the support of children, illness and accidents, were most frequently cited in appeals for poor relief, while settlement disputes and bastardy cases also account for a fair proportion of letters.[74] On the whole, the letters were written by another party on behalf of the applicant, and the good character of the applicant was frequently cited in support of their case, as claimants sought to establish themselves as proper and deserving objects of relief. In January 1826, for instance, a letter was written on behalf of Mrs (later Widow) Clark from Holy Trinity, Cambridge. The writer of the letter explained that her current allowance of 4s. did not provide subsistence and argues that due to her 'very great industry and other excellent qualities', and the fact that she had three children to support, the eldest girl of whom was unable to get a place because she 'suffers from a complaint', she deserved a higher pension.[75] When in January 1831 Widow

---

[70] Snell, *Parish and belonging*, ch. iii.
[71] Sokoll, *Essex pauper letters*.
[72] Studies include Sokoll, *Essex pauper letters*, and 'Old age in poverty', and 'Writing for relief: rhetoric in English pauper letters, 1800–1834', in Gestrich, King and Raphael, *Being poor in modern Europe*, 91–111; Sharpe, 'The bowels of compation'; King, 'Sickness and old age'; A. Tomkins, 'Men's pauper letters', in S. King, T. Nutt and A. Tomkins (eds), *Narratives of the poor in eighteenth-century England*, i, London 2006, 1–125, 205–97, and 'Women and poverty', 152–3, 167–8; Jones, 'I cannot keep my place without being deascent'; and King, 'I fear you will think me too presumtuous'.
[73] Snell, *Parish and belonging*, 87–9; King, 'Friendship, kinship and belonging'.
[74] One letter is dated 1760, another 1809, the rest are after 1815: letters to the overseers, BLARS P70/18/4/3–55.
[75] Ibid. P70/18/4/31.

Clark's pension was reduced by the Shefford overseer to 4s., she wrote requesting 6s. The author of the letter wrote describing her as 'exceedingly afflicted' by the deduction, and that 4s. was 'impossible to do with'. The overseer was told that she needed 7s. during the winter, but she could 'do with less afterwards or be removed'. The writer said of her that 'she certainly is a most deserving woman'.[76] Threatening to return home, as Widow Clark did, and with all the resulting cost, was a common ploy by non-resident paupers in their request for assistance. This strategy reveals there was a process of negotiation between pauper and overseer rather than a one-sided decision by an overseer whether to grant assistance. In 1824 one man asked for relief to be sent to the parish where he had a job, otherwise he would come home.[77] Sarah Spencer cited her age as a reason for relief and deployed another strategy: that of deference. In October 1815 she wrote from Canterbury, Kent, stating that her allowances of 2s. 6d. per week was not sufficient. She was eighty-six and needed a woman in 'to do for her', and requested that if the overseer granted her a trifle more, she would be very thankful.[78] Individual letters could deploy more than one strategy – and sometimes conflicting ones at that – in their authors' attempt to secure assistance.[79] Although the system was largely stacked against them, such strategies did give the poor some real bargaining power.

James Humberstone's reason for distress was unemployment which had resulted in rent arrears. As in many of the other letters, his excellent character was also highlighted. David Godsmark, his employer, wrote on behalf of his employee in February 1817:

> I Write to inform you that James humberston is in very great distress his being out of imployment part of the Winter and has not been able to earn sufficient to support his family and keep his rent paid up he expects to have his goods taken from him for rent therefore he would be much oblige to you if you Would send him some money to pay his rent. he owes about 2£5$^s$ he is now in my imployment & he is a very good Working Man & I think he would not Wish to trouble you if he Could possibly help it. I therefore hope you will Essist him. I am Sir, your obe$^t$ S$^t$, David Godsmark.[80]

Humberstone's appeal for assistance did not have the outcome he would have preferred: although the parish did send the money for the rent, the overseer then arranged to have the family sent home and their goods sold. The overseers' accounts do not record any payments to him again until 1822, when he was once again being sent relief out of the parish.

---

[76] Ibid. P70/18/4/46.
[77] Ibid. P70/18/4/26.
[78] Ibid. P70/18/4/10.
[79] See, for example, Sokoll, 'Writing for relief'.
[80] Letters to the overseers, BLARS, P70/18/4/13.

Appeals for help in meeting in medical expenses were common in Shefford, as elsewhere.[81] When James Clarke hurt his leg badly in Cambridge in October 1825 the overseer of the parish within which he resided wrote to Shefford about his 'sad accident', that he was in the hospital and that he had a large family to support. His family were chargeable to Shefford and he had five children and another on the way. His friendly society was giving him 9s.–10s. a week, but it was not enough. His wife was 'unable to do any thing but provide for her family'.[82] When George Allen met with a serious accident in Bedford in August 1830, the local overseer wrote to Shefford stating that Allen was very ill in the infirmary and that he needed assistance 'in his illness'; five months later the parish was still sending money to him in Bedford.[83] The surgeon William Blower wrote on behalf of a man named Henry from St Paul's, Bedford, in 1830, stating that he was 'confined to his bed by a dangerous illness, and that he requires great attention'. Presumably the authority of the surgeon would help with the application.[84] In February 1825 a letter was written to the Shefford overseer requesting medical assistance and extra cash for Widow Wildman 'who is very ill in her stomach &c & keeps her Bed'. She had been ill 'a full fortnight' and the overseer was reminded that she had children to support.[85] Another letter was sent to the Shefford overseer on Widow Wildman's behalf a year later. She had remarried, but continued to receive a pension of 3s. a week on behalf of her children, but, she complained, 'neither can do any things at present towards their livelihood'. Her oldest boy was being apprenticed to a carpenter and she asked for £2 or £3 towards the cost.[86]

Pauper letters add another dimension to what can be found out about individuals in the overseers' accounts and make it possible to see whether appeals were successful. The cases of Ann Cannon and William Richardson illustrate this. Ann Cannon received a pension in 1795–6, and then disappeared from the accounts until 1811. Between 1811 and 1828 she received a regular pension of around 1s. a week, sent to her in large instalments to Stoke Newington, Middlesex. It does not appear that these payments were sent automatically: on several occasions Ann Cannon had to write requesting assistance. In October 1815 she wrote asking for 15s. stating that she was in 'Grate Wants', and two years later she pleaded 'please send me what is due to me'. On one occasion she asked for a 'Little Some of Money', 12s. or 13s. in advance, 'for I am very Much Distressed' and for the overseer to take it out

---

[81] Sokoll, *Essex pauper letters*; S. King, '"Stop this overwhelming torment of destiny": negotiating financial aid at times of sickness under the English old poor law, 1800–40', *Bulletin of the History of Medicine* lxxix (2005), 228–60, and 'Sickness and old age'.
[82] Letters to the overseers, BLARS, P70/18/4/30.
[83] Ibid. P70/18/4/43, 45.
[84] Ibid. P70/18/4/36.
[85] Ibid. P70/18/4/28.
[86] Ibid. P70/18/4/32.

of future money.[87] In 1828 she appears to have been very ill, for the doctor, Mr Layman, was paid £3 4s. 6d. on her behalf. In the second case, William Richardson first came to the Shefford overseer's attention in 1801 when he was examined and removed, yet between 1804 and 1806 he received odd payments, and between 1811 and 1814 a regular allowance was sent to him at Bedford. In March 1817 he wrote to the Shefford overseer requesting relief because he was 'in a bad state'. A year later the overseer at Shefford was informed that Richardson was in the infirmary, and it was said of him that 'he has neither work nor money'. When he came out of the hospital he stayed with a man, who wrote requesting an allowance, and Richardson also asked for his rent to be paid. By July 1818 it appears Richardson had died and there was a final appeal for the 'Rent for late W$^m$ Richardson'. Although he received financial assistance until 1814, none of these later appeals were met from the overseers' purse.[88] It was not inevitable that once aid was granted it would be continued. William Richardson's experience seeks to highlight the precarious nature of relief for the non-resident.

Scrutiny of pauper letters reveals something of the interaction between claimant and overseer that went into securing poor relief. An analysis of the overseers' accounts alone only reveals those who were successful applicants, whereas pauper correspondence includes some who were not, and the letters reveal the 'process', 'negotiation' and 'strategic space' by which a pauper claimed assistance. James Taylor found that in Kirkby Lonsdale relief was closely linked to the perception of the character of the person or family receiving it; this explains the references to good character in the Shefford correspondence.[89] From her analysis of the Hall family's letters, Pamela Sharpe believes that it was important for the poor to be seen to be impoverished. When the overseers referred to the poor, she argues, their concern was often more with their clothes and external appearance than whether they had bread or not. There were frequent references to nakedness, lack of cleanliness and whether the poor were 'decent and sweet'.[90] More recently, Peter Jones has shown how paupers stressed in their letters images of nakedness, decency and the ragged child.[91] Clothing was a significant proportion of spending in kind. This emphasis on external appearance and respectability, argues Sharpe, suggests that the very invisibility of the poor who wrote to the parish worked to their disadvantage. The signifiers of being a member of the deserving poor were still face-to-face. The Hall family's experience of non-resident relief suggests that this type of assistance was often irregular

---

[87] Ibid. P70/18/4/8, 12, 18, 52.
[88] Ibid. P70/18/4/14, 20/1–23.
[89] J. S. Taylor, 'Voices in the crowd: the Kirkby Lonsdale township letters, 1809–36', in Hitchcock, King and Sharpe, *Chronicling poverty*, 109–26 at p. 120.
[90] Sharpe, 'The bowels of compation', 87–108.
[91] Jones, 'I cannot keep my place without being deascent'.

and on many occasions the first to be cut.[92] The sheer weight of correspondence indicates the nagging required of overseers by paupers if they were to remain visible and proper objects of relief.

Paupers living in the locality did not necessarily have to abide by the overseer's decision on assistance. There was a higher level to which the poor could resort in the process of relief negotiation – the local magistrate. The horizons of the politics of poor relief expanded outside the parish boundaries. Paupers were frequently willing to go over the heads of parish overseers in their quest for relief to Samuel Whitbread, sitting in his justice rooms in Southill. Benjamin Bland, for instance, complained in December 1814 that the parish did not allow him sufficient income. He was in his seventies, and infirm, and his wife was sixty-seven. The parish allowed him 6s. a week for working on the roads, out of which he had to find 1s. a week in rent. Whitbread ordered the overseers to pay his rent as well.[93] When Campton's overseer threatened William Coulson with turning him out of his house, Whitbread reminded the overseer that he had to give Coulson due notice.[94] On the other hand, paupers did not always improve their material circumstances with a trip to Whitbread's justice room. Elizabeth Newman approached Whitbread to request further relief for her father Thomas Stephens, 'unable to walk hither'. The overseer had allowed him 3s. 6d. for ten weeks and had then reduced the sum. Whitbread ruled that the overseers had been 'justified in so doing'.[95]

The poor with the least power were those passing through the parish – identified in Campton and Shefford's overseers' accounts as 'travelers', 'gypsys', 'Irish', 'vagrants', 'soldiers' and 'sailors' – most of whom passed though with a pass. One contemporary commented that Irish and Scots vagrants in the Bedfordshire parish of Maulden were given 2s. 6d. 'to walk the stage'.[96] In Campton and Shefford such strangers were usually given a small cash sum of a few shillings, although those who were ill were frequently given a little more and, in January 1809, £4 6s. 8d. was spent on 'Goods and Attendance on the Gypsies being Ill with Small pox' in Campton. Many more strangers passed though Shefford than Campton: there were forty-four cases of individuals or families in Campton (1767–1834) but 1,650 in Shefford in half as many years (1794–1829). On occasion, food was provided at Shefford poor house or short-term lodgings paid for. In both communities pregnant female strangers were hurried on their way: they were provided with cash and, if necessary, transport in a carriage, in an attempt to prevent the birth of a bastard who would take its settlement in Campton or Shefford.

---

[92] Sharpe, 'The bowels of compation', 87–108.
[93] *Whitbread's notebooks*, entries 1053, 1055.
[94] Ibid. entry 570.
[95] Ibid. entries 659, 669.
[96] *Poor law report*, 238–9.

Although the poor law provided relief for those wandering, these were surely the most firmly excluded by the parochial officers and the wider community.

## Attitudes to poverty

In the hierarchy of poor law authority, between the overseer and the magistrate, was the parish vestry. While relief was distributed on a day-to-day basis by overseers, parish policy was made by the vestry and overseers had to answer to this body. Every Easter ratepayers assembled to elect churchwardens, overseers of the poor and a surveyor of the highways, but until 1819 other vestry meetings were called at the discretion of the parish officials.[97] At the Easter meeting of 1811 the Shefford vestry resolved that its overseer was to call an early evening meeting on the first Monday of every month in order to have his accounts inspected 'by the parishioners' or suffer a penalty, which indicates that the vestry were keen to retain control over parish policy and expenditure.[98] Each Shefford vestry meeting was attended by a small core of ratepayers of between four and twelve men.[99] This means that decisions were made by a small number of inhabitants for a population of 763 in 1831. Parish vestries were frequently self-replicating with the same individuals reappearing year after year, and this was largely also true in Shefford.[100] However, unlike other, largely rural and tightly controlled parishes, the vestry in Shefford was not run by any elite: vestry members were not only drawn from the higher ratepayers but included some individuals rated at the lowest levels, at below £5. Mr Layman, the parish surgeon, sat on the vestry, as did one woman, Mrs Phipps.[101]

Usually parish vestries were concerned to keep the cost of assistance to a minimum.[102] In Shefford, entries on decisions concerning poor relief were usually entered in the vestry minutes when relief was to be cut rather than awarded. In March 1819, for instance, pensions were reduced or stopped altogether to the following paupers: 'Ann Bowers 1 Shilling p$^r$ Week less; Braybrooks Wife 1 Shilling p$^r$ Week less; W$^m$ Young Widdow 2/6 p$^r$ Week less; Bland Child to have no more allow.'[103] Only those allowed new relief and those whose relief was to be reduced or stopped altogether feature in the vestry minutes; unfortunately, applicants who failed to secure relief are not mentioned.[104] In 1834 it appears that there was a hardening of attitudes to

---

[97] Eastwood, *Governing rural England*, 36.
[98] Shefford vestry minutes, BLARS, P70/8/1, Easter 1811.
[99] Ibid.
[100] Botelho, *Old age*, 21.
[101] The vestry members (in the vestry minutes) were linked to the ratepayers' books.
[102] Ottaway, *Decline of life*, 196–7.
[103] Shefford vestry minutes, BLARS, P70/8/1, entry for 25 Mar. 1819.
[104] King has located records which allow for the calculation of the numbers of applicants who were refused (see pp. 11–12 above): 'Making the most of opportunity', 232–4.

the poor on the part of the vestry, perhaps in anticipation of the poor law reforms of that year. In January, for instance, Widow Hayes's pension was discontinued until she made an application to a magistrate. In March it was decided that 'the Overseer make enquiry personally at Henlow respecting the condition of Huckly family and report whether their allowance can be reduced', and in April George Smith was hauled before a magistrate for 'defrauding the Parish in relief'.

The authority of the magistracy was above the overseer and vestry. Samuel Whitbread was justice of the peace for the east Bedfordshire hundreds of Biggleswade, Wixamtree and Clifton (which included Campton and Shefford), as well as a Foxite Whig and MP for Bedford Borough from 1790. He was also an overseer of the poor for his own parish, Southill, and he attended quarter sessions regularly. He was an active member at Westminster and presented a number of important bills regarding a minimum wage (1795, 1800) and the poor laws (1807).[105] He was an important player in his roles as JP and as a member of parliament. Attitudes towards the poor underwent a fundamental transformation during this period, based partly upon concern at spiralling relief costs, but also due to a much wider intellectual shift encompassing the idea of political economy, utilitarianism and Malthusianism. Whitbread is critical to this story, not least because his local experiences informed his views on national policy. In the later war years Whitbread was one of only a few who offered serious resistance to Malthus' gloomy predictions. Malthus' work was of profound influence upon the architects of the New Poor Law; as Mark Blaug has commented, this was 'a generation drunk on Malthusian wine'.[106] Whitbread's starting-point was radically different from that of Malthus because of his insistence that his practical experience as a magistrate offered a more certain framework for developing new policies than the theory of political economists.[107] Indeed, Whitbread had stated that when reading Malthus' *Essay* a man had to 'place a strict guard over his heart

---

[105] *A bill to explain and amend so much of an act, made in the fifth year of the reign of Queen Elizabeth, intituled, 'An act containing divers orders for artificers, labourers, servants of husbandry, and apprentices,' as empowers justices of the peace at, or within six weeks after, every general quarter sessions held at Easter, to regulate the wages of labourers in husbandry*, PP 1795, xcvii. 97, 9 Dec. 1795; *A bill to explain and amend so much of an act, made in the fifth year of the reign of Queen Elizabeth, intituled, "An act containing divers orders for artificers, labourers, servants of husbandry, and apprentices," as empowers justices of the peace to regulate the wages of labourers in husbandry*, PP 1800, cxxvii.127, 13 Feb. 1800; D. Rapp, *Samuel Whitbread (1764–1815): a social and political study*, London 1987, 211–13; *Whitbread's notebooks*, introduction at pp. 7, 9; Fulford, *Samuel Whitbread*, 76; Eastwood, *Governing rural England*, 125; Poynter, *Society and pauperism*, 171–2. Debates in the House of Commons on Samuel Whitbread's bill to regulate the wages of labourers in husbandry, on 12 Feb. 1796 and 11 Feb. 1800, are reproduced in Aspinall and Smith, *English historical documents*, 415–19.
[106] Blaug, 'Myth of the old poor law', 153.
[107] Eastwood, *Governing rural England*, 125.

lest it become hardened against the distress of his fellow creatures'.[108] Other critics wrote against the 'revolution in the public mind' on the subject of pauperism associated with Malthusian views.[109]

As a magistrate in east Bedfordshire Whitbread sat almost daily in his justice room, frequently starting the day at 8 a.m. in his dressing gown. Between September 1813 and February 1814 he held sessions on 110 days out of 182 days. He took notes on the proceedings in his own hand.[110] One contemporary, Lord Upper Ossory, had noted dryly that, 'Bedfordshire used to be called Whitbreadshire.'[111] Whitbread was heavily involved in the region on a range of issues. He promoted various improvements in the county, from a new gaol and bridewell, to a new guildhall and market houses, a new bridge over the Ouse at Bedford, the paving of streets and provision of roads, the opening of Bedford infirmary and a lunatic asylum, the provision of schooling for the poor.[112] He also asked for reports from local doctors on the causes of death, especially among children, and surveyed parish provision of medical care.[113] By 1809 he had a school in Shefford. Whitbread welcomed Lancaster's new general schools, but another of his ambitions was to educate children to be able to read the Scriptures and he was a founder member of the Bedford branch of the Auxiliary Bible Society which distributed subsidised Bibles. His contributions to hospitals, the poor, schools and societies averaged £400–£600 a year.[114] Furthermore he kept a careful watch on conditions in local workhouses and was also concerned about the state of local housing. He ordered improvements to be made in both.[115] His local experience with workhouse conditions informed his desire, expressed in his 1807 bill, to set strict rules for the better regulation of all workhouses.[116]

Most of the cases he heard in his justice room involved the poor laws. In the last four months of 1813, for instance, half of the complaints that came before him were concerned with poor law matters.[117] His attitude has been described as 'quick sympathy for genuine hardship and dismissal of unsuitable claims'.[118] Recent work by Peter King on his notebooks underlines

---

[108] Rapp, *Samuel Whitbread*, 212–13.
[109] Poynter, *Society and pauperism*, 171–2.
[110] Rapp, *Samuel Whitbread*, 147; *Whitbread's notebooks*, introduction at pp. 7–8. Whitbread's notebooks survive for the periods Dec. 1810–Dec. 1811 and Sept. 1813–Dec. 1814.
[111] Fulford, *Samuel Whitbread*, 78n.
[112] Rapp, *Samuel Whitbread*, 127–31, 231.
[113] Fulford, *Samuel Whitbread*, 77–8; Williams, 'Practitioners' income'.
[114] Rapp, *Samuel Whitbread*, 231 n 2; *Whitbread's notebooks*, introduction at pp. 25–6. In Campton and Shefford 54 people requested Bibles and Testaments: *Whitbread's notebooks*, entry 452n.
[115] *Whitbread's notebooks*, introduction and entries 71, 72; Godber, *History of Bedfordshire*, 427–9.
[116] *Bill for encouraging industry*, 8–9.
[117] Rapp, *Samuel Whitbread*, 147; *Whitbread's notebooks*, introduction at pp. 7–8.
[118] *Whitbread's notebooks*, introduction at p. 12.

this benevolence.[119] King finds that direct pauper appeals accounted for 20 per cent of the cases that Whitbread heard and that they were brought by paupers from nearly fifty parishes. It is possible to quantify how successful such appeals were: Whitbread made judgements favourable to claimants in a very large proportion of cases, at two-thirds, and in only a tiny fraction of cases did he order a reduction of poor relief. Moreover, King finds that in almost all cases overseers followed his instructions. Within his jurisdiction the reactions of the parish authorities to Whitbread's judgements were 'positive and deferential'. Such an analysis reveals that Samuel Whitbread exercised considerable power over parish overseers and vestries, and it also highlights how the system of pauper appeals allowed the poor to circumscribe the power of the parish elites, who were their employers and vestry members, by recourse to magistrates. Indeed, King describes the appeals system as a 'strategic weapon' for the poor.

In parliament Whitbread was a driving force for social reform, in particular with regard to education for the poor, establishing a minimum wage and in overhauling the poor law. His experience in Bedfordshire had persuaded him that parliament could intervene effectively to protect the living standards of the poor and, he believed, this was of more value than abstract intellectual ideals; he argued that, 'the deductions of reason were confuted by experience'.[120] Like David Davies, Whitbread was convinced that a minimum wage would guarantee the industry and the moral well-being of the poor, even though this ran counter to prevailing economic theory. The poor harvests of 1794 and 1795 and the apparent economic distress of the labouring poor helped to inform his Minimum Wage Bill of 1795, under which he had hoped to empower magistrates at quarter sessions to fix a minimum wage for agricultural labourers. It was defeated primarily due to Pitt's promise of a new poor law bill and, of course, prevailing political economics which opposed regulation of wages.[121] Whitbread's bill received only lukewarm response even from his own party, Fox was especially cool, and it was lost on a delayed second reading. Pitt's Poor Law Bill of the following year was never formally debated in parliament and, due to the considerable criticism it received, was abandoned.[122] Whitbread reintroduced his Minimum Wage Bill in 1800, but it failed once again. The failure of these bills brought an end to the legislative attempts to meet the problems of scarcity and instead policy remained in the hands of local magistrates.[123]

During the rest of the war years Whitbread was the major advocate of poor law reform. His *Bill for promoting and encouraging industry amongst the*

[119] King, 'Rights of the poor and the role of the law'.
[120] Rapp, *Samuel Whitbread*, ch. v; Eastwood, *Governing rural England*, 118–19.
[121] Eastwood, *Governing rural England*, 118–19.
[122] Ibid; Poynter, *Society and pauperism*, 62–76.
[123] Poynter, *Society and pauperism*, 76. For the policy of Speenhamland see chapter 2 above.

*labouring classes of the community, and for the relief and regulation of the necessitous poor* of 1807 proposed reform of the administration of the poor laws. On 19 February he spoke to the House of Commons on 'how to reduce the sum of human vice and misery, and how to augment that of human happiness and virtue' and his performance was described as 'very long, elaborate and animated'.[124] The bill failed, partly due to its complexity and also because poor law reform invoked such fierce debate. Contemporary opinions were so confused and contradictory that gaining any degree of agreement was extremely fraught.[125] J. R. Poynter argues that this was the last attempt by a private member to revise the whole poor law system and that the day of reform by the individual had passed: 'Whitbread's bill was not merely a failure, it was almost an anachronism.'[126] Although the bill was lost, it provoked a new wave of pamphleteering; Whitbread had raised the urgent question of political control over the management of the poor. A decade later his ideas bore fruit in the Sturges Bourne Acts of 1818–19.[127]

Whitbread argued against Malthusian proposals for the abolition of the poor law, advocating reform instead, if only as a 'sure and legal refuge' for those in extraordinary need. He only hoped that 'by taking proper steps' the poor law might 'hereafter become almost obsolete'.[128] He sought both some restriction of relief and to provide new schemes by which the poor might free themselves of the need for relief; as Poynter suggests, Whitbread was groping towards the twin principles of less eligibility and self-help that later came to define New Poor Law policy.[129] One great innovation that he proposed was a national system of education; he advocated the establishment of schools in every parish, paid for out of the poor rates, and free for the children of labourers. His belief that educating the poor would improve their morals and reduce pauperism was new enough to be controversial.[130] Whitbread also proposed a system of rewards and penalties. He sought to empower magistrates at quarter sessions to give a reward to those labouring men who had brought up six or more children to a certain age without parochial relief, up to £20, plus a coat, a hat or a certificate, while the idle poor could be committed to a house of correction and, he even advocated the badging of the criminal poor. A system of rewards was already operating in Bedfordshire: the duke of Bedford's Agricultural Society gave rewards to those men who brought up the largest families without recourse to parish assistance. In 1803, for instance, Thomas Lawrence of Shillington was awarded 5 guineas

---

[124] Eastwood, *Governing rural England*, 118–19; Wrigley and Souden, 'Introduction', 7–8; Fulford, *Samuel Whitbread*, 180.
[125] Poynter, *Society and pauperism*, 207–22.
[126] Ibid. 207.
[127] Eastwood, *Governing rural England*, 125–7.
[128] Poynter, *Society and pauperism*, 208–9.
[129] Ibid, 207–22.
[130] Ibid; Rapp, *Samuel Whitbread*, ch. v; Fulford, *Samuel Whitbread*, ch. xiv.

for having brought up nine living children without poor relief.[131] Whitbread also wished to establish a National Poor's Fund as a place for saving by the poor.[132]

The influence of ideas of less eligibility can be seen in Whitbread's proposal that relief to the deserving able-bodied poor should not result in a higher income than they could earn by independent industry.[133] He suggested that the parish could hire out the able-bodied unemployed, but their allowance should be less than the prevailing average wage.[134] He wished to place restrictions on entitlement and suggested that a householder should only gain a settlement by five years' residence provided that he did not receive relief and was not convicted of any crime.[135] Yet he did not see the workhouse as the place to enforce any principles of less eligibility; he actually wanted to bring the poor out of workhouses wherever possible. The bill did not attempt to abolish them, but Whitbread argued that they were both expensive – 'it hath been found by Experience, that the Expence of maintaining poor Persons in Workhouses is much greater than the Expence of maintaining such poor Persons at their own Habitations'[136] – and demoralising places for their inhabitants. He had sought to regulate them as JP at the local level, and now he sought closer regulation in his bill and a relaxation of the Workhouse Test Act.[137] Although Whitbread was unsuccessful, magistrates were given increasing powers to regulate workhouses a few years later.[138]

The other great innovation in his bill, and the one that was to rouse the wrath of Malthus, was the revival of the power of parishes to build cottages for the poor at the expense of the poor rates. Whitbread complained that, 'the poor are greatly distressed for habitation and large families are compelled to live in single rooms, or in outhouses or places unfit for the inhabitation of men', because of the rise in population and in the expense of building. This would also facilitate less use of the workhouse.[139] Thus, it is evident that Whitbread was particularly concerned with the accommodation for the poor, either in their own homes or within local workhouses. Other proposals that he put forward included extending rating to personal property and stock in trade, to exempt cottagers and to increase the vestry representation of large landowners. His bill also advocated the submission of accounts to quarter sessions, and that any parish rating for a three-year period at more than double the county average would have to seek a special dispensation from

---

[131] Godber, *History of Bedfordshire*, 420.
[132] Poynter, *Society and pauperism*, 207–22.
[133] *Bill for encouraging industry*, 6–7.
[134] Rapp, *Samuel Whitbread*, ch. v; Fulford, *Samuel Whitbread*, ch. xiv; Poynter, *Society and pauperism*, 207–22.
[135] Poynter, *Society and pauperism*, 207–22.
[136] *Bill for encouraging industry*, 3, 8–9.
[137] Poynter, *Society and pauperism*, 207–22.
[138] Ibid. 187.
[139] Ibid. 207–22.

justices. These suggestions would have extended the control of the gentry over local government.[140]

Malthus took objection to parts of Whitbread's bill and he had his reply, *The amendment of the poor laws, a letter to Samuel Whitbread, Esq. M. P., on his proposed bill*, ready just five weeks after the bill had been read in parliament.[141] It was the only pamphlet that he wrote on the poor law.[142] Malthus praised much of the bill, but he sought to defend himself against the charge of hard-heartedness and he attacked Whitbread's suggestion that parishes provide cottages. He argued that the difficulty of obtaining cottages mitigated against early marriages, thereby limiting the increase in population that otherwise might be expected from the poor laws, and thus that the provision of cottages would be a direct incentive to marry young and imprudently.[143] Instead of one-eighth of the population then on relief, Malthus predicted that Whitbread's proposal for 'a sufficient number of tenements' would lead to an increase of between one-third and one-half on poor relief because it would encourage early marriage, increase population, decrease the wages of labourers and 'render the condition of the independent labourer absolutely hopeless'.[144] Whitbread replied to Malthus to allay his fears, stating that parish officers would only be empowered, not compelled, to build cottages during conditions of 'strong necessity'. He gave the example of a parish contiguous with his parish of Southill, where the want of accommodation had led to 'great indecency' and, by the building of a few cottages, 'I should hope to produce the moral and physical good effects which are obvious; & to excite an ambition amongst the Labourers to obtain these more comfortable Habitations; but I do not think one creature would thereby be added to the population of the Parish.'[145] After the defeat of the bill Whitbread remained active locally in poor law issues and he also became increasingly involved in the Royal Lancastrian Institution, but he became disillusioned with poor law reform. He died in 1815.[146]

After the end of the Napoleonic wars, social relations in the county were strained. In 1816 the duke of Bedford's steward, Salmon, complained that forty years previously able, willing and industrious men would shudder at the idea of parish relief, but this was no longer the case, although he did recognise that earnings were frequently inadequate.[147] Parish work schemes

---

[140] Eastwood, *Governing rural England*, 125–6.
[141] T. R. Malthus, 'The amendment of the poor laws, a letter to Samuel Whitbread, Esq. M.P., on his proposed bill', in *Works of Malthus*, iv. 5–19.
[142] Poynter, *Society and pauperism*, 213.
[143] Malthus, 'Amendment of the poor laws', 8.
[144] Rapp, *Samuel Whitbread*, ch. v.
[145] Samuel Whitbread to T. R. Malthus, 5 Apr. 1807, in *T. R. Malthus: the unpublished papers in the collection of Kanto Gakuen University*, ed. J. M. Pullen and T. Hughes Parry, Cambridge 1997, i. 80–5.
[146] Poynter, *Society and pauperism*, 207–22.
[147] Godber, *History of Bedfordshire*, 416.

were often blamed for the deterioration in relations between landlords, tenant farmers and labourers. In 1819 the duke himself sought to put an end to the roundsman system in the county, describing it as 'destructive of the moral energies of the labourer and injurious to the interests of the farmer'.[148] Complaints were also voiced about the setting to work of gangs of unemployed labourers on the roads. Redbornstoke justices stated in a petition presented to parliament in 1829 that such work produced in the minds of labourers 'a general and settled feeling of hostility'.[149] Indeed, during the 1820s and 1830s there was on-going unrest in the county with labourers demanding the raising of wages and damaging parish property, and constables being targeted. Parish overseers were roughly handled in Eaton Socon in 1828 and Eaton Bray in 1829 and parish property (five wheelbarrows and five tar bags) was destroyed at Millbrook.[150] There were also arson attacks on ricks and farms. In Keysoe in 1822 labourers approached farmers 'with intent to alarm and terrify ... and by threats and menaces' to get wages raised.[151] In response, the duke's agent, Crocker, visited his tenant farmers trying to persuade them to employ more men. There was tension between these farmers and the duke and Crocker complained that, 'The farmers do anything but help; as fast as we take them on, they discharge.'[152] There was widespread concern about disorder among working men. In Shefford in March 1830 it was resolved by the vestry that 'Constables be instructed to remove all idle Boys and disorderly Persons assembling and congregating at the corner of the street' and such concern was well founded: three years later constables were attacked in the town.[153]

This situation of unrest exploded into the Swing Riots of 1830–1 that engulfed much of the south and east. The unrest was characterised primarily by incendiarism and attempted incendiarism, machine-breaking, wage riots and anonymous threatening letters.[154] Eric Hobsbawm and George Rudé placed Bedfordshire outside the main area of rioting, in what they characterised as the 'grey zone of unrest', but more recent research has uncovered many more disturbances country-wide and within Bedfordshire.[155] Incendi-

[148] Ibid.
[149] Ibid. 417.
[150] Armstrong, *Farmworkers*, 71.
[151] Godber, *History of Bedfordshire*, 417–19.
[152] Ibid.
[153] Shefford vestry minutes, BLARS, P70/8/1; Godber, *History of Bedfordshire*, 418.
[154] M. Holland (ed.), *Swing unmasked: the agricultural riots of 1830 to 1832 and their wider implications*, FACHRC publications, Milton Keynes 2005, 5. See also P. Jones, 'Swing, Speenhamland and rural social relations: the "moral economy" of the English crowd in the nineteenth century', *SH* xxxii (2007), 271–90, and 'Finding Captain Swing: protest, parish relations, and the state of the public mind in 1830', *IRSH* liv (2009), 429–58.
[155] E. J. Hobsbawm and G. Rudé, *Captain Swing*, London 1969, 175; Holland, *Swing unmasked*, appendix 1 at pp. 261–80; appendix 2 at pp. 281–94. Hobsbawm and Rudé found 1,475 incidents in England, whereas Holland found 3,283 incidents in England, Scotland and Wales: *Swing unmasked*, 5. See also A. Charlesworth, 'The Captain Swing

arism, wage strikes and attacks on constables continued in the county after 1831.[156] Tensions between landowners, tenant farmers and labourers were running very high and the disturbances were one way – an extreme way – for the poor to negotiate better living conditions. During the rioting in Bedfordshire there were fires, threats to parsons, assaults and wage riots.[157] In early December 1830 there was a two-day wage riot at Stotfold, towards Baldock on the Hertfordshire border. A few days later the movement shifted to the other side of the county, to Flitwick, a village near to Woburn, where between thirty and forty men, armed with sticks and bludgeons, went around the parish asking the farmers for 'more money'.[158] There is evidence of incidents in an additional eighteen parishes in the county.[159] In the 'Rural queries' sent out in 1832, local correspondents attributed the riots to 'unemployment' (Maulden), 'distress and unemployment' (Meppershall), 'antipathy of paupers to overseers, game preservers and thrashing machines' (Sharnbrook), 'the parish system [of poor relief]' (Southill-cum-Warden) and 'the game laws' (Willington).[160] In Blunham-cum-Muggerhanger men used the threat of incendiarism to demand poor relief: '[Incendiarism] has been threatened in Vestry where relief has been refused; and the relief has, in consequence, been granted.'[161] Thomas Batchelor, rector of Lidlington, commented that 'of a violent revolution ... the riots and burning of 1830, &c, were premonitory symptoms'.[162] In the face of such unrest poor relief expenditure remained high, in Campton as well as the county more generally.[163] It was a short-term victory for the poor, however: the Swing Riots have been widely viewed as the final nail in the coffin of the old poor law, signifying as they did the breakdown in social relations in wide swathes of the countryside. They helped to contribute to the rapid ushering in of the New Poor Law which had, argues Keith Snell, 'surely the most harmful and socially damaging effect on rural class relations in the south and east of any nineteenth-century legislation'.[164]

The parish vestry was central to the formulation of parochial poor law policy and within the local politics of the poor rate. The vestry made relief decisions on individual paupers, oversaw the overseers' accounts on a monthly basis, and chose to pay for the increasing poverty problem by rating

---

protests of 1830–1', in A. Charlesworth (ed.), *An atlas of rural protest, 1548 to 1900*, London 1983, 151–4, and Armstrong, *Farmworkers*, 72–7.
[156] Apfel and Dunkley, 'English rural society', 49–50.
[157] Hobsbawm and Rudé, *Captain Swing*, 149.
[158] Ibid. 149–50.
[159] Holland, *Swing unmasked*, appendix 1 at pp. 261–80; appendix 2 at pp. 281–94.
[160] 'Rural queries'.
[161] Hobsbawm and Rudé, *Captain Swing*, 81.
[162] *Poor law report*, appendix D, 'Labour rate', 6.
[163] See chapter 2 above.
[164] Snell, *Annals of the labouring poor*, 137.

an increasing number of inhabitants who were drawn from further down the social scale.

Strain is evident in this localised system from at least the late 1790s. Relief costs and the number of paupers were rocketing. The vestry responded with a range of schemes, from child allowances and food subsidies, to the introduction of medical contracts and infirmary subscriptions, to unemployment payments and make-work schemes. Parish officials began to rate the poorer sort in the knowledge that, after 1795, rating no longer conferred settlement for those renting under £10. Those who were most likely to default on their rates and who were most likely to need poor relief at some later point were those whose entitlement was most circumscribed; these inhabitants were to pay into the poor rate but they were not entitled to draw from it in the future. Although the social distance between ratepayers and the poor contracted with the extension of rating, an inability to acquire settlement through ratepaying at the lower level ensured that the distinction between ratepayers and paupers was maintained. The vestry also restricted eligibility through the active application of the settlement laws, through the process of examination and removal and the moving on of strangers. The parish did recognise that the settled poor living outside the parish qualified for non-resident relief and costs could be substantial; nevertheless, such relief could be infrequent, casual and contested. The very nature of the old poor law with its reliance upon face-to-face connections worked to the disadvantage of those living elsewhere.

However, the parish vestry did not hold all the power within the politics of the parish. The poor were not altogether powerless and they could negotiate, cajole and threaten through the strategies that they employed in their letters back to the parish, as well as going over the heads of parish officials to the magistrate who might find in their favour. If all else failed, in the last resort they might turn to unrest and riot. However, this was a period where the politics of poverty was particularly contested at both the parochial and the national level. The local and the national came together in a unique way in east Bedfordshire in the person of Samuel Whitbread. He drew upon his experience of the living conditions of the poor within his jurisdiction of east Bedfordshire to inform his own and wider opinion upon minimum wages and the administration, function and future of the old poor law. He was a crucial participant in the wider intellectual and political discussion of its reform.

# 4

# *Gender, Life-Cycle and the Life-Course*

Poverty was gendered and overwhelmingly life-cycle related. This chapter presents research on the life-cycle and life-course nature of poverty, drawing upon the pauper biographies of almost 250 pensioners, qualitatively and longitudinally. At least 85 per cent of all pensioners were elderly individuals or elderly couples, couple-headed families or lone parents, and a few were orphans. A snapshot approach might reveal a greater variety of reasons for the receipt of poor relief, over and above regular weekly pension payments and to those not suffering a life-cycle crisis, particularly sickness.[1] However, in terms of the sheer weight of expenditure and the duration of relief, life-cycle-related pensioners dominated relief lists throughout the period. Gender was also particularly important. Access to regular poor relief was heavily gendered: many more women were relieved than men. Young widows and unmarried mothers accounted for more than four-fifths of lone parent pensioners and elderly women were more than twice as likely to be relieved as old men. However, by the end of the period elderly men became increasingly vulnerable as they were marginalised from an over-stocked labour market. A significant number of those relieved long-term, of those experiencing heavily pauperised life-courses, were also women. The extent to which kin were able to assist their poor relatives, as well as whether one generation passed on their poverty to the next, are also significant factors in a life-cycle approach to poverty.

## Life-cycle, life-course and poverty

Parish overseers under the old poor law offered relief at the key life-course poverty points: clothing, boarding out and apprenticeship for children; supplementary cash and payments in kind for families 'overburdened with children' at times of specific economic hardship and for lone women with young children; and substantial welfare packages (weekly pensions, fuel,

---

[1] Healey's analysis of three censuses of the poor for Bolton, Lancashire (in 1674, 1686 and 1699), reveals that life-cycle poverty was a significant determinant of poverty, in particular old age, but also that other reasons were also important, especially the breakdown or failure of the nuclear family and illness. Healey defines lone parents with children as not in life-cycle crisis, whereas this book places them at the same life-cycle stage as couple-headed families but suffering the additional hardship of being headed by just one parent: 'Poverty in an industrializing town'.

medical care) for the aged.² The redistribution of children between households served useful functions. Boarding out orphans and young members of families with too many children to support with other parish residents provided much needed additional income for the receiving households whilst relieving their families of origin. Pauper apprenticeship served the same function as domestic service and service in husbandry: surplus children in poorer households were moved to households which required their labour. Pauper apprenticeship trained adolescents in a trade, as well as usually giving them a new place of settlement (and thus eligibility for any future poor relief).³

Some families 'overburdened with children' had received poor relief during the seventeenth and eighteenth centuries, but more general assistance to this category of the poor only became more common at the very end of the eighteenth century.⁴ While the secondary literature assumes the widespread allocation of relief to families headed by a married couple from 1795, such assistance was in fact far more sporadic and limited. Broken families, however, who had lost their male breadwinner, and young widows with children were a significant and expensive category of the deserving poor. It was acknowledged that young and old widows were unlikely to be able to support themselves in the absence of their husbands and that poor relief to these women was necessary in a society which paid women in work far less than men. Unmarried mothers became an increasingly prominent group of recipients as illegitimacy rose sharply over the late eighteenth and early nineteenth centuries. In the rural parish of Abson and Wick near Bristol, for instance, Mary Fissell found that unmarried mothers made up nearly 11 per cent of recipients of poor relief and accounted for 23 per cent of poor law expenditure.⁵

The elderly were generally deemed deserving. There was a strong association of the age of sixty with old age, but poor relief was only paid to the elderly when their chronological and functional attributes coincided, that is, once they were beyond working.⁶ In the Cambridgeshire parish of Linton

---

² See also Snell, *Annals of the labouring poor*, ch. iii, and King, *Poverty and welfare*, chs vi–vii.
³ Wall, 'Leaving home'; A. Kussmaul, *Servants in husbandry in early modern England*, Cambridge 1981; Sharpe, 'Poor children as apprentices in Colyton', and *Population and society*, 256–70; Hindle, 'Waste children?'; J. Lane, *Apprenticeship in England, 1600–1914*, London 1996; Honeyman, *Child workers in England*; Levene, 'Parish apprenticeship'.
⁴ Wales, 'Poverty, poor relief and the life-cycle', 353; Newman Brown, 'Receipt of poor relief', 411; Hampson, *Poverty in Cambridgeshire*, 178–9; Hindle, *On the parish?*, 273–4; Ottaway, *Decline of life*, chs v–vi; Sharpe, *Reproducing Colyton*, 247.
⁵ Fissell, 'The "sick and drooping poor"', 40. See also Levene, Nutt and Williams, *Illegitimacy*.
⁶ Ottaway, *Decline of life*, 21, 26; Thane, *Old age*, ch. i; Smith, 'Structured dependence of the elderly'. It appears that in the sixteenth and seventeenth centuries contemporaries regarded the age of 50 as the onset of old age: Pelling, 'Old age, poverty, and disability', 78; Botelho, *Old age*, 12–13.

at the end of the seventeenth century, pensioners were 'very Ancient and decreppid', 'Aged and past worke', 'aged and lame', 'bed Read' [bedridden], 'decrepid and past labour'.[7] In pauper letters the elderly poor were represented as 'poor helpless creature[s]' who could 'just creep about'. The picture is one of growing debility, being unable to do hard work, episodes of illness, weakness and fatigue, the exhaustion of body and soul.[8] Susannah Ottaway found that the average age of all male pensioners was around seventy, which was, she argues, a common marker of male dependency.[9] In Shefford in 1809 Prudence Adams was allowed a pension of 3s. 6d., 'in consequence of her Age and Infirmity', when she was aged sixty-five.[10] David Thomson has argued that by the mid-nineteenth century high proportions of both men and woman received parish pensions in their old age, and that these allowances were in fact old age pensions, but E. H. Hunt has disputed the extent to which such payments were given as of right to the elderly, rather than as 'disability' payments as the aged grew more infirm, or as income supplements for those still able, at least partly, to work for their own livelihood.[11] There was no real concept of 'retirement' in the eighteenth and nineteenth centuries. In fact no age was ascribed in law until the Old Age Pensions Act of 1908, and this was at the advanced age of seventy.[12]

This life-cycle of alternating periods of poverty and prosperity also has implications for the ability to pay poor rates; it would be reasonable to expect periods of exemption from paying the rates, or indeed receipt of poor relief, to coincide with parenthood and old age. Historians have speculated that ratepayers were willing to pay the poor rate because one day, if they fell on hard times, they too might require poor relief.[13]

## Childhood

In Campton and Shefford children with at least one parent were frequent recipients of poor relief, but very few were orphans who had lost both parents; indeed there were only seven such in Campton and six in Shefford, which seems remarkable.[14] It is only through analysis of the pauper biographies

---

[7] Hampson, *Poverty in Cambridgeshire*, 178–9.
[8] Sokoll, 'Old age in poverty', 143–5.
[9] Ottaway, *Decline of life*, 201–2.
[10] Shefford vestry minutes, BLARS, P70/8/1, 28/04/1809.
[11] D. Thomson, 'Provision for the elderly in England, 1830 to 1908', unpubl. PhD diss. Cambridge 1980, 20, and 'The decline of social welfare'; Hunt, 'Paupers and pensioners, 407–30.
[12] Thane, *Old age*, ch. xi; B. Harris, *The origins of the British welfare state: social welfare in England and Wales, 1800–1945*, Basingstoke 2004, 159–60.
[13] See King, 'Pauper inventories', 182.
[14] There were many more orphans in Aldenham, Hertfordshire, in the seventeenth century: Newman Brown, 'The receipt of poor relief', table 12.3 at p. 412.

that it becomes clear that so few children were without both parents. This probably reflects the fall in adult mortality towards the end of the eighteenth century.[15] The other children were members of families, either couple-headed or headed by lone parents, and so their relief histories have been analysed as part of those types of households. In at least four instances of relief to orphans, prior to being orphaned, their widowed parents had received regular relief to bring up their children. On the deaths of those lone parents, their children continued to receive regular relief through payments, often for boarding out with what would now be termed foster families. Jenny Cherry, for instance, received relief for herself and her children for two years until her death in July 1782. The parish paid for her funeral and then boarded out the orphans with Elizabeth Godfrey for the next thirteen years. The cash sums declined over the years as the children grew up and were able to work. The orphans were also clothed by the parish in September 1786 at a cost of £1 9s. 2d. Likewise, Ann Dilly received a pension until she died, leaving her daughters Ann and Elizabeth dependent on the parish. They were allocated a pension for six years, as well as regular help by four carers, clothing and shoes, and they were provided with lace, pins and cushions so that they might earn something by lace-making. In many cases children were provided with the tools of a trade, indicating that all children were expected to earn what they could from a fairly early age and that overseers sought to fulfill the aims of the Elizabethan legislation to set the poor, including children, to work. In a further instance, William Lansberry, a married man with six children, found himself in a similar situation. While his wife was alive he received occasional relief from the parish between 1786 and 1791, but, when his wife became ill while giving birth to their seventh child in March 1794, William was allocated a pension. His wife and new baby died within weeks and William's pension continued until his own death in January 1796, leaving his six children – Thomas, 19, William, 16, John, 13, Ann, 10, Sarah, 8, and Elizabeth, 6 – orphaned. His dependent children (most probably the four youngest) were boarded out with Ann Herbert, a widow with seven children of her own (aged 7, 14 and another five aged over 16), and herself a regular pensioner between 1792 and 1822, until her death.[16] The parish paid for the upkeep of the children until each of them reached the age of fifteen. Others, such as Randall's children, Smith's children and Elizabeth Squire, had lost their mothers, and either the parish was relieving their fathers by boarding them out or their fathers had also died and they were in fact orphans. In two cases bastard children were also fostered out.

A number of the foster parents were employed by the parish at other times as well, to look after other children or for parish work, and some

---

[15] Wrigley, 'British population during the "long" eighteenth century', 79–80; Wrigley, Davies, Oeppen and Schofield, *Family reconstitution*, ch. vi at pp. 280–93.
[16] The fourth case is that of Mary Bland, a widow with one child, who died and left her child on the parish.

also recipients of poor relief themselves at some point in their life-courses. Foster parents were either paid in addition to their pensions (and boarding payments never replaced poor relief for them) or they were never in receipt of any other parish pay. Their poor law 'careers' as fosterers are similar to those of the other carers and nurses employed by the Campton and Shefford authorities.[17] Some had considerable experience. J. Clark, for instance, acted not only as a foster parent to Dilly's orphaned children, but was also paid by the authorities to care for their mother Ann Dilly in her last illness, as well as Widow Lincoln, Sarah Lincoln and Richard Roberson in the period before they died. She was paid 6d. a week for 'doing for' Sarah Lincoln and Richard Roberson for three months each, 1s. for 'waiting' on Widow Lincoln and 1s. 6d. per week for 'doing for' Ann Dilly and then her children. One of the orphans, Ann, was also cared for by a carer called Pine and also by Mary Barber, who was another very experienced nurse and carer.[18] Mary Smith was employed not only to foster Smith's children, but also for doing the laundry at Shefford's workhouse, sitting up with Kempson's child, and attending the Saunders family.

Caring for boarded-out children could pay well: Ann Herbert earned 4s. a week for sixty-four weeks in 1796–7 for the Lansberry children, in addition to her weekly pension of 2s.; and Elizabeth Lincoln was also paid 4s. a week for the board of Randall's orphans on top of her weekly payments of 2s.–3s. These sums were far higher than the pay for many other nursing and caring duties, but this was in part to recompense households for the costs associated with taking in a child.[19] The average boarding-out sum was 2s. 8d. The only formal, written agreement that survives dates from April 1767. It was agreed between the parish of Campton and Henry Stringer that he would care for Frances Cooper: 'Henrey S agreed with pr Cam to giv FC new pear shous Boad washing mending Login Larn Speen Linine, 1 yr', but unfortunately no contract sum is given. In another case Ann Gore was paid between 1s. 6d. and 2s. per week to foster William Herbert's 'natural child'. Nelly, the illegitimate child of Mary Gobby and Richard Lincoln, was born in September 1777. Four months later her mother was gravely ill and the parish provided her with fuel, drops, bread and beer, and nursing by Jemima Johnson and Ann Hayes (both experienced nurses). When Mary died the parish immediately boarded Nelly with Ann Hayes, and then with Ann Allen, until the baby died aged 11 months. Both foster mothers were paid between 1s. and 2s. 6d. per week. For Ann Hayes these sums were in addition to her own pension, but they were the only payments to Ann Allen. Indeed, in at least six cases foster parents were never recipients of poor relief in their own right. This demonstrates how money raised from the poor rates could benefit people other than paupers in a given community. However, in five instances,

---

[17] Williams, 'Caring for the sick poor'.
[18] Ibid. 162, and the entry for Mary Barber at p. 168.
[19] Ibid. 156–7.

foster parents were also receiving weekly pensions and the parish authorities might have placed the children with them in order to give them some more sorely needed income. The Cherry children were boarded with Elizabeth Godfrey immediately upon their mother's death and, although Elizabeth only started to receive relief once she had begun to foster the Cherry orphans, she received not only a regular weekly pension of between 3s. and 3s. 6d. but also lump sums for boarding the children. There is also evidence to suggest that overseers were paying parish officers in other parishes (non-resident relief) for the boarding of children.[20]

Somewhat surprisingly, parish officers rarely apprenticed orphaned or poor children. In only two cases in Campton, and only one in Shefford, were children apprenticed. In Campton, between November 1785 and April 1786, John Burrige's three children William, aged 14, Mary, 12, and George, 10, were bound apprentices at a cost to the parish of £2 17s. 9d. Decades later, in June 1827, fifteen-year-old Robert Jude was bound by the parish at a cost of £2 and they paid a further 9s. 6d. for two shirts and a pair of stockings for him. Robert was the illegitimate son of Mary Jude, who also had an illegitimate daughter, Sally, who was a year older. Mary managed to bring up her two children without any other recourse to the parish. In Shefford Henry Kempston was apprenticed in January 1815 to James Elliot, a blacksmith, of nearby Shillington. He was a 'poor boy' aged 18 whose parents James and Ann Kempston were 'not able to maintain him' (indeed, they were one of the few couple-headed families who required substantial relief). He was apprenticed for just three years. In 1818 the overseers of Shefford and of Shillington were in negotiations over Henry's settlement and between 1821 and 1822 the overseers of Shefford relieved him for periods of unemployment and paid him to dig gravel. In the register of parish apprentices he is the only entry.[21] The reluctance of overseers to apprentice children might confirm Keith Snell's argument that apprenticeship was in decline by the later eighteenth century, although the more recent research by Katrina Honeyman and Alysa Levene suggests that, more generally, many parish officers did continue to apprentice substantial numbers of pauper children in the later eighteenth and early nineteenth centuries, particularly to the industrialising regions, but also in craft-type training.[22] However, contemporary comment suggests that in Bedfordshire as a whole, poor children were rarely apprenticed: the

---

[20] Large lump sum payments are paid for children to men such as Mr Arch, Mr Johnson, Mr Hare, Mr Phipps, Mr Tear and Mr Berbet, who are likely to have been overseers in other parishes. These were probably boarding out sums.
[21] Shefford apprenticeship records, BLARS, P70/14/1–4. The only other indenture is for 1698.
[22] Snell, *Annals of the labouring poor*, chs v, vi; Honeyman, *Child workers*; Levene, 'Parish apprenticeship'. The number of children being apprenticed remained high in Colyton, Devon, with 84 children apprenticed in the period 1750–99 and 192 between 1800 and 1837. However there was a decline in apprentices living-in: Sharpe, *Reproducing Colyton*, 259.

Revd Dr Hunt JP, vicar of Willington and rector of St Peter's and St John's, Bedford, told the Commission on the Poor Laws (published in 1834) that 'The parishes near Bedford are not much in the habit of binding out poor children as apprentices, except occasionally an infirm or crippled child, to a tailor or to some sedentary trade.'[23]

## Parenthood

Relief to couple-headed families was restricted in value and in duration to periods of specific economic crisis. Either there was sufficient employment/income for these men and women at other times and thus they had no need of relief, or married couples found it much harder to qualify for it. Only a handful of long-term pension recipients were couple-headed families over the entire period: the Lennard family (ten years and eleven months), the Blands (fourteen years and three months), the Stevens (sixteen years), the Kempstons (ten years and six months) and the Savages (eleven years). In both communities, most families received less than £7 a year in regular poor relief. Some were allocated between £7 and £14, but only a few received payments higher than £14 a year. In the case of one family only – Ann and James Kempston of Shefford – were payments so high that the parish must have been their main source of income and the sums that they received were quite exceptional. Their average annual payment was £18 and between 1812 and 1820 it never fell below £14, and was as high as £28 in 1813 and £25 in 1814. The parish apprenticed their son Henry in January 1815, when he was eighteen, and they also had an older son of nineteen and two daughters of fifteen and four. Ann had another baby in the following November. In Campton, John and Mary Lennard received comparable sums, but only for the years 1824 (£30) and 1825 (£28); in other years they received around £10. Similarly, Charles and Mary Bland, Henry and Mary Clarke and Thomas Stevens's family were all given sums as high as £15–£20 in specific years, but they more commonly received far less.

These parishes favoured relief to lone parents, and particularly those headed by women. The rise in illegitimacy over the eighteenth and early nineteenth centuries meant that unmarried mothers became a more prominent category of recipient. Although a similar number of women were regularly relieved in the two parishes (eight in Campton, seven in Shefford), the proportion of lone parents that they represented in Shefford (37 per cent) was double that of Campton (16 per cent). The parish examined pregnant single women and restricted its commitment to those with a settlement. Elizabeth Stevens, for instance, was examined when she was seven months pregnant. Her son Thomas was baptised in February 1807 and she then

---

[23] *Poor law report*, appendix C, 377.

received a weekly pension of 2s. Mary Barnet, on the other hand, was in a less secure position. She was pregnant and her husband had been absent for three years. The parish overseers of Shefford approached Samuel Whitbread for advice about removing her.[24] Where possible, to indemnify the parish against the costs of bastardy, orders of affiliation were taken out on putative fathers and bastardy bonds were set up.[25] Before 1800 weekly allowances to unmarried mothers were usually around 1s., a sum which rose to 1s. 6d. around 1800, while after 1800 the usual payment was 2s. However, in the case of four women their payments were tailored and fluctuated according to need. The parish paid for the lyings-in of only three unmarried mothers. It is possible that affiliation orders ensured that the putatative fathers paid these costs directly.[26] Dr Hunt commented that a pension of 'Eighteen pence a week added to a peasant girl's own earnings furnish a bare subsistence for child and mother', but he also indicated that employment opportunities in lace-making and straw-plaiting largely prevented the abandonment of infants or the mothers going away into service.[27]

Another legal strategy to circumscribe the long-term responsibility of the parish for any bastard children was the encouragement of, and sometimes forced, marriages of the parents. This is in contrast with the policy of some parochial officers in the seventeenth century who sought to prevent the poor from marrying.[28] Of the twelve weddings paid for by the overseers for Campton and Shefford, one was of a couple with an illegitimate child, three were of couples where the bride was definitely pregnant, and in six cases there is evidence to suggest the bride was already pregnant. The grooms-to-be and putative fathers were gaoled in the local bridewell and legal warrants and/or affiliation orders were issued; the banns were read; and the overseers paid for the ring, the licence, other marriage fees and expenses, and, sometimes, food and beer. Weddings and their legal costs were not cheap. Most weddings cost between £4 and £5, but that between Elizabeth Hart and John Darling came to a staggering £14. No doubt zealous parish overseers sought to free the parish of any future expenses, hoping that marriage would curtail bastardy expenses. In five instances all poor relief stopped with the marriages and it is likely that many of these couples left Campton and Shefford, most probably for the new husbands' parishes of settlement. In two cases, however, the couples remained in the communities, had large families, and continued

---

[24] *Whitbread's notebooks*, entry 936.
[25] In Campton affidavits were taken out on three men; in Shefford eight bastardy bonds, one examination and one affiliation order are extant for the period 1742 to 1830: bastardy records, BLARS, P70/15/1–11.
[26] See Nutt, 'The paradox and problems', and 'Paternal financial responsibility'.
[27] *Poor law report*, appendix C, 405.
[28] S. Hindle, 'The problem of pauper marriage in seventeenth-century England', *TRHS* 6th ser. viii (1998), 71–89; Broad, 'Parish economies of welfare', 993–5.

to receive occasional relief, although another two couples also had large families but did not require any further parish assistance. Although the parish did not pay for their wedding, marriage between Patience Whittemore and Jonas Heathfield signalled the end of their poor relief payments. In July 1825, when Patience was seven months pregnant, Campton paid 11s. 6d. for an order of affiliation against Jonas. They then paid Patience 2s. a week for the next five months until, in March 1826, the couple married and all poor relief ceased. They went on to have another four children. In another case, the parish authorities were not so successful. In October 1806 Richard Brice was committed to a bridewell while the banns were read in Bedford St Paul's church. The pair did not marry, however, and Brice paid 2s. a week in child support for a short period (ten weeks) before he disappeared from the records, most probably because he absconded.

There are just a small number of instances in Campton and Shefford where women recorded more than one illegitimate birth. It was relatively rare for a woman to have more than one bastard infant, although it was more widespread in the late eighteenth century than earlier, and particularly in agricultural communities.[29] Unmarried mothers became a more prominent category of poor relief recipient as illegitimacy rates rose rapidly in the second half of the century and reached a high point in the 1820s.[30] Ann Mintle gave birth to her son John Williams in 1765 and her daughter Mary Hickes the following year. If the second names given to these children were the surnames of their fathers, then this would indicate that they had different fathers. Eight women gave birth to two illegitimate children, with only one woman, Hannah Gibbons, giving birth to three and another, Sene Madde, to five. Having more than one bastard child did not necessarily make women more likely to require poor relief: only two of the eight women having two children came onto poor relief. It is, of course, possible that the women avoiding parish dependency were cohabiting with the fathers of their children, a situation which was particularly prevalent in the early nineteenth century.[31] Hannah Gibbons never came to the attentions of the

---

[29] P. Laslett, K. Oosterveen and R. M. Smith (eds), *Bastardy and its comparative history: studies in the history of illegitimacy and marital nonconformism in Britain, France, Germany, Sweden, North America, Jamaica and Japan*, London 1980; S. King, 'The bastardy-prone sub-society again: bastards and their fathers and mothers in Lancashire, Wiltshire, and Somerset, 1800–1840', in Levene, Nutt and Williams, *Illegitimacy*, 66–85.

[30] P. Laslett, 'Introduction: comparing illegitimacy over time and between cultures', in Laslett, Oosterveen and Smith, *Bastardy*, 1–70. The age at marriage in Campton-with-Shefford and Southill fell nearly four years for men from 27 in the first half of the seventeenth century to 23 in the first half of the nineteenth century, while the age for women fell nearly three years from 25 to 22: Campton-with-Shefford and Southill family reconstitution.

[31] J. R. Gillis, *For better, for worse: British marriages, 1600 to the present*, Oxford 1985, ch. vii. See also Levene, Nutt and Williams, *Illegitimacy*, 12, 82, 99, 116, 154; Crawford, *Parents of poor children*, 93–5.

parochial officers, but Sene Madde and her children were long-term recipients of parish assistance. The two women who gave birth to illegitimate twins, Elizabeth Odell in 1781 and Elizabeth Savage in 1825, were both recipients of parish pensions.

Sene Madde of Shefford was untypical. Of her five children, Harriet was born in June 1789, Benjamin in May 1792, Aaron was born and died in July 1796, and Thomas was born in March 1798. It appears that she had another baby in August 1797, when the midwife was paid on her account, but the infant does not appear in the baptism register and most probably died shortly after birth. Sene was a regular pensioner at the start of the accounts in 1794, receiving 4s. a week, and sizeable sums were paid for her rent. Her pension was highly responsive to her circumstances and rose and fell over the years: in July 1795 her pension increased to 5s.; a year later it fell to 4s. again; from November 1799 the dole increased to 5s., then 6s., and then 8s.; her stipend was not reduced until two and a half years later, when it fell to 6s.; from May 1804 her weekly allowance rose and fell, rising to 7s. 6d. and then falling over the next three years to 5s., 4s., 3s. Over the next seven years it fell steadily from 4s. 6d. in January 1807 to just 1s. by July 1813. She also received wine and port and 2lbs of pork. She was examined as to her place of settlement twice, once in April 1796 when she was pregnant with Aaron and again in January 1807. The expenses of Aaron's delivery and his burial were paid for by the poor law. Sene provided services for the parish and this earned her precious extra cash. She was paid an extra 1s. for housework at the workhouse and for caring duties. A vestry meeting in September 1809 decided that 'Maddy Senna to be Allowed Weekly 2s/ as having 2 Children & 1s/ for the Care of the Poor'. When Widow Jane Stevens died Sene asked the vestry if she might have her clothes, which were new six months previously, and the vestry allowed her request.[32] She was also paid as a parish carer, nursing Spencer, attending Baldwin, and arranging the funeral of Thomas Priest. Sene left the records in 1814, with no explanation. Even if her life story is untypical, what Sene's pauper biography does reveal is the central role of the poor law in her makeshift economy: the overseers provided her with poor relief and income from parish work. Sene's children also received poor relief in their own right; in the 1790s and 1800s they received clothing and shoes on many occasions. In November 1816, when he was twenty-four, Benjamin received occasional cash payments and food and drink during an illness. In the following month he was examined as to his settlement and he and his wife Phoebe were removed.[33]

This was a period during which illegitimacy rates were historically high, as was the propensity of unmarried mothers to give birth to more than one bastard. Peter Laslett termed this phenomenon the 'bastardy-prone

---

[32] BLARS, P70/8/1, 22 Sept. 1809; 20 Mar. 1810.
[33] Quarter session minutes, ibid. QSM 26/1817, 69.

subsociety' and the concept has been revisited more recently by Steven King, who argues that a small number of families accounted for a large proportion of bastard births.[34] However, given that illegitimacy was so pervasive, it has also been argued that society more generally, rather than a subsection, was bastardy prone.[35] In Campton there was one family where four generations of women had illegitimate children, but this is hardly sufficient evidence of a bastardy-prone subsociety. In 1763 Mary Herbert delivered her illegitimate daughter, also Mary. In the first week of January 1793 this Mary gave birth to her own 'base-born' daughter, Clark, and the parish authorities paid the £2 lying-in costs. Thereafter the mother and child received a weekly pension of 1s. 6d., which rose to 2s. during the high price years of 1800–3, before returning to its previous level. The pension ceased in 1806, when Clark was thirteen. Clark returned to the relief rolls once again, however, when she gave birth to her own bastard child, in October 1814, at a cost to the parish of £5. She did not automatically receive a weekly allowance, only becoming a regular recipient from November 1817, when she received a weekly allowance of 2s. and then 1s., until April 1824 when her child was ten.[36]

## Widows and widowers

Widowhood brought a great many women onto poor relief: both young and middle-aged widows with dependent children to support and much older, now solitary, elderly widows.[37] Indeed, Susannah Ottaway argues that, 'Among the so-called "deserving poor", old women, especially widows, had a particularly privileged place in the minds of their eighteenth-century contemporaries, and thus it is clear that there was a gender component to the nature of an old person's entitlement to poor relief.' For much of the seventeenth and eighteenth centuries it was much more acceptable to give an elderly woman a weekly dole than an aged man.[38] Widows were one of the most deserving categories of recipients since they were not the architects of their own situation. The economic position of widows in Bedfordshire might not have been as severe as in other places, however. The participation of widows

---

[34] P. Laslett, 'The bastardy-prone sub-society', in Laslett, Oosterveen and Smith, *Bastardy*, 217–46; King, 'The bastardy-prone sub-society again'; Reay, *Microhistories*, 188–97, 210–12.

[35] A. Levene, T. Nutt and S. Williams, 'Introduction', in Levene, Nutt and Williams, *Illegitimacy*, 1–17 at pp. 12–13.

[36] An affiliation order was obtained from Samuel Whitbread: *Whitbread's notebooks*, entry 1076.

[37] Wales, 'Poverty, poor relief and the life-cycle'; Newman Brown, 'The receipt of poor relief'; Smith, 'Widowhood and ageing'.

[38] Ottaway, *Decline of life*, 179–80. Widows were far more likely to have been in receipt of a parish pension in Aldenham, Hertfordshire, in the seventeenth century: Newman Brown, 'The receipt of poor relief', 412.

in the labour force was high in the nearby parish of Cardington in the snapshot years of 1782 and 1851. At the earlier date some 80.9 per cent of young widows (aged between twenty and thirty-nine) worked, falling only slightly to 70 per cent by 1851. The participation rate of older widows (those over sixty) was lower, at 40 per cent in 1782, but this increased sharply to 72 per cent in 1851. Of course, the radical amendment of the poor laws occurred between these two dates and this may have pushed more women into work in 1851, thus providing further evidence of the severity of the New Poor Law. The amount that these women might earn was falling after 1782 with the collapse in spinning in Cardington. Lace-making replaced it but it was much more poorly paid.[39] However, in Campton and Shefford straw-plaiting, which was better paid than lace, occupied a great many women.[40]

In Campton and Shefford fifty-six widows of various ages were allocated regular weekly pensions for which there is sufficient information to assess the point at which they became pensioners: whether at the point of widowhood, whether before widowhood (as part of a couple or family), or long after their husbands had died.[41] To a large extent findings for Campton and Shefford support those of previous studies to the effect that most of the widows coming on to the relief rolls in their own names did so at the point of widowhood (62 per cent). However, a significant proportion of these women had already been on relief as part of a couple before the death of the husband (an additional 23 per cent). Some husbands had been on relief for a short time (up to nine months) during their growing infirmity and final illnesses and the payments then continued to the new widow. Other husbands had been parish recipients for anything up to ten years, with an average of four and a half years.[42] After the burials of their spouses, these widows simply continued a pattern of receiving relief already established in the family. Of the remaining widows, 11 per cent had been in receipt of parish relief at some much earlier point earlier in their lifetimes, while 4 per cent only came to collect a pension long after they were widowed, when they themselves were elderly.

Of those widows and widowers who had either received regular poor relief at some point earlier in their families' life-cycles or who were already in receipt of a parish pension when their spouses died, in six cases relief was in the form of child allowances. This is what might be expected for some, since

---

[39] Saito, 'Who worked when', table 9.3 at p. 221.
[40] See chapter 1 above.
[41] Only those widows and widowers who spouses' dates of deaths could be ascertained, and compared with the date of first pension, were included. In 14 cases (from a total of 56) widows probably only came onto relief at the time of their husbands' burials, since no firm dates could be established. These are calculations for pensioners only and do not include those husbands and wives who received occasional relief in the months before the husbands' deaths.
[42] These figures do not include those in receipt of a pension for up to nine months before the husbands' deaths.

many were families who would then require a continuation or a reinstatement of relief once the household head had died. This was the case for Ann Hayes, Lucy Newman, Mary Clark and Mary Leonard. Mary Clark's family received child allowance payments in 1799–1801 and 1805–6, and at the point of her husband's burial in 1814. Mary then received her own pension, which continued after her children had grown up and flown the nest, and into her old age. In 1834, at the age of sixty-three, she was still in receipt of a pension. Mary Leonard's family had also received child allowances previously, in 1817, before she came onto continuous relief from 1821. Elizabeth Knight's poor relief career was slightly different, since she and her husband Thomas received child allowance payments between December 1799 and March 1802 and again for two years and eight months between 1816 and 1819. From April 1827 Elizabeth and Thomas received a pension as a couple in their old age. When Thomas died in January 1829 Elizabeth continued to receive the pension in her own name, now as an aged widow. The only widower in a similar position was Thomas Smith, whose family was allocated an allowance between December 1800 and April 1802. Although his wife Mary had died eight months later, Thomas did not come onto regular relief until 1819, in his middle age.

Widowers, too, could find themselves in similar situations, but in much smaller numbers. There were fourteen widowers who received parish pensions and, of these, seven (50 per cent) came on to the relief rolls at the point of their wives' deaths. One such was William Newman, who received a pension and help from Lucy Townsend in order to help him to care for his three small children. In two cases husbands had already been in receipt of parish payments for some time before their wives died; in another two cases widowers had received relief at some earlier point in their lifetimes; and in three cases widowers only came on to the relief rolls at a much later date when they were elderly and received pensions until they died.

### Old age

The elderly were particularly favoured as poor relief beneficiaries. Women were favoured over men: 53 per cent of the pensions given to the elderly were allocated to old women, as opposed to 19 per cent to old men, and the remaining 28 per cent to elderly couples. By the period under consideration here, this was not necessarily due to differentials in male and female life expectancy: in the first half of the eighteenth century women had a higher life expectancy at birth than men, but in the second half of the century there were big gains in male life expectancy and men surged ahead. In old age the advantage in life expectancy of women was very modest.[43]

---

[43] Wrigley, Davies, Oeppen and Schofield, *Family reconstitution*, 298–307.

**Table 12**
**Age distribution of elderly pensioners at the start of their pension, Campton and Shefford, 1760s–1830s**

| Age | per cent |
|---|---|
| 60–4 | 37 |
| 65–9 | 33 |
| 70–4 | 12 |
| 75–9 | 12 |
| 80 or over | 6 |
| [70 or over | 30] |

*Source:* Campton overseers' accounts, BLARS, P18/12/1–2, X514/1–3; Shefford overseers' accounts, P70/12/1–2; Campton and Shefford family reconstitution.

*Notes:* This calculation excludes those already on relief at the start of the overseers' accounts (since their age at first pension is not known) and also excludes widows who came on at their husbands' deaths if the husband was already in receipt of a pension (since they had previously benefited from a couples' pension). The figures include eight wives of elderly couples on relief together.

Historians of old age have argued that there was no set 'pensionable' age under the old poor law and that those at the other end of the life-course were expected to work until infirmity overtook them.[44] The level of wages and the types of work one did were adjusted according to a worker's ability and this was influenced by their age.[45] Samuel Whitbread expected men in their seventies to work if they were able to do so.[46] In Campton and Shefford most of the elderly coming onto long-term relief did so in their early sixties (37 per cent) but another third were between sixty-five and sixty-nine and the remaining 30 per cent were aged seventy or older (*see* table 12). William Russell and James Austin were both in their eighties (eighty-two and eighty-three respectively). Benjamin Bland was employed by the Shefford overseer to 'paddle on the road' at 6s. a week when he was in his seventies and his wife, aged sixty-seven, was 'infirm and can do very little'.[47] However, even the definition of 'able-bodied' was flexible and fluctuated with economic circumstances, as elderly men were increasingly marginalised from the overstocked labour market in Campton and Shefford after 1815 and were pushed onto long-term relief.

---

[44] Ottaway, *Decline of life*, ch. i; Thane, *Old age*, ch. i.
[45] R. Wells, *Wretched faces: famine in wartime England, 1793–1801*, Sutton 1988, 17; Hitchcock, King and Sharpe, 'Introduction' at p. 10.
[46] *Whitbread's notebooks*, entries 542, 1055.
[47] Ibid. entries 1053, 1055.

## Pauperised life-courses

Analysing the pauper biographies over the individual's entire life-course and the family's life-cycle reveals that there were long-term paupers, as well as paupers who were relieved for more than one period. Almost one-fifth of pensions in the two communities endured for between five and ten years (medium-term pensions), and 16 per cent in Campton and 18 per cent in Shefford were given for ten years or longer (long-term pensions). In Campton the four longest pension durations were for thirty, thirty-four, thirty-seven and forty-three years, while in Shefford the longest pension was for twenty-nine years (although the overseers' accounts are only extant for thirty-four years and some pension terms might therefore have been truncated). There was, therefore, a small, but significant, number of paupers who received weekly pensions for relatively long periods. In addition, there were those individuals who were in receipt of a pension two or three times during their lifetimes. The life-courses of all these recipients were heavily pauperised. The richness of their stories will become apparent; the combination of their long-term relief histories and the family reconstitution means that in many cases a great deal is known about them. Some of the most interesting and illuminating life histories are those far less easy to quantify.

In both Campton and Shefford around 16 per cent of pensioners received a pension twice in their life times. Some of these had only a small break between periods of continuous payments, but others had longer gaps. Most received two short-term pensions: in just over two-thirds of cases in Campton and half in Shefford, both pension periods were for less than five years. The remaining third received at least one medium- or long-term pension. There are no easy generalisations about the pauper careers of these individuals and families; they were extremely varied. Three pauper biographies illustrate this. William and Mary Barber, for instance, were on relief in their old age. Both received occasional relief for illnesses between 1812 and 1817, and then in 1818 William received a weekly pension for them both for nine months, accompanied by extra payments for clothing, shoes, bedding and fuel. After a short break in relief, Mary died and William came back on to the relief rolls as a widower, first because he was ill and then his relief was upgraded to a weekly pension. In contrast, Henry Clark was allocated a child allowance at the turn of the century for his children Francis and Sarah (aged four and two respectively). Henry reappeared on to the pension lists just before his death in 1814 and his widow then received her own parish pension. William Allen's biography is very complicated. His mother Jemima was examined with regard to her settlement when she was five months' pregnant with him, since she was unmarried. Jemima had another bastard child, Sarah, six years later, who died when she was two years old. That same month, William, now eight years old, came on to relief and received a pension for eight months. Five months after his pension started, Jemima married Cornelius Johnson, in February 1797; Cornelius already had five children between the ages of eleven and nineteen and Cornelius and Jemima had another three children together. It is not clear whether William was living with the family. William received a further pension when he was aged eleven for seven months and thereafter he received occasional relief until he was sixteen, primarily clothing and shoes (at a cost of £5 10s.) and his mother was paid for washing and mending for him. Although William's poor law story ends there, the Johnson family's does not. The family received child allowances payments around 1800 for their other son, James. When Cornelius died in May 1805, Jemima and her dependent children started to draw a pension, which lasted for eight years, and at one point her rent was paid. Her youngest son, James, also received weekly relief in his own right and the parish paid for the burial of one of the children. Jemima was even given straws to teach her children to plait. William Allen's story, and that of his mother Jemima and step-father Cornelius, illustrates not just a complicated family history but also reveals the flexibility, responsiveness and tailored nature of parish relief.

In Campton four individuals received a pension for three periods. Mary Goodship, Sarah Odell and Sarah Lansbury were all solitary, middle-aged women and the first two women were allocated relief again in their old age. Mary Goodship received pensions for nine months, then for a separate period of three years, and then for six months up until her burial. Sarah Odell's three pension periods ran for fifteen months, ten months and then for fifteen years and three months. Sarah Lansbury's pension arrangements were similar: her first pension lasted for eighteen months, the second for three years, and finally she received a weekly sum for twenty-four years and two months. The third pension periods were of long duration for Sarah Odell and Sarah Lansbury. The final pensioner, Frederick Gregory, received a pension when he was a widower with children and another two later in life when elderly; his pensions payments were for six months, nine months and four years.

The lists of those receiving medium-term parish pensions – for between five and ten years – were dominated by those towards the end of their lives: 41 per cent of these pensioners in Campton were elderly and 47 per cent in Shefford. In Campton, one-fifth of those receiving medium-term pensions were lone parents. This suggests that the expectation of the parish was to support lone parents for up to ten years, after which time the children might be able to earn something. Rowntree estimated that primary poverty lasted for around ten years during parenthood. The commitment of the parish to other children – orphans and those boarded out – was also usually medium-term. However, there was an important group whose histories were not life-cycle related: a fifth of medium-term pensioners were solitaries and this highlights the fact that the parish also paid such relief to another group.

Individuals and their families in receipt of long-term weekly sums – for more than ten years – were closer to being 'lifetime' paupers rather than life-cycle ones. Because these recipients were on relief for so long, more than half of them changed their family category whilst receiving their pensions.

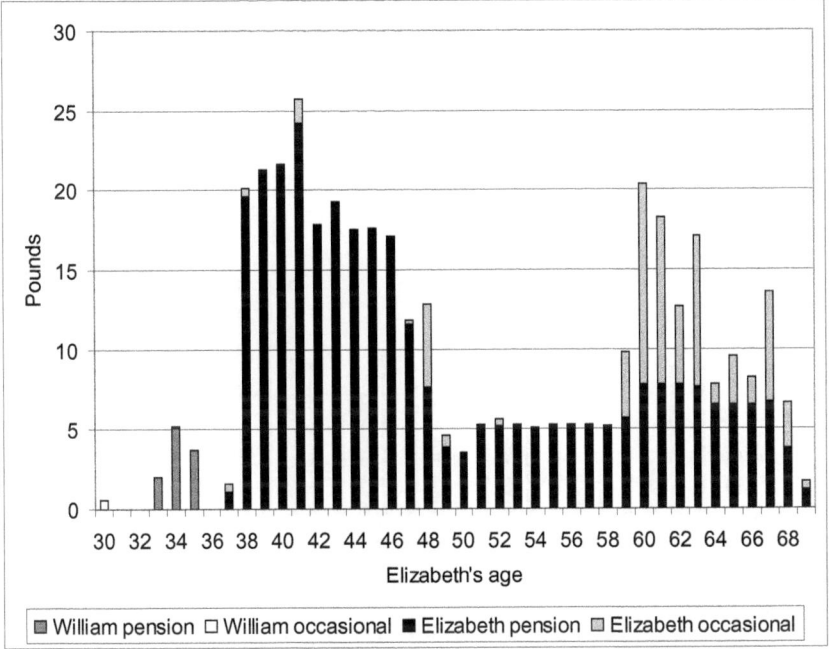

Figure 12. Pauper careers of William and Elizabeth Newman

In Campton, a significant proportion (30 per cent) started their relief careers as families or lone parents and their pensions continued into their old age without the break we might expect when their children had flown the nest and before the infirmity of old age crept in. There was some aspect to their lives that kept them on poor relief week after week, year after year, for more than a decade. Elizabeth Newman (see figure 12) and Ann Hayes, for instance, first came on to the relief rolls with their husbands and children. Relief continued to them after their husbands died, leaving them middle-aged widows with dependent children, and they remained pensioners even after their children were grown up and on into their old age. The poor law careers of Ann Herbert, Mary Thompson (see figure 13) and Esther Merryweathers (see figure 14) were very similar.

Just over one-third of long-term paupers were elderly, and a third of these were elderly couples who, when their spouse died, continued to receive their own pension. All of those relieved for more than twenty years were women. Solitary men and women also accounted for a small but significant group of long-term paupers. Elizabeth Bryant received a pension for nearly thirteen years, while Hannah Merryweathers, the unmarried incapacitated adult daughter of Esther Merryweathers, was on relief for eleven years (and she was still on at the end of the accounts, in 1834, and recorded as a pauper in the 1841 census) and she was a frequent patient at Bedford Infirmary.

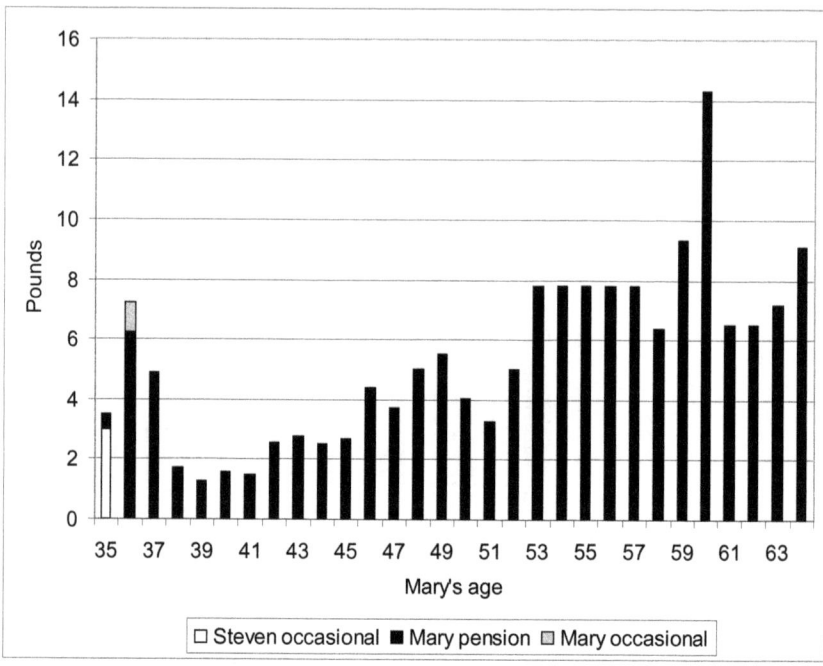

Figure 13. Pauper careers of Steven and Mary Thompson

For those paupers experiencing such long-term poverty, the only way off relief was death. Indeed, most of those receiving pensions in seventeenth-century Norfolk died on the parish.[48] In the Bedfordshire communities, however, the picture was more complicated. One-third of all pensioners (however long they were on relief) died on relief, and, for those in receipt of a pension for over five years, the figure was higher at 41 per cent in Shefford and 50 per cent in Campton. However, this still means that most pensioners did not die on relief. In one-fifth (Shefford) and one-quarter (Campton) of the cases where pensioners did die on relief, these individuals had also been pensioners at an earlier point in their life-courses. Even for the elderly, therefore, admittance to the relief rolls was not necessarily for the rest of their lives.[49] These figures reveal a somewhat more varied picture of the poor relief careers of beneficiaries than suggested by Tim Wales's smaller study. In the seventeenth century there were far fewer paupers and more were elderly than in Campton and Shefford in the later eighteenth and early nineteenth century. Death was not the only way off regular poor relief for most. Between

[48] Wales, 'Poverty, poor relief and the life-cycle', fig. 11.1 at pp. 362–4.
[49] Nine of the pensioners who were allocated a pension for more than one period were elderly (25% of those on relief more than once).

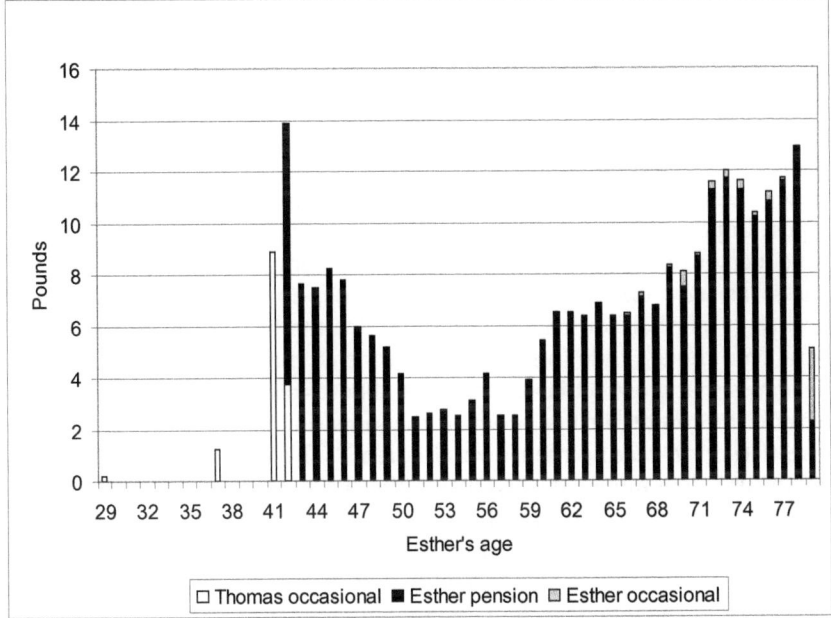

Figure 14. Pauper careers of Thomas and Esther Merryweathers

half and two-thirds of the regularly relieved did not die on the parish, but became independent of the parish once again.

There are other ways in which poverty might be conceptualised. One such is inherited poverty. Barry Stapleton found that a large proportion of the poverty relieved by charity in Odiham, Kent, between 1650 and 1850, could be described as such.[50] In contrast, in the Bedfordshire communities the vast majority of poverty was not inherited by children from their parents: in 68 per cent of cases there was no poverty link between consecutive generations of the same family. Those children who did fall into poverty in their adult years did so primarily due to life-cycle reasons, at the point in their life-course when they had their own children. There is little evidence of any pauperised 'under-class'.

### Kin and community

Another key theme is the relative strength of kinship ties.[51] Household structures and links between kin are important because of the implications

[50] Stapleton, 'Inherited poverty'.
[51] For recent contributions to this debate see R. M. Smith and N. Tadmor (eds), 'Kinship in Britain and beyond from the early modern to the present', *C&C* xxv (2010), special issue.

for poor relief. To what extent did the parish step in to fill the void of inadequate familial assistance? Due to the predominance of the nuclear (couples and their children), rather than the extended, household of pre-industrial populations and the high rate of geographical mobility, it has been argued that kinship ties were weak.[52] It has been suggested that households suffered 'nuclear-hardship' and that the collectivity had to provide material assistance.[53] The concept of 'nuclear family hardship' refers to the difficulties imposed upon individuals when they live in nuclear families.[54] Hardship is a product of disruption to the nuclear family unit, in Richard M. Smith's words, 'brought on by the death of a spouse, unemployment, sickness or senility – such that households found it difficult to be economically self-sufficient even though their formation rules insisted that couples should be so'.[55] He argues that grown children were not able to care for their elderly parents because the parent became needy at the same time as the couple's resources were tied up in rearing their own children.[56] The demographic availability of kin also determined the extent of the 'kinship universe'. Between the mid-seventeenth century and the early nineteenth century the average age of widowhood for women increased from 47.4 to 53.3. This meant that by the early nineteenth century widows had greater numbers of surviving children, siblings and grandchildren and therefore potentially more effective kin support. However, as Richard Wall points out, this also meant that there were more kin whom an individual might need to assist across generations.[57]

On the other hand, it has been argued by others that many households actually went through an extended phase or were close to, if not actually living with, numerous kin. Extension of the household could be a short-term arrangement for impoverished labouring families and up to three-quarters of households could be related to at least one other in the village or in an adjoining settlement.[58] Nevertheless, the lack of kin who were able to help might push a family on to poor relief. One of Mary Fissell's principal arguments is that many of those receiving poor relief in Bristol in the eighteenth

---

[52] P. Laslett, 'Family, kinship and collectivity as systems of support in pre-industrial Europe: a consideration of the "nuclear-hardship' hypothesis", C&C iii (1988), 153–75; Smith, 'Some issues'.
[53] Laslett, 'Family, kinship and collectivity', 153; Smith, 'Some issues', 73.
[54] Laslett, 'Family, kinship and collectivity', 153.
[55] Smith, 'Some issues', 73.
[56] Ibid. See also R. Wall, 'Economic collaboration of family members within and beyond households in English society, 1600–2000', C&C xxv (2010), 83–108 at p. 94.
[57] Ibid. 95.
[58] See Reay, Microhistories, 83–5, 163, 167; R. O'Day, *The family and family relationships, 1500–1900: England, France and the United States of America*, Basingstoke 1994, ch. i. On the elderly see Ottaway, *Decline of life*, ch. iv, and Thane, *Old age*, ch. vii. See also the work of D. Cooper and M. Donald on kin and social networks among the residents of the Old Tiverton Road, Exeter: 'Households and "hidden" kin in the early-nineteenth-century England: four case studies in suburban Exeter, 1821–61', C&C x (1995), 257–78.

century were lacking support from kin and friends.[59] Steven King has tested this supposition by dividing the poor into those who were 'kin-rich' and those who were 'kin-poor'. The kin-rich were linked by blood or marriage to at least two other people in their locality, while the kin-poor were not linked to any others. The latter came into contact with the parish at an earlier age and tended to stay on relief for longer. The kin-rich were a mixture of the chronic life-cycle poor, who were rich in kin but endemically poor, and the accidental poor, such as the sick.[60] King and others have also argued that assistance from relatives was a significant part of the makeshift economy and that help might come from the extended family, thus keeping families off formal relief.[61] In law, parents were responsible for their children, and sons and unmarried daughters could be held responsible for their parents, but only to provide monetary payments, not shelter. Grandparents were liable for grandchildren, but not vice versa, while married daughters and their husbands were not chargeable for their parents. Brothers, sisters, aunts, uncles, nephews and nieces could not be held responsible for one another.[62]

One way to explore the issue of the availability of kin in Campton and Shefford is to calculate the proportion of elderly pensioners who had adult children (from the family reconstitution) who might be expected to offer some support to their parents. The elderly formed the core of recipients and were frequently the highest cost. Of course, not all of those children who had been baptised in these communities and were now grown up would have continued to live near by; many would have moved away from the parish during apprenticeship or service, in search of other employment or upon marriage. As Richard Wall highlights, from the point of view of elderly parents the important criterion would have been the proximity of the nearest child. It would seem that the availability of kin was relatively high in east Bedfordshire. In the nearby parish of Cardington in 1782 a third of parents had a child resident in the same parish and nearly half of all married sons lived within five miles.[63] The proportion of elderly pensioners who had

---

[59] Fissell, 'The "sick and drooping poor"', passim, and *Patients, power, and the poor*, 101, 105.
[60] King, *Poverty and welfare*, 169–70.
[61] See the chapters in King and Tomkins, *The poor in England*.
[62] D. Thomson, 'I am not my father's keeper: families and the elderly in nineteenth-century England', *Law and History Review* ii (1984), 265–86 at pp. 268–70; 'Welfare and the historians', in L. Bonfield, R. M. Smith and K. Wrightson (eds), *The world we have gained: histories of population and social structure*, Oxford 1986, 355–78 at p. 365; and 'The welfare of the elderly in the past: a family or community responsibility?' in Pelling and Smith, *Life, death and the elderly*, 194–221; Smith, 'Some issues'; and Hindle, *On the parish?*, 49–50. Bonfield discusses the evolution of the law between about 1601 and the eighteenth century in 'Seeking connections between kinship and the law in early modern England', *C&C* xxv (2010), 49–82 at pp. 72–6.
[63] Wall, 'Economic collaboration', 97. Wall also assess the extent to which family members supported each other financially and the extent of co-residence. On co-residence in the eighteenth century see also Ottaway, *Decline of life*, 116–40, 150–71, 209–11.

grown up sons and daughters was 63 per cent in Campton and 58 per cent in Shefford. Only one-third of adult children in the two communities could be linked to their own marriages, indicating that many must have married in other parishes.[64] The proportion of the elderly with surviving adult children was high, which indicates that most of the elderly were apparently not kin-poor, and yet these elderly pensioners were receiving long-term financial aid from the parish. Around 30 per cent of the elderly in both parishes could not be linked to the family reconstitution, which might indicate that they were 'kin-poor', although these individuals may well have had family living in neighbouring parishes or further afield.[65]

There are other instances where family members can be glimpsed providing assistance in consultation with the parish authorities. Prudence Adams was allocated a pension of 3s. 6d. with her son promising Shefford's vestry 'that no further incumberance shall attend this Parish'.[66] It is not clear if this means that she was living with him or merely that her son was responsible for any further financial help that she required. It seems that her son kept his promise, since Prudence received the stipulated 3s. 6d. per week. This sum later declined to 3s., then fell back further to 2s., but there were no other payments to her. The vestry minutes are clearer in the case of Ann Bird. About the time that her husband deserted her it is recorded that, 'It is resolved that the relatives of Ann Bird shall be Allowed 18$^d$ p$^r$ Week providing they keep her under there Care', which is suggestive of co-residence. The overseers' accounts reveal that Ann Bird was resident in Shefford at this date, aged about sixty-two, and already in receipt of a pension. Thereafter she was paid as an out-resident, which indicates that she moved out of Shefford and presumably in with her relatives in another parish. Perhaps she was no longer able to remain independent due to failing health. She had three adult children in their thirties and one in his twenties. Before this decision Ann had been receiving considerably more – 3s. per week and 13d. worth of food, so the overseers saved money from her changed circumstances. The lump sums continued until her death in 1817. Susannah Ottaway comments that assistance to an elderly person by an adult child is mentioned only rarely in poor law and vestry records, but, where it is, there often appears to have been some negotiation between the son or daughter and the parish.[67] Family responsibility was one factor considered by Samuel Whitbread when making decisions on levels of relief. In one

---

[64] This was a time when only 10% of people never married: Ottaway, *Decline of life*, 165.
[65] These individuals did not marry or have their children baptised in Campton or Shefford.
[66] Shefford vestry minutes, BLARS, P70/8/1, 28 Apr. 1809; 22 Sept. 1809.
[67] Ottaway, *Decline of life*, 152–4, 175. Many of the elderly men and women who had surviving children did live with their offspring. Old women were more likely than men to live in homes headed by their children, while older men were more likely to head households containing unmarried children.

case where a wife wanted relief in 1814 because her husband was in prison for snaring, Whitbread records that she was receiving 2s. a week for herself and 2s. for each child; he advised the overseer to 'apply to the fathers on both sides for assistance'.[68] He was tough on men who deserted their wives and families and he sent them to prison to await quarter sessions orders.[69] The household listing for Cardington, Bedfordshire, in 1782 suggests that co-residence was uncommon since just 6.6 per cent extended to include kin or three generations.[70]

Another source of assistance between kin that is visible to historians is caring duties paid for by the parish. In Campton, most carers were unrelated to those for whom they cared, but on occasion a woman was also paid to assist a sick member of her family, and some carers were employed only to care for a relative. In most of the cases, married daughters were employed to nurse or wash for their sick or infirm mothers, such as Ann Whittemore, who was paid 4d. a week for washing for her mother, Widow Devereux, for twenty months. But there were other instances where assistance was given to sisters and grandmothers. In Shefford it was far rarer for relatives to be paid to care for one another and in only one instance does this appear to have taken place, in March 1820, when Eleanor Seamour and Mary Seamour were paid 14s. 10d. for 'doing for Wid Elizabeth Seamour in her illness and after decease'.[71] Similar cases can be found in the other Bedfordshire parishes of Luton and Aspley Guise, as well as in Essex, Dorset and Devon.[72] Once married, daughters were no longer legally obliged to support their parents, but there is clear evidence here that they were doing just that.[73] The evidence seems to suggest that relatives were paid to go into the homes of their kin to care for them, rather than that their elderly or sickly kin were living with them, but without a household listing for Campton and Shefford, actual living arrangements cannot be ascertained. Such payments have been interpreted by historians as reinforcing familial obligation, since

---

[68] *Whitbread's notebooks*, entry 795.
[69] Ibid. entries 744, 885.
[70] *Inhabitants of Cardington*, 33.
[71] This statement assumes that these women were related because they shared a surname.
[72] P. Bell, 'Early health care in Luton and Dunstable', *Bedfordshire Magazine* xix (Autumn 1984), 229–36 at p. 231; J. Walmsley 'Provision for the non able-bodied poor in the eighteenth and early nineteenth centuries: some evidence from three Bedfordshire parishes', *The Local Historian* xx (1990), 9–19 at p. 13; Ottaway, *Decline of life*, 97, 157, 230; P. Sharpe, 'Gender-specific demographic adjustment to changing economic circumstances: Colyton 1538–1837', unpubl. PhD diss. Cambridge 1988, 186. Ottaway found that in Terling, Essex, where kin were paid to care for one another, daughters nursed mothers, while in Puddletown, Dorset, sisters, mothers and nieces as well as daughters were paid by the overseers to look after their family members. The two examples that Sharpe gives of care between relatives in Colyton are of daughters caring for mothers.
[73] Thomson, 'I am not my father's keeper', 268–70; Bonfield, 'Seeking connections', 72–6.

overseers realised that financial responsibility between labouring households was difficult to maintain.[74]

What are the implications that are to be drawn from such evidence? It is clear that there was mutual assistance between relatives that was financially supported by the parish; however, this was relatively limited. Many of the elderly who had adult sons and daughters were receiving long-term relief from the parish. There are two possible explanations for this. The first is that adult children were themselves too poor to assist their ageing parents and, indeed, many grown up children did have young families themselves.[75] Susannah Ottaway notes that 'those old men and women who were most in need of assistance (the aged poor) had children who were unlikely to have the wherewithal to offer them support'.[76] That more families required relief during this period supports such an explanation. This was a period when child allowances were given and under-employment became a persistent problem. Another explanation, which is not incompatible with the first, is that families were not generally expected to be financially liable for elderly relatives. Despite the explicit statement within the old poor law that children should accept responsibility for their parents, David Thomson has found (and drawing upon evidence from Bedfordshire) that the law was relatively rarely implemented.[77] In contrast, however, there are pauper letters for Essex which reveal that overseers did sometimes pursue this avenue to relieve the rates.[78]

In summary, the overwhelming evidence from Campton and Shefford confirms that life-cycle poverty accounted for the majority of parish spending, in terms of pensions and relief in kind. However, there were small but significant groups which did not fit into this neat typology: solitary men and women and, in particular, long-term 'lifetime' paupers or those who were pensioners at a number of stages over the life-course. These life-courses were heavily pauperised. Poverty was experienced in a diversity of ways and poor relief was tailored to the needs of the recipients, in terms of 'customised care packages' of assistance to each pauper rather than standardised pensions.[79] Campton and Shefford relieved far, far fewer middle-aged couples with children than were recognised by Rowntree as in primary poverty in York in 1899 (anywhere up to three-quarters of those in poverty), despite the fact that there was a larger proportion of children in the population

---

[74] Fissell, 'The "sick and drooping poor"', 43; R. M. Smith, 'Charity, self-interest and welfare: reflections from demographic and family history', in Daunton, *Charity*, 23–49; J. Finch, *Family obligations and social change*, Cambridge 1989, ch. ii; Anderson, *Family structure*.

[75] Smith, 'Structured dependence', 424–5.

[76] Ottaway, *Decline of life*, 155.

[77] Thomson, 'I am not my father's keeper', and 'Welfare of the elderly', 196–200. Barker-Read also found this in five parishes in Kent: 'Treatment of the aged poor', 60–1, 273–86.

[78] Sokoll, *Essex pauper letters*, letter 379 at pp. 360–1.

[79] Ottaway, *Decline of life*, 189, 205.

earlier in the century.[80] Instead, Campton and Shefford's overseers sought to relieve the poverty of broken families before that of complete families: widows and widowers with children, and unmarried mothers. This must have meant that only a proportion of all children who were potentially in poverty were relieved, those in lone-parent families prioritised over those living in couple-headed families. This does not necessarily mean that couple-headed families were not poor, merely that their poverty was not always recognised by the formal poor law system. The clear winners were the elderly, who were relieved in large numbers, frequently long-term, with relatively generous pensions and the lion's share of relief in kind. Such welfare packages were not automatic, however, and an individual had to be past work in order to qualify. Of all adults receiving relief, women were favoured over men. Women accounted for the majority of lone parents and a large share of the elderly. This surely confirms that women were more likely to experience poverty than men, due to their poorer earning power and the difficulties of raising children alone. It must also suggest that there was a strong cultural belief in the deserving nature and dependency of women. Under the old poor law it seems that the parish was willing to shoulder the burden of poverty for some of these women; under the New Poor Law, however, women without male providers were viewed far more ambiguously.[81]

## Life-cycle, life-course and ratepaying

Ratepayer biographies reveal that couples and families made up the majority of ratepayers.[82] At the start of their ratepaying careers 27 per cent were young

---

[80] This figure includes 'chief wage earner out of work' (2.31%), 'irregularity of work' (2.83%), 'largeness of family' (22.16%) and 'in regular work but at low wages' (51.96%). The other causes of primary poverty were 'death of chief wage earner' (15.63%) and 'illness or old age of chief wage earner' (5.11%): Rowntree, *Poverty: a study of town life*, 120–1.

[81] P. Thane, 'Women and the poor law in Victorian and Edwardian England', *HWJ* vi (1978), 30–51. On the issue of how women were treated under the old and new poor laws see also Tomkins, 'Women and poverty'. Nigel Goose offers a different perspective to Thane in 'Poverty, old age and gender in nineteenth-century England: the case of Hertfordshire', *C&C* xx (2005), 351–84.

[82] Ratepayer biographies have also been assembled, so that it is possible to comment on their family circumstances. Almost two-thirds of them could be linked to the reconstitution, which indicates that these individuals recorded vital events in Shefford and we can, therefore, know something of their family circumstances when they were paying rates. It was more difficult to get information on the family circumstances for non-linked ratepayers, however, since for these there was no internal evidence on family structure in the rate books as in overseers' accounts. Some long-term ratepayers cannot be linked to the reconstitution, which either indicates that they recorded no vital events or that they lived elsewhere and paid for property in Shefford. William Long was one such whose property was valued at between £10 and £18 10s. for a cottage, land, meadow and a shop.

or middle-aged couples and 42 per cent had families.[83] Of course, many of the couples went on to have families (58 per cent). All these couples started to pay rates at marriage or shortly after, indicating that a significant section of the parish was deemed capable of paying rates at the point of setting up their own independent households. Edward and Mary Franklin, for instance, married in November 1812 and started paying the rates a year later when they had their first baby. They continued to pay the rates while they had a further three children. Thus many of these households could afford to pay parish poor rates even when they were at Rowntree's second primary poverty phase. In a small number of cases men, such as Thomas Kennings, were single when they started to pay rates but they too married and had children.[84]

Ratepaying continued into old age with over one quarter of those liable being over the age of sixty, Rowntree's third poverty phase. Elderly ratepayers could be part of couple-headed households, or could be widows or widowers. The proportion of ratepayers who were widowers was small (2.5 per cent), while 10 per cent were widows who continued to pay the rates after their husbands died; up to 8 per cent were elderly but some 2 per cent were not, with children under the age of fifteen. In two cases sons took over paying the rates from their fathers, presumably because they inherited the land and buildings that were being assessed. In another case, Henry Stonebridge paid rates, as did his son Henry and his daughter Mary when they married. For those with sufficient means, the life-cycle did not impact upon them to the point where they no longer qualified to pay the rates. However, ratepaying could be relatively short-term which suggests three possibilities: the migration of families from Shefford, a high turnover of ownership or tenancy, or that some families were no longer able to pay. Ratepayers could become exempt from paying the rates, no longer be assessed or they could come to require poor relief themselves.

It has been argued that ratepayers were willing to pay their rates because they, too, might require poor relief at some point in their lives.[85] Everyone had a settlement and in this period even the better off might sink into parish-dependent poverty through old age, illness, disability, insanity, bankruptcy or unemployment.[86] It was not uncommon for old men and women who had been small tradesmen or tenant farmers to fall into dependence upon the parish.[87] Robert Ray believed that his father should be relieved by

---

[83] These percentages are of ratepayers where familial circumstances are known.
[84] Some households in Aldenham stopped paying poor rates at this stage in the life-cycle, while in Kent a number of households were exempted from paying the poor rate if they kept their elderly parents: Newman Brown, 'Receipt of poor relief', 415; Barker-Read, 'Treatment of the aged poor', 277.
[85] See chapter 3 above.
[86] Snell, *Parish and belonging*, 103.
[87] Wells, *Wretched faces*, 17; Hitchcock, King and Sharpe, 'Introduction', 10.

the parish of St Botolph's, Essex, because he had been a ratepayer: 'my Father Paid Rates and Taxes to the Parish of St Botolfs a Great number of Years to help Support others and he is now entitled to that which he receives'.[88] In the Bedfordshire parish of Eaton Socon, at the beginning of the eighteenth century, John Cooper was paying rates, but, by 1733, he was receiving relief.[89] There is evidence of a similar pattern in Shefford. One-fifth of all ratepayers (fifty-eight) received some form of poor relief.[90] Ratepaying and relief receipt might be distinct and separate life-cycle stages, but they might also run in parallel. A small minority of ratepayer-paupers were women (13 per cent), just as a small proportion of women were ratepayers (16 per cent).

In 29 per cent of cases ratepayers received poor relief after they had stopped paying rates; 19 per cent were allocated occasional relief and 10 per cent regular weekly pensions.[91] These individuals contributed to the rates during middle age and then received relief later in life; the impact of alternating periods of prosperity and poverty on their lives can clearly be seen. Newman Brown found similar instances in Aldenham, Hertfordshire, in the seventeenth century.[92] After 1815 unemployment was an important reason for receipt of occasional relief by previous ratepayers. Over one-third of ratepayers receiving some form of occasional relief did so because of unemployment. Some were provided with parish work, such as digging gravel, or were sent to work for local farmers. In 14 per cent of cases rate-paying was interrupted by a period in the militia and their families received relief while they were away. Thomas Kennings, for instance, paid rates between 1805 and 1807. His family then received militia payments while he was away in the period 1809–10, and his ratepaying duties resumed between 1811 and 1820.

While it might be expected that relief would come after ratepaying, the two actually overlapped in almost half of all cases. Thirty-four per cent of such 'ratepayer-paupers' were given occasional relief whilst also paying the rates, such as John Godfrey, who paid rates throughout the period 1803–20 and yet was given poor relief of 2s. 6d. in August 1812 and three weeks' cash in February 1817 during a brief spell of illness. Samuel Ebdon's ratepaying and relief history is more complex. He received occasional cash for five months before the ratepayer books start and then paid rates from 1803 until 1805. During late 1804 he was given 2s. 6d. poor relief for six weeks, whilst still paying his rates. In March 1805 one poor rate was paid for by the

---

[88] Sokoll, *Essex pauper letters*, letter 379 at pp. 360–1.
[89] Godber, *History of Bedfordshire*, 366.
[90] The Shefford ratepayer books have been nominally linked with the overseers' accounts (which overlap for the periods 1803–17 and 1819–20) to create 'ratepayer–pauper' biographies.
[91] In some cases it cannot be known for certain that poor relief came after (and was not parallel with) ratepaying because the ratepayer books end in 1820 and poor relief was given after that date. In the remaining cases relief was paid before the ratepayer books started in 1803.
[92] Newman Brown, 'Receipt of poor relief', 415.

parish and he was recorded as excused the poor rate thereafter. He was given occasional relief again in October 1806, July 1808 and November 1809 until June 1810, in which period his three children and wife were ill and died.

Perhaps more surprisingly, ratepayer-paupers could also be allocated weekly pensions whilst they were paying rates. This happened in 15 per cent of cases. Thomas Rogers, for instance, paid poor rates between 1803 and 1805 and then again between 1807 and 1820. He was a pensioner from 1817, while he was paying rates, and received 5s. a week, and thus his pension and ratepaying overlapped between 1817 and 1820 at least. When Thomas's wife Alice reached her final illness care and food were paid for by the parish and when she died in July 1821 the overseer paid the £1 12s. 6d. for her funeral. Pension payments stopped with Alice's death, but Thomas was allocated a pension in his own right from 1824 at the reduced level of between 1s. and 3s. Paul Slack found the similar case of a widow in Temple parish, Bristol, in 1696 who paid a rate of ½d. per week and received a weekly pension for the poor children for whom she cared.[93] Some of those with overlapping ratepaying and relief histories also received additional relief later in life.

Austin Bowers's ratepayer-pauper biography highlights that individuals' histories could be complex and that they could fall into more than one category. He paid rates between 1813 and 1820, but no sum was actually collected in December 1816 and January 1817. He received occasional relief (cash, clothing, provisions) whilst paying rates – in 1813, 1814, 1819, 1820 – and after the ratepayer books end – in 1821, 1823 and 1824 (cash, unemployment pay). From October 1824, when he was aged sixty-five, he was allocated a regular weekly pension of 3s. 6d., plus payments for washing and mending, until his death, his funeral also being paid for by the parish, in August 1826. There are here a number of overlapping roles – ratepayer, then ratepayer-pauper, followed by a period of dependency upon the parish in old age.

Another form of occasional relief in kind was either exemption from ratepaying or the payment of the poor rates for the individual by the parish, as in the case of Samuel Ebdon. If individuals helped in this manner are included then the numbers relieved – and defined as 'poor' – increase. Another forty-nine ratepayers (18 per cent) were either excused paying their rates or were recorded as not actually paying anything on at least one occasion. The parish paid the rates at some point for nine of the ratepayer-paupers and an additional nine paupers had their rates paid, either to parishes other than Shefford or to Shefford outside the period of the ratepayer books, and so they might also count as 'ratepayer-paupers'. Unfortunately Campton's ratepayer books do not survive, but the overseers' accounts record thirty-three individuals as having their poor rates paid by the parish. These people can therefore be counted as ratepayer-paupers and added to a wider group of

---

[93] Slack, *Poverty and policy*, 178–9.

'poor'. Benjamin Hewitt requested that his rate arrears be paid by his settlement parish, St Peter's, Colchester, when he was out of work in Whitton, Suffolk: 'Sur i hav sent you a few lines to in form you that i have but a little work now and they come to me for the poors rate from last mickelmas and i cannot pay it and they sommods me on the hall this week and i must pay it with in a few days or els they will destress me for it so i hope you will send me a little money.'[94]

Identifying a cross-over between rate-paying and receiving relief, and calculating its prevalence, lends support to the argument that ratepayers must have been aware that they, too, might require relief one day. In over half of cases ratepayers received irregular assistance from the parish at crisis points in their lives, whilst one-quarter of ratepayers qualified for weekly pension payments, some for years. In addition, almost another fifth were excused ratepaying at some point. As ratepaying increasingly extended down the social scale to the less well-off in the market town over this period, awareness of their own potential need might have underlined the need to support the poor in Campton and Shefford and also shows that the poor rate and parish relief did not create rigid status distinctions.[95]

Childhood, parenthood and old age were expensive points in the life-course for parish officials in both Campton and Shefford. This underscores the life-cycle nature of poverty and its continuity from at least the early modern period to the modern day. But there is also evidence of considerable change. In terms of the aged during the eighteenth century, Ottaway found that, certainly at the end of the eighteenth century, there was a heavily gendered element and that it was markedly more acceptable to give an elderly woman a weekly dole than an aged man.[96] However, as the mid-nineteenth century approached it became equally acceptable to give an elderly man a weekly pension. This was in large part due to structural changes in the economy in the south and east that resulted in large numbers of agricultural labourers being thrown out of work. For preference farmers employed married men with dependants and overseers of the poor were prepared to support older men, who were no longer capable of heavy full-time work but were not yet totally dependent. The criteria for eligibility as a deserving object of relief had, from wider economic necessity, moved in their favour. Of course, it was never inevitable that parish officials would support these men; they could simply have chosen to offer supplementary and sporadic relief. However, farmers dominated vestry politics and they were able to manage local labour markets through the application of the poor law. Dominance by the farming community was not welcome to those ratepayers who were not employed in agriculture, who felt that they were subsidising such schemes.

[94] Sokoll, *Essex pauper letters*, letter 466 at p. 427.
[95] Slack, *Poverty and policy*, 178–9.
[96] Ottaway, *Decline of life*, 237–41.

There was continuity and change with regard to other groups of recipients. Families were relieved in larger numbers, as identified in the older economic histories of the old poor law, but the pauper biographies provide strong evidence that such relief was restricted to economic crises and was largely supplementary in nature. There was no widespread resort to Speenhamland-style allowances. The huge shift in welfare provisioning in favour of families, assumed as a given in the secondary literature, is simply not evident at the micro-level. Lone parents, and mothers in particular, were the 'broken families' that parish officials were willing to support in large numbers and with more generosity, and there are clear implications that the parish replaced absent male household heads. After the Poor Law Amendment Act guardians were more ambivalent in their support for women without husbands.[97] But it is also clear that the highest numbers of broken families, like couple-headed families, were also relieved in times of economic crisis.

For a substantial minority poverty endured for longer than any single life-cycle crisis, however, and these individuals and families remained on relief for significant periods. Their poverty was much closer to 'lifetime' poverty. There is, however, little evidence here of poverty being passed from one generation to another or of a developing under-class. It seems that kin were unwilling or, as is more likely, largely unable to assist their poor relatives. There is some evidence of assistance between kin through caring roles or residential arrangements, but it is clear that the community played a far more significant role in relief of economic distress and that relief policy in Campton and Shefford was far closer to the community end of the welfare continuum than the familial.[98]

---

[97] Thane, 'Women and the poor law'.
[98] Thomson, 'Welfare and the historians'.

# 5

# Work, Unemployment and the Makeshift Economy

That the poor law played a central part in local labour markets, as well as in the household economies of the labouring poor, is widely acknowledged. Crucial issues were the relief of unemployment, the setting of the poor to work, and the nature of the makeshift economy. There was widespread seasonal un- and under-employment of men and boys in agriculture in the cereal-growing regions after 1813; evidence for this in Campton and Shefford is to be found in the 'masculinisation' of the relief rolls. While most unemployed adult men and boys received only occasional payments in cash and kind, elderly men were increasingly reliant on regular poor relief as overseers sought to alleviate the surplus labour problem by siphoning off this group of working, but increasingly infirm, men. The post-war period was characterised by a proliferation of make-work schemes for the unemployed, while the parish also employed local people in a wide range of other parish tasks. After earnings, poor relief provided the core of the wider 'economy of makeshifts' by which the poor put together a living, but the makeshift economy also encompassed a diverse range of other resources and self-provisioning activities.[1]

## Unemployment and make-work schemes

Widespread winter unemployment in rural agricultural parishes has been dated to the period after 1813. One of the worst years was 1816 since the unemployment problem was aggravated by the discharge of troops. There was a temporary recovery in 1817 and 1818, but thereafter under- and unemployment increased again until the 1830s. In the words of Alan Armstrong, 'the distress seemed all but incurable'. Norman Gash has estimated that men were on parish allowances for three to five months of the year at below Speenhamland standard rates.[2] The worst cases of seasonal unemployment were in the south and east of England; seasonal fluctuations affected the

---

[1] King and Tomkins, *The poor in England*; Williams, 'Economy of makeshifts'. For definitions and discussion see chapter 1 above.
[2] N. Gash, 'Rural unemployment, 1815–34', EcHR vi (1935), 90–3 at p. 92; Armstrong, *Farmworkers*, 63–4, and 'The influence of demographic factors on the position of the agricultural labourer in England and Wales, c. 1750–1914', AgHR xxix (1981), 71–82.

pastoral areas of the north and west far less, where livestock provided year-round work. Periods without work affected adolescent boys as well as adult men. Un- and under-employment had a depressing effect on wages. In some areas the worsening economic situation in agriculture was aggravated by deteriorating opportunities for women and children's work, but in others, such as Bedfordshire, the problem must have been alleviated to some extent by the high demand for women and children in lace-making, straw-plaiting and hat-making.[3]

The issue was discussed in many of the parliamentary papers of the early nineteenth century. The *Select committee on labourers' wages* of 1824 asked parishes about the extent of relief to able-bodied men and in 1832 the Poor Law Commissioners stated that winter unemployment was common in Buckinghamshire, Bedfordshire, Cambridgeshire, Kent, Sussex, Essex and Surrey.[4] It was even argued that the increase in crime in agricultural districts was due to low wages and unemployment.[5] In Bedfordshire in 1830 T. P. Macqueen claimed that of ninety-six prisoners in Bedford gaol, seventy-six were of good character and only driven to crime by sheer want.[6] In 1817 the government had responded to the post-war distress with an act to provide loans for public works and parish relief. It has been argued that the significance of this act was its acknowledgement of the obligation of government to combat unemployment, the establishment of the regular practice of making government loans for public works, and the desire to raise the level of employment.[7] However, in terms of the provision of parish employment, its impact was minimal: most loans were given to canal companies, turnpike trustees and some public utilities.[8] Make-work schemes were instead provided at the level of the parish and paid for either out of the poor rates or the rates of the surveyors of the highways.

In both Campton and Shefford there was a large increase in the numbers of men and adolescent boys granted occasional relief for periods without work, particularly after 1815 (*see* figure 15). In the straw-plaiting trade younger children (aged between five and nine) of both sexes were generally employed in large numbers, but whereas older girls (aged between ten and fourteen) remained in the trade adolescent boys tended to graduate to agricultural labour.[9] In Toddington in Bedfordshire in 1867 it was noted that, 'At the age of 10 or 12 most of the boys exchange plaiting for farm work, but resume plaiting when severe weather or a scarcity of work prevents

---

[3] Armstrong, *Farmworkers*, 63–8; Godber, *History of Bedfordshire*, 449.
[4] Gash, 'Rural unemployment', 92; 'Rural queries', pt I, xxx.1.
[5] Gash, 'Rural unemployment', 91–3.
[6] Godber, *History of Bedfordshire*, 420.
[7] M. W. Flinn, 'The Poor Employment Act of 1817', EcHR xiv (1961), 82–92 at pp. 82–3, 85.
[8] Ibid. 88–90.
[9] Goose, 'Straw plait and hat trades', 105. See also chapter 1 above..

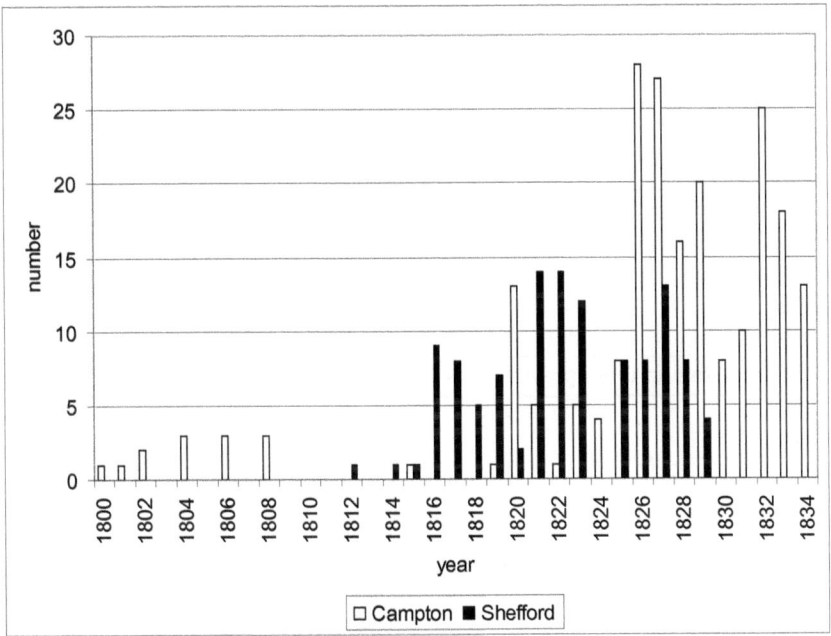

Figure 15. Number of unemployed men and boys, Campton and Shefford, 1800–34

them from labouring in the fields.'[10] However, from records of unemployment it would appear that older boys in Campton and Shefford did not return to straw-plaiting, either because it was considered 'women's work' or because local overseers were prepared to top-up or replace their earnings. In Campton and Shefford this meant that, after 1815, they were increasingly unemployed for some part of the year. The censuses between 1841 and 1901 record higher levels of male employment in the straw-plaiting and hat trades in Bedfordshire than in other straw counties, and this might reflect the continuing poverty problem as well as the determination of the Poor Law Guardians to withhold outdoor relief from able-bodied males.[11]

Payments to adult men and boys could be for just odd days without work (under-employment) or could be for a week at a time without work. In around one-third of cases the payments were for up to seven days without work while all other payments were for a week at a time or longer. Adult males were paid around 1s. per day when they had no work and there are frequent comments by the overseers of 'making up' a week's pay, which reveals that a system of allowances-in-aid of wages had been implemented. The unemployed accounted for a significant proportion of the increase in the

---

[10] This is cited in Goose, 'Straw plait and hat trades', 105.
[11] Williams, 'Economy of makeshifts'; Goose, 'Straw plait and hat trades', 100, 105.

### Table 13
### Numbers of the unemployed and unemployment expenditure, Campton and Shefford, 1800s–1830s

|  | Campton % | Shefford % |
|---|---|---|
| Numbers unemployed as a proportion of occasional recipients | | |
| 1800s | 16.7 | |
| 1810s | 4.1 | 13.8 |
| 1820s | 41.0 | 25.8 |
| 1830s | 44.8 | |
| Spending on unemployment as a proportion of occasional spending | | |
| 1800s | 4.6 | |
| 1810s | 2.0 | 6.9 |
| 1820s | 30.4 | 19.5 |
| 1830s | 33.4 | |

*Source:* Campton overseers' accounts, BLARS, P18/12/1–2, X514/1–3; Shefford overseers' accounts, P70/12/1–2; Campton and Shefford family reconstitution.

numbers of all those occasionally relieved: almost 45 per cent of occasional recipients in Campton by the 1830s and nearly 26 per cent in Shefford during the 1820s (see table 13). In 1826 twenty-eight men and boys were relieved in Campton (12 per cent of the male population), while in Shefford fourteen men and boys were relieved in 1821 and 1822 (4 per cent of the town's male population). It is evident that the problem was much greater in the agricultural parish than in its neighbouring market town.[12] Under- and unemployment persisted in Campton into the 1830s; it is unfortunate that there is no data for Shefford after 1828.

Figure 15 reveals that some men were unemployed in Campton before and during the French wars. Elsewhere there is evidence of increasing unemployment from as early as the 1770s. In Essex, Cambridgeshire and Berkshire occasional grants to able-bodied men unable to find work begin to appear more regularly from that decade.[13] However, the impact of unemployment was much greater after the wars ended. The northern Bedfordshire parish of Eaton Socon was relieving unemployed men in 1794, but the problem was particularly severe after 1818; between 1794 and the 1830s there was an eight-fold increase in the number of men relieved.[14] In central Bedfordshire parishes the highly seasonal availability of work during the 1830s pauperised a large number of families and rates of unemployment were reported at

---

[12] *Abstract of census returns*, 1831.
[13] This is quoted in Huzel, 'The labourer and the poor law', 771.
[14] Emmison, *Eaton Socon*, 50–60.

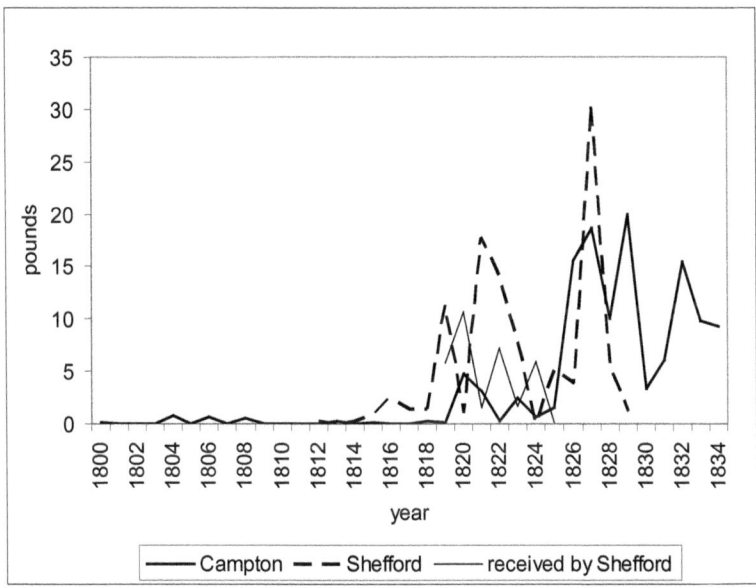

Figure 16. Cash payments to the unemployed and for make-work schemes, Campton and Shefford, plus receipts for work done in Shefford, 1800–34

between 3 and 25 per cent.[15] In Ampthill between 1826 and 1830 labourers were fully employed only at harvest-time; the parish experienced surplus labour for three-quarters of the year. The exact period of full employment varied each year depending on the weather and the number of labourers without work outside the harvest also varied.[16] Nevertheless, there was a core of men regularly out of work in the winter months: of those named in the winter of 1826–7, 60 per cent were named again two years later and 40 per cent three years on. In the Hundred of Redbornestoke, which included Ampthill, 523 men from thirteen parishes were recorded as, 'almost wholly on the hands of the overseers' in 1829.[17]

Figure 16 shows the cost of unemployment on the parish purse and the peak years of spending in the two communities: 1826–9 and 1832–4 in Campton, and 1819, 1821–2 and 1827 in Shefford. Payments associated with unemployment accounted for up to one-third of all casual expenditure in Campton and up to one-fifth in Shefford (see table 13). What must be kept in mind through this discussion, however, is that although the welfare net was being thrown ever wider to accommodate a greater number of unemployed men and boys, in terms of expenditure such recipients were rela-

---

[15] Williams, 'Economy of makeshifts', 23, 30.
[16] Boyer, *Economic history*, 91–3.
[17] Armstrong, *Farmworkers*, 64.

tively inexpensive when compared to pensioners. Despite George Boyer's contention that, 'the major function of poor relief in rural parishes from 1795 to 1834 was the payment of unemployment benefits to seasonally unemployed agricultural labourers',[18] the major function of poor relief in these two communities continued to be regular pensions to the elderly and to lone parents.

Although unemployment in both communities was highly seasonal, it was most notable in Shefford, where grreater numbers of men and boys collected unemployment pay in December, January, February and March, and fewer in August and September. In Campton, however, the shortage of work was so serious that labourers were unemployed in the summer as well as the winter. This was no longer just an issue of winter unemployment. In many other Bedfordshire parishes the sheer scale of the problem was such that labourers were out of work during part of the summer, but seldom during the hay-time or harvest.[19] In 1829 Campton's overseer paid seven unemployed men their 'Expences to the Hay County' so that they might find work elsewhere. The central Bedfordshire parish of Westoning had such a severe problem with the unemployment of agricultural labourers in the mid-1830s that up to 77 per cent of labourers were without work during the winter months and the average working year was just twenty-two weeks.[20]

Pay for parish work varied enormously and was sometimes very low. The overseers paid labourers by the day for 'doing the rounds' of the parish farmers, at between 3d. and 6d. per day, but of course such relief was topping up other payments from the farmers. Gravel work and stone picking was paid at piece rates (by the yard), for instance, '30 yards of Gravil at 9$^d$ Per yard'. Boys were paid less than adult men. Other parish work in Shefford for the unemployed included hoeing potatoes at the poor house. Without records of the cash payments made by farmers it is impossible to calculate the full amount paid to unemployed men and boys and to determine whether, as suggested by Norman Gash, the combination of wages and poor relief was below Speenhamland rates. Prevailing wage rates in the county were between 6s. and 9s. in 1824 and 9s. in 1834. Payments for a week without work were as low as 2s. 6d. and as high as 9s.; and so it appears that for some men allowances compared favourably with wages while for others they were pitiful, making it is difficult to generalise.[21] The household budgets for the parish of Westoning reveal that where the husband and father faced periods of unemployment the families were overwhelmingly pauperised: in 1834 more than 90 per cent of families received poor relief and these allowances accounted for 42.8 per cent of household income. Westoning's overseers

---

[18] Boyer, Economic history, 15.
[19] 'Rural queries'. For unemployment even during the harvest see Hobsbawm and Rudé, Captain Swing, 73–4.
[20] Williams, 'Economy of makeshifts', 30.
[21] Idem, 'Poor relief, labourers' households and living standards', table 5 at p. 507.

did not only relieve nuclear families: although twenty-seven couple-headed families with children were relieved, ten young single men, three elderly, men middle-aged couples and one single middle-aged man were also given allowances.[22] The situation was not so severe in either Campton or Shefford, however, which is perhaps indicative of better management of the local parish labour markets by their vestries and local farmers.

All unemployment payments in Campton and Shefford were made to males; it was never specified in the account books that women received cash for periods out of work. In Essex in the first half of the eighteenth century women received occasional payments for temporary periods without work, but by the end of the century, with the collapse of spinning, women were no longer recognised as being 'out of work' and no longer qualified for payments.[23] Keith Snell has argued that women were increasingly marginalised from the more highly paid harvest work and were relegated to the more poorly paid spring-time agricultural activities; this meant that they were more likely to be unemployed between July and February and least likely in the spring months of March–June.[24] In Campton and Shefford occasional payments to women displayed the opposite tendency and were highest in the winter months and lowest in August–October. If women were not relieved when out of work it might be that occasional payments simply reflected the seasons and more occasional relief was distributed in the winter. Moreover women in Bedfordshire need not necessarily have had to resort to poorly paid agricultural work (if indeed they could get it given the high levels of male unemployment) since they were employed in large numbers in lace-making and straw-plaiting. The highest earnings in straw-plaiting were to be had in the spring, and so women would choose this work over women's relatively poorly paid spring-time field activities.[25] James Turner commented upon such work in the county in the mid-1830s: 'The women and children were employed in making lace and plait, and would get more money in that way than in the fields, employed by the farmers; and so many boys and men being out of work, I should say that the women and children were not

---

[22] Idem, 'Economy of makeshifts', 31.
[23] P. Sharpe, *Adapting to capitalism: working women in the English economy, 1700–1850*, London 1996.
[24] Snell, *Annals of the labouring poor*, ch. i. There is a debate between Snell and Landau on the significance of the timing of settlement examinations: N. Landau, 'The laws of settlement and the surveillance of immigration in eighteenth-century Kent', *C&C* iii (1988), 391–420; Snell, 'Pauper settlement'; Landau, 'The eighteenth-century context of the laws of settlement'. The detail of this debate is not relevant here because in 1795 the settlement law (35 Geo III c.101) was amended so that removal could take place only when a person became actually chargeable to the parish, rather than when a person was merely thought 'likely' to become chargeable, and it is the period after 1795 which is the focus of attention here.
[25] Sharpe, *Adapting to capitalism*; Verdon, *Rural women workers*, ch. v. See also chapter 1 above.

employed in the fields.'[26] The most common by-employment for unemployed men in Westoning was also straw-plaiting, which, once the skill had been learned, could be easily picked up and put down between jobs. Another was travelling with a basket, but this paid very little, at most 1s. a week.[27]

Unemployment relief did not come without strings attached, and make-work schemes were adopted in both communities. The late eighteenth and early nineteenth centuries was a period of considerable innovation in terms of social policy at the local level. Work for the parish was primarily agricultural, such as weeding, wheeling logs, stone picking, and the roundsman system, and labourers were employed to work on the roads, undertaking tasks such as digging, wheeling and sieving gravel. In October 1829 in Shefford it was 'Resolved that all Persons applying for work to be employed on the Church paths, or in any way the Overseer may think proper.'[28] The most popular work scheme was gravel work and stone picking, followed by the roundsmen system and the repair of the roads. Unemployed men had been set to work on the roads from as early as 1773, and it seems to have been a common experience in the early nineteenth century. In the Warwickshire parish of Tysoe, men were regularly so employed, while in Berkshire unemployed men were given work at the gravel pit, peat pit or on the roads.[29] In the parish of St Botolph's, Colchester, a resolution was passed in May 1826 that those who applied for relief and were able to work were to be employed on the roads.[30] Many of the Bedfordshire parishes responding to the 'Rural and town queries' in 1832 used labourers to repair the parish roads and the unemployed were also set to work on the gravel pit.[31] Work on the roads could pay less than work as roundsmen.[32] Turnpike trusts and parishes built and maintained their local and county roads by means of the low wages of the seasonally unemployed rural labourer. Indeed, reports claim that never before had the notoriously impassable roads of southern England been in a better state of repair than in the early 1830s after several years of regular attention from pauper labourers.[33] However, the futility, inefficiency and brutality of road work were deeply resented by farm labourers.[34] Shefford

---

[26] *Select committee on poor law amendment act: twenty-sixth and twenty-seventh reports*, PP 1837–8 xviii, pt II.281, C359, report 26, 5, 7–8.
[27] Williams, 'Economy of makeshifts', 41–2.
[28] Shefford vestry minutes, BLARS, P70/8/1.
[29] A. W. Ashby, 'One hundred years of poor law administration in a Warwickshire village', in P. Vinogradoff (ed.) *Oxford studies in social and legal history*, Oxford 1912, iii. 146–62; S. W. Taylor, 'Aspects of the socio-demographic history of seven Berkshire parishes in the eighteenth century', unpubl. PhD diss. Reading 1987, 371.
[30] Sharpe 'The bowels of compation', 97.
[31] Boyer, *Economic history*, 21; *Poor law report*, XXV, XXVI, appendix B (2), 'Answers to town queries', 2h.
[32] Godber, *History of Bedfordshire*, 417.
[33] R. G. Cowherd, *Political economists and the English poor laws*, Athens, OH 1977, 143–4; Oxley, *Poor relief in England and Wales*, 117.
[34] Cowherd, *Political economists*, 143.

managed to claw back some of the financial outlay of parish work by getting their unemployed to work for others (*see* figure 16), but the amount that was reimbursed was small. Furthermore, the 'real' cost of work on the roads is under-recorded in Campton and Shefford, since the surveyors' accounts also note payments to men for work by the day on the roads. These accounts do not survive after 1815, when the unemployment problem was particularly acute, but it is clear that additional revenue was found from these funds and that surveyors thus subsidised the costs of the unemployed.[35]

The 'roundsman' system was only explicitly referred to in Campton in 1801 and 1804 and in Shefford between 1816 and 1820, but it is likely that it is hidden within the more general entry of 'work' in the overseers' accounts. A contemporary and local version of the system is given by Thomas Batchelor, the Lidlington farmer, in the *Report to the Board of Agriculture* (1808) (although he does not describe overseers 'topping up' wages):

> When a labourer can obtain no employment he applies to the acting overseer, from whom he passes on to the different farmers all round the parish, being employed by each of them after the rate of one day for every 20 l. rent. The allowance to a labourer on the rounds is commonly 2d. per day below the pay of other labourers.[36]

The roundsman system was not new in the nineteenth century and had been used to organise the labour of the unemployed in the county in the previous century. It was reported in Turvey in 1734, Toddington in 1758, Caddington in 1781, Eaton Socon from the 1780s, Lidlington in 1808 and in many other parishes.[37] Dissatisfaction with the practice was expressed in 1819. At the Epiphany quarter sessions of 1819 a general resolution was passed which had been proposed by the duke of Bedford. It was resolved that

> 1st. That the System of Roundsmen or of paying Laborers a certain portion of the wages of their Labour out of the Parish Poor Rates, which has too long prevailed in this County, is destructive of the Moral Energies of the Laboror, and equally injurious to the Interests of the Farmer, who has a right to expect a fair and adequate portion of Labor from the Hands employed on his farm.
> 2nd. That in order to discourage this pernicious practice, We recommend to the several Magistrates in this County, within their respective Divisions, not to allow any sums which shall after the first day of February next, to so paid out of the Poor Rates, in the Overseer's Accounts.

---

[35] Campton surveyors' accounts, BLARS, P18/21, 1794–1815.
[36] This is cited by Emmison, *Eaton Socon*, 50–1.
[37] Ibid. Emmison gives a list of Bedfordshire parishes using the roundsman system at p. 61 n. 146. Parishes are also recorded using make-work schemes in east Bedfordshire in *Whitbread's notebooks*, entries 839, 780, 781, 782, 32, 73, 23, 32, 73, 778–82, 814, 934. Eden records roundsmen in Northamptonshire in the mid-1790s: *The state of the poor*, i. 571.

3rd. That a sufficient Number of these Resolutions be printed and circulated forthwith and advertised in the Northampton Mercury and Bedford Gazette.'[38]

None the less there is evidence that the system continued in Shefford, as well as in Eaton Socon and other Bedfordshire parishes.[39] There is no evidence of the operation of the labour rate in either Campton or Shefford, but other Bedfordshire parishes resorted to this system for short periods of time in the 1830s.[40]

The parish authorities in the two communities responded to the problems posed by male unemployment in differing ways: while in both parishes many men and boys were given occasional relief and provided with work, in Campton a much larger number of older men was given regular weekly pensions. Indeed, 80 per cent of the pensions given to elderly couples date after around 1813. This shift might be seen as unexpected given that populations at the time were youthful. It is possible that the younger segments of the population were migrating out of the parish in search of better employment prospects, and leaving the aged behind. Yet there is abundant evidence in the overseers' accounts – in the form of unemployment relief – that adolescent boys and young fathers were staying put. The most plausible explanation for the rising proportion of elderly pensioners is economic: older men were being discriminated against in the labour market. In an over-stocked labour market older men were increasingly marginalised. They were slowly withdrawing from paid employment and their pensions might be interpreted as a mixture of long-term unemployment benefits and recompense for increasing infirmity. Such men were most likely to be physically worn out and suffering from chronic sickness, but still capable of some work. Before the problems of over-supply of labour these men had not been regarded as beyond work, but they now found that they were. Parish overseers would rather have relieved these men than younger men with families, whose claims to poor relief were especially unwelcome, and contemporaries certainly believed that male heads of families were favoured by farmers to keep them off the rates.[41]

Of those receiving a payment for unemployment in Shefford, the majority were between the ages of twenty-one and fifty, the 'most-economically productive' age groups (see table 14). However, nine were fifty and over, and one, Thomas Gobby, was in his eighties. Austin Bowers, Benjamin Bland and Thomas Gobby (see table 15) were three older men who received a mixture of the odd cash payment, clothing and food, and cash when out of work. As each became more infirm they were given weekly pensions that were intended to offset the diminishing market value of their labour; these men were no longer able to earn enough to support themselves but were not

---

[38] Emmison, *Eaton Socon*, 53.
[39] Ibid. 60–1; Godber, *History of Bedfordshire*, 416.
[40] *Poor law report*, appendix (D), 1–9.
[41] Ibid.

## Table 14
### Ages of the unemployed in Shefford, 1800–34

| Age | number |
|---|---|
| 'boys' or 'sons' | 5 |
| 15–21 | 2 |
| 21–50 | 16 |
| 50s | 6 |
| 60s | (2) |
| 70s | 1 |
| 80s | 1 |
| 'old' | 1 |
| not able to ascertain age | 17 |
| Total | 49 |

*Source:* Shefford overseers' accounts, BLARS, P70/12/1–2; Campton and Shefford family reconstitution.

*Note:* parentheses denote a man who received relief when he was in his fifties and sixties.

yet so infirm that they required full support. In 1813 and 1814 Benjamin Bland received some sporadic relief from the parish. In December of 1814 he took advantage of the pauper appeals system and complained to Samuel Whitbread who recorded that

> Benjamin Bland of Shefford complains that he has not sufficient allowance from the parish; he is more than 70, his wife 67; he is infirm and can do very little; the parish employ him to paddle on the road; they allow him 6s out of which he pays 1s a week rent. Ordered the parish to pay the pauper's rent in addition to the weekly allowance of 6s.[42]

Benjamin continued to do some work towards his upkeep until a year before he died, at the age of eighty-three.

An increase in elderly dependence has been found for other parishes in the south from the later eighteenth century onwards. In the Essex parish of Terling and the Dorset parish of Puddletown Susannah Ottaway finds that there were rises in the numbers and proportion of the aged receiving poor relief in the late eighteenth century, particularly older men: 'For the aged poor, the safety net offered by the Old Poor Law had been thrown wider in this period, but it was also weakened in strength by the economic hardships of the late eighteenth century.'[43] Richard M. Smith found a similar

---

[42] *Whitbread's notebooks*, entries 1053, 1055.
[43] Ottaway, 'Providing for the elderly', 409.

## Table 15
### Three case histories of Shefford's older 'unemployed' in the early nineteenth century

| Austin Bowers aged fifty-four in 1813 | | Benjamin Bland aged sixty-four in 1806 | | Thomas Gobby aged fifty-six in 1817 | |
|---|---|---|---|---|---|
| 1813 | clothing | 1806 | Ill | 1817 | cash, work |
| 1814 | cash, clothing | 1813 | cash | 1818 | cash, roundsman, unemployed, clothing |
| 1819 | provisions, cash | 1814 | cash | 1819 | cash, unemployed, clothing, ill, work |
| 1820 | provisions, cash | 1815 | cash, unemployed, roundsman | 1820 | work, cash, washing and mending |
| 1821 | cash, unemployed | 1816–17 | cash, unemployed, roundsman, ill | 1821 | work, washing, cash, provisions, ill |
| 1822 | cash, unemployed, roundsman | 1818–20 | pension | 1822 | ill, washing, clothing, unemployed |
| 1823 | work | 1821 | pension, unemployed | 1823 | cash, washing, clothing, work |
| 1824 | cash, pension, cash | 1822 | pension | 1824 | pension, washing, work |
| 1825 | cash, washing and mending, pension | 1823 | pension, unemployed | 1825 | pension, washing and mending, work |
| 1826 | pension, burial aged sixty-seven | 1824 | pension, ill, burial aged eighty-three | 1826 | pension, washing and mending, burial aged sixty-five |

*Source:* Campton overseers' accounts, BLARS, P18/12/1–2, X514/1–3; Shefford overseers' accounts, P70/12/1–2; Campton and Shefford family reconstitution.

masculinisation of pensioner populations in a number of parishes by 1780.[44] It seems extremely likely, based on the findings for Campton and Shefford, that pensioner populations became even more masculinised after the end of the Napoleonic Wars in the south and east. Certainly, the difficulty for older men only partially fit for work is a theme which pervades many of the Essex pauper letters across the early nineteenth century.[45] At the time of his first letter in 1818, William James, who was sixty-five, and his wife, who was seventy, were finding his earnings insufficient. He was an unskilled day labourer doing a wide variety of jobs. He was growing infirm and complained to the overseers of being unable to do hard work, of his illnesses, his weakness and fatigue. 'My strength, and all my faculties', he wrote in the summer of 1823, 'fail me very fast ... for many weeks past, sometimes work, & sometimes none, my Earnings have been but small ... I find health and strength decaying fast, so that when I have a little work to do, I find myself, through Age, and fatigue, incapable to perform it.'[46]

Many of the letters in the Essex collection mention that an elderly person was still working but not able to subsist without drawing poor relief, either due to insufficient earnings or because they could not find employment due to their age. One man, J. Berry, complained in the summer of 1818 that, 'they will not Employ a Old Hand. while they can get Plenty of young ones'.[47] William James referred to the 'dead state of Employment' in the 1820s and that, 'work is slack and meanly paid for. and I am not Able to do a days work as I have done'.[48] There are other letters describing the discrimination against the aged in a labour market flooded with younger competitors.[49]

After 1834 relatively high proportions of the elderly continued to be given outdoor relief in Bedfordshire despite the change in the law.[50] David Thomson has found that, on any one day in 1844, half of all men and two-thirds of all women over the age of seventy were regular paupers in Ampthill Union and that their pensions were sufficient for their maintenance.[51] Campton and Shefford were two of the parishes within this Union. E. H. Hunt has disputed Thomson's characterisation of these payments as 'old age pensions' and has suggested that these payments would be more accurately

---

44 Smith, 'Charity, self-interest and welfare', 39–40.
45 Sokoll, *Essex pauper letters*, and 'Old age in poverty'. See also King, 'Sickness and old age'.
46 Sokoll, 'Old age in poverty', 144–5.
47 Idem, *Essex pauper letters*, 389.
48 Ibid. 389–489.
49 Ibid. 614.
50 Thomson, 'Provision for the elderly', 20. Several of his themes are elaborated in his 'Decline of social welfare'; 'Welfare and the historians'; 'I am not my father's keeper'; 'Workhouse to nursing home: residential care of elderly people in England since 1840', A&S iii (1983), 43–67; and 'The overpaid elderly', *New Society*, 7 Mar. 1986, 408–9.
51 Idem, 'Provision for the elderly', 20, and 'Welfare of the elderly', 202.

described as 'disability pensions' for men and 'widows' pensions' for women.[52] Relief paid to men in their sixties was justified in the records because they were 'out-of-work', 'looking for work', 'worn-out by work' or 'past work'.[53] Hunt argues that full maintenance by the parochial authorities was more likely to be granted in places where the labour market was over-stocked and Bedfordshire was such a place.[54] Elderly men were also over-represented in the new union workhouses in the neighbouring county of Hertfordshire in 1851.[55] Thus it appears that male unemployment became an increasing problem in the south of England from the later eighteenth century onwards, that it was particularly severe from the end of the Napoleonic Wars, and that it persisted into the 1850s at least. Older men, who were less able to compete with younger men, and who were less expensive to relieve than a entire family, were the casualties of the over-stocked agricultural labour market and were pushed either onto outdoor relief or into the union workhouse. The Poor Law Amendment Act did not cut assistance to these men, but the introduction of the New Poor Law did result in a relocation of relief for them from their own homes to the workhouse.

### Other parish work

Make-work schemes for the unemployed were just one form of work provided by the parish authorities in Campton and Shefford. In particular, the poor law was a significant employer of medical services – nurses, carers and medical practitioners – as well as paying families for the boarding out of children, and others for the making and mending of clothing distributed to the poor. The running of the poorhouses also generated small-scale jobs, while local shopkeepers and other providers also benefited by supplying a wide range of goods for the poorhouses and for distribution as outdoor relief, particularly food and fuel. A distinction needs to be drawn between work provided for the poor, such as the roundsman system or road work, and other jobs generated by the administration of the poor laws, such as the contracted medical practitioner. In addition, there was a third type of parish work where necessary jobs were given to those who were still independent of parish relief.

One of the key aims of the Elizabethan poor laws had been the setting to work of the able-bodied poor and the apprenticing of poor children, all functions which the authorities of Campton and Shefford attempted to fulfil. As

---

[52] Hunt, 'Paupers and pensioners', 415.
[53] Ibid; Thomson, 'Provision for the elderly', 95–6.
[54] Hunt, 'Paupers and pensioners', 415–16.
[55] N. Goose, 'Workhouse populations in the mid-nineteenth century: the case of Hertfordshire', *LPS* lxii (1999), 52–69, and 'Poverty, old age and gender'. On the impact of demography upon agricultural labourers in the nineteenth century see Armstrong, 'Influence of demographic factors', 75–6, and *Farmworkers*, ch. iii.

part of this they assisted in the purchase of items for work or paid for instruction, usually for children or adolescents. In 1767 the orphaned Cooper girls were provided with 15d. worth of yarn; they were in their teens and their weekly pension sums of 21d.–30d. were obviously intended to supplement this work. Campton's overseer paid 16s. 10d. for 'Mary Clark two Children 2 pillows Bobbins Cotton thread parchment two horses for Lacemaking' and Widow Newman was paid 10s. to teach them. Likewise, £1 12s. was spent by Shefford's officials on lace-making items and instruction by Mrs Roberts in order to teach Steven's girl to make lace. Straw-plaiting was also encouraged: 10s. was paid 'for Larning Humberstone four Children to plat'. Large numbers of children and women were engaged in both these trades in east Bedfordshire in this period and children could be employed in both from the age of four.[56] Bedfordshire was known for its lace and straw schools and there is evidence here of the parish paying to get children started in these activities and so relieve the burden of the rates.

At the appropriate age, poor children might also be apprenticed, but there were very few instances of this in Campton and Shefford. This might reflect the decline in apprenticeship after the later eighteenth century which has been charted by Keith Snell; however, the research of Katrina Honeyman and Alysa Levene shows a counter trend for the same period. Honeyman argues that substantial numbers of pauper apprentices were sent to the workshops and factories located in industrialising areas, while Levene has shown that pauper appentices continued to be bound out to craft and traditional manufacturing placements.[57] To find work for older children and obtain a settlement for them elsewhere the parish authorities might also resort to putting out adolescents into service. Although there are few direct references to this in either Campton or Shefford, the evidence from the provision of full sets of clothing to adolescents suggests that they were being kitted out in preparation for service. In March 1833 there is an explicit reference in the vestry minutes: it was decided that the 'Boy of Widow Haddow be supplied with a suit of clothes to fit him for a Place in the employ of Stokes at Bedford, and that in consequence the allowance of 1/ per week be stopped in future'.[58] The pace at which farm service contracted is still a matter of debate within the historiography, with the most recent scholarship suggesting that this form of hiring survived for longer in the south and east, and within particular localities, than was previously thought and that it remained both resilient

---

[56] Goose, *Berkhamsted region*, 34–46, and *St Albans and its region*, 47–9, 70–4, 76–7; Cunningham, 'Employment of children', 137, 140–2.
[57] Snell, *Annals of the labouring poor*, chs v–vi; Honeyman, *Child workers in England*. Levene finds that 76% of pauper apprentices in a range of London parishes were bound out to traditional and newer manufacturing occupations: 'Parish apprenticeship', 927.
[58] Shefford vestry minutes, BLARS, P70/8/1.

and adaptable to capitalist agriculture.[59] However, despite the evidence of the persistence of pauper apprenticeship and farm service the employment prospects of adolescent boys in Campton and Shefford had worsened considerably, with few apprenticed or going into service, coupled with a rise in the number of boys unemployed in field work. They had been thrown into an unstable, casualised and increasingly saturated proletarian labour market.[60]

Carers and nurses accounted for the largest category of parish 'employees'.[61] The commitment of parishes to medical poor relief grew over the eighteenth century and generated work for carers and nurses as well as for contracted medical practitioners. Campton's overseers employed seventy carers over a sixty-seven-year period, while the overseers in Shefford employed thirty-two carers over thirty-four years. Care work in the two communities encompassed skilled nursing and more general forms of care and help with practical tasks, such as washing. Overseers of the poor did not make hard and fast distinctions between different forms of care, and often just referred to someone 'doing for' someone else – the term 'doing for' covered helping with household chores, doing the laundry, and nursing. In the two parishes the vast majority of care work was for 'doing for', 'attendance', 'looking after', 'care', 'nursing', 'washing' and 'cleaning'.[62] Other tasks were nursing women after childbirth, sitting up through the night with those acutely ill or dying, laying out the dead and helping with the funeral, and boarding out children. Similar forms of nursing and care work were provided in the other Bedfordshire parishes of Aspley Guise, Marston Morteyne, Northill, Eaton Socon, Luton and Dunstable.[63]

Most carers and nurses were women (three-quarters), but a small number of men were also employed. While women carers undertook the full range of task work, most of the male carers were paid on odd occasions just to attend other men, such as John Godfrey, for example, who was paid 3s. for

---

[59] For Berkshire, Norfolk, Nottinghamshire, Oxford, Somerset, Staffordshire and Sussex see Howkins and Verdon, 'Adaptable and sustainable?'; for Hertfordshire see Goose, *St Albans and its region*, 109–14; 'Farm service in southern England in the mid-nineteenth century', *LPS* lxxii (2004), 77–82; and 'Farm service, seasonal unemployment and casual labour in mid nineteenth-century England', *AgHR* liv (2006), 274–303; for Buckinghamshire see Leigh Shaw–Taylor, 'Family farms and capitalist farms in mid nineteenth–century England', *AgHR* liii (2005), 158–91; for Devon see Jean Robin, *The way we lived then*, Aldershot 2000, 50–4; and for the north see A. J. Gritt, 'The census and the servant: a reassessment of the decline and distribution of farm service in early nineteenth-century England', *EcHR* liii (2000), 84–106.
[60] In Hertfordshire in 1851 districts of economic vitality were associated both with higher levels of farm service and of casualisation, whereas seasonal unemployment was generally higher in the least dynamic areas: Goose, 'Farm service and seasonal unemployment'.
[61] Williams, 'Caring for the sick poor'.
[62] In the Norwich census of the poor for 1570, nursing came under the terms 'keeping' and 'helping': M. Pelling, *The common lot: sickness, medical occupations and the urban poor in early modern England*, London 1998, ch. viii.
[63] Williams, 'Caring for the sick poor'.

'Attend$^g$ Edw Hargrave' in 1816. It is likely that even when men engaged in caring tasks, they did not wash linen or scrub floors. The gendered division of labour probably pertained even where men carried out other parts of the nursing task.[64] Another way of putting the poor to work would be to employ those already on poor relief as carers, and thereby reduce the financial outlay.[65] The biographies of carers reveal that although around half of them received poor relief at some point in their lives, the proportion who were in receipt of poor relief at exactly the same time as they were employed in care work was just one-fifth in Campton and just over one-quarter in Shefford. Furthermore, in the vast majority of cases such employment did not alter the amount of their weekly pensions but was an additional payment. In 1807, for instance, Ann Collip was paid to care for Mary Ingram for four weeks. Ann was paid 2s. 6d. for nursing Mary and 3s. 9d. for doing the family's laundry. These payments were in addition to her weekly pension of 1s. 6d. It is significant that pensions were not adjusted to take into account the amount earned in care work: these carers were not earning their keep. In this regard, care work was not a make-work scheme like the roundsman system.

Carers in these two parishes can be placed into several different groups. Many carers were employed only once or twice, while others received a mixed bag of payments for care work and poor relief over the years, and a third group of needy women were allocated caring jobs so that they might earn a little more in some weeks. There was also a fourth small group of more 'professional' and skilled nurses, who nursed lying-in women and assisted during epidemics. Alice Arnold, for instance, was paid £2 1s. in 1781 for nursing Sarah Briant for a month following the birth of her son, and Thompson earned two guineas for around three weeks' attendance on those afflicted with the smallpox during an outbreak of the disease in Campton in 1832. Boarded-out children could bring in sizeable sums to the receiving households, at approximately 4s. a week: Ann Herbert earned 4s. a week for sixty-four weeks in 1796–7 boarding out Lansberry's children. However, the going rate for other care work was far less. Only small sums could be earned by sitting up with the ill and dying, generally 6d. per night. Washing was even more poorly paid at between 3d. and 9d. a week. More substantial sums could be made 'nursing' and 'attending', up to 8s., but payments for these tasks fluctuated between 1s.–2s. and 7s.–8s. per payment, and it is unclear from the account books how many weeks' work these larger payments were intended to cover. Moreover, care work had a seasonal aspect, with the least spent on it in the summer months and the most from October through to April.

The making and mending of clothing and bedding was another form of parish employment and there are many instances of local women being paid

---

[64] Pelling, *Common lot*, ch. viii.
[65] Fissell, 'The "sick and drooping poor"', 43; Walmsley, 'Provision for the non able-bodied poor', 13.

to perform these tasks at rates that varied between 4d. and 7s. 4d (see table 3). Servicing of the poor house also provided women with opportunities to clean the building or furniture within it or wash laundry. Mary Smith, for instance, was paid 1s. 6d. for washing at the Shefford poorhouse and Sene Madde, who had five bastard children, was regularly paid for 'doing for' the poorhouse, as well as caring for the sick. The poorhouse generated other maintenance jobs, such as whitewashing, glazing, the fixing or provision of new furniture or other goods, and providing fuel and food. Such jobs provided additional earnings to the family economies of the labouring poor and were just one facet of the makeshift economy.

## The mixed economy of social welfare and the makeshift economy

The survival strategies of the labouring poor consisted of a combination of poor law and charitable provision, together with a wider economy of makeshifts. What was the availability and value of such resources in the two Bedfordshire communities of Shefford and Campton, and how did they insersect with the poor law? Earnings of some form were the most important element in the family economy, hence the availability of employment opportunities at the local level was crucial.

All members of labouring families contributed earnings where they could. During the seventeenth and eighteenth centuries there was a growing reliance upon waged labour rather than self-employment and other self-provisioning activities.[66] Husbands usually contributed the most in earnings, but the proportion attributable to wives and children could be substantial, and was crucial in supporting families through the poverty cycle.[67] In Bedfordshire there were very high levels of participation by women and children in the labour market, predominantly in spinning, lace-making and straw-plaiting. In 1782 in the parish of Cardington, nearby to Campton and Shefford, married women recorded participation rates of 82 per cent for those aged between twenty and thirty-nine and 51 per cent for those aged between forty and fifty-nine, and girls were also employed in wage labour from a very early age. The participation rates of female workers remained high in the 1851 census, despite the collapse in spinning, as women and children had turned to lace-making instead.[68] The evidence from household budgets on the proportion contributed by wives and children in Bedfordshire is somewhat contradictory. Nicola Verdon's estimate for 1832 is the highest, at 13 per cent for

---

[66] Botelho, *Old age*, 74; J. Humphries, 'Household economy', in Floud and Johnson, *Cambridge economic history*, i. 238–67.
[67] Humphries, 'Household economy', 257–62.
[68] Saito, 'Who worked when', table 2 at p. 16.

women, a massive 42 per cent for children, and the remaining 45 per cent by men.[69] Such levels are confirmed by the budgets for the parish of Clophill in 1795, where the earnings of wives and children represented 42 per cent of household income.[70] However, in seven parishes in central Bedfordshire for 1834, women and children contributed a much more modest proportion – at between 12.5 and 27.6 per cent combined.[71] This is still slightly higher than those found more generally by Sara Horrell and Jane Humphries for low-wage agriculture at this time, at 18–22 per cent.[72] The proportion of earnings contributed by women and children to the household budgets collected by Horrell and Humphries is probably so low because all the 'low-wage agriculture' areas have been placed into one category by the occupation of the male household head. It is not possible to break down their sample by occupation and chronology and also by region. Nigel Goose suggests that this explains why the (higher) participation rates and earnings that he finds for the straw-plait and hat trades of Hertfordshire are not reflected in Horrell and Humphries's findings for low wage agriculture and this argument can be extended to Bedfordshire. He finds that earnings from the straw and hat trades could account for a substantial proportion of household income, adding between 4s. and 11s. per week in 1851, particularly in parishes where the trade was heavily dominant.[73] Female and child labour was central to the household economies of the labouring poor in Bedfordshire and the wider lace-making and straw-plaiting regions.

In the context of discussion of the economy of makeshifts it is important that earnings were not always paid in cash, but occasionally in kind and by exchange. Plaiters reported that 'we get a bit of plait, and we take it and get a pottle loaf, or two pottle loaves, for our plait'. A similar observation was made about lace-making in the northern parish of Eaton Socon in 1817: 'there is great difficulty in selling the lace at all without taking it out in goods in return; they cannot get ready money for their lace; they are obliged to take shop goods in return'.[74] This suggests that those employed in lace-making and straw-plaiting in certain areas had less negotiating power than those similarly employed in plaiting in the south of the county.

Charity was another – sometimes alternative, sometimes complementary – avenue of welfare assistance. The key feature of charitable provision was its variability from one location to another.[75] John Broad and L. A. Botelho have

---

[69] Verdon, 'Rural labour market', figure 6 at p. 317.
[70] Eden, *State of the poor*, iii, cccxxxix (5 budgets).
[71] Williams, 'Economy of makeshifts', table 5 at p. 34.
[72] Horrell and Humphries, 'Women's labour force participation', table 2 at pp.102–3.
[73] Goose, 'Working women', 21, and 'Straw plait and hat trades', particularly pp. 113, 117.
[74] Williams, 'Economy of makeshifts', 33, 36.
[75] Broad, 'Parish economies of welfare'.

emphasised that charitable funds could provide a significant complement to rate-based relief in three southern communities and two Suffolk parishes respectively.[76] In Campton, however, charitable assistance was relatively restricted. In 1823 annual relief was just £4 11s. 10d. in cash from Ellard's and Kelynge's charity and the Poor's Stock and another charity distributed two-penny loaves once a year.[77] Such sums compare very unfavourably with those of poor relief expenditure. Shefford had a feoffment estate, settled by Robert Lucas in the sixteenth century, for the maintenance of the town's bridges, causeways and highways, the surplus from which was to be given to the poor. In 1823 it was reported that 'There has been no overplus of revenue applied for or given to the poor of Shefford, for very many years', yet in 1867–8 charitable income in the town was reported at a substantial £139 15s.[78] This figure compares far more favourably with parish spending in Shefford, which was between £150 and £300 in the first three decades of the nineteenth century (see figure 2). Unfortunately no other records survive, but it would certainly appear that far more charitable relief was available in the market town. This could, perhaps, explain in part the lower levels of relief. Mary Barker-Read also found that there was far more charitable provision in the town of Maidstone than in the largely rural Kentish parishes of Cowden and Wrotham.[79]

Despite the restricted financial nature of charitable relief in Campton, records do survive for the parish's Ellard's and Kelynge's charity and analysis of these reveals the characteristics of charitable beneficiaries and their overlap with poor relief recipients.[80] The money of this charity was raised as interest upon capital of £48 'in the hands of William Ellard of Mepsal upon Bond' and an additional pound was paid by John Kelynge Esqr of Ampthill 'according to the last will & Testamt of the Revd Mr Antelminells Kelynge late Rectr' of Meppershall. Further money was added to the charity from communion money. The sums were distributed by churchwardens, curates and overseers of the poor once a year on the first Sunday after 5 November 'amongst poor and indigent persons of the parish, according to their several wants, and the size of their families'.[81] 'Communions Moneys' was also given out in Shefford in 1711; this is the only instance that has been found of

---

[76] Ibid; Botelho, Old age.
[77] Commission of inquiry into charities, 7.
[78] Ibid. 8–9; General digest of endowed charities for counties and cities mentioned in fourteenth report of charity commissioners, PP 1867–8, lii, pt II.1, C.433, 6.
[79] The annual income from charities devoted to relief of the poor in 1817 was £1 0s. in Cowden (rural), £39 15s. in Cranbrook (some urban with a large rural hinterland), £1,485 0s. in Maidstone (urban), £104 18s. in Tonbridge (some urban with a large rural hinterland), and £219 2s. in Wrotham (rural): Barker-Read, 'Treatment of the aged poor', 287–311, and particularly table 7.3 at p. 302.
[80] Campton charity records, BLARS, P18/25/14 1711, 1726–87. Barker–Read terms these types of charities 'small charities': 'Treatment of the aged poor', 304–6.
[81] Campton charity records, BLARS, P18/25/14; Commission of inquiry into charities, 7.

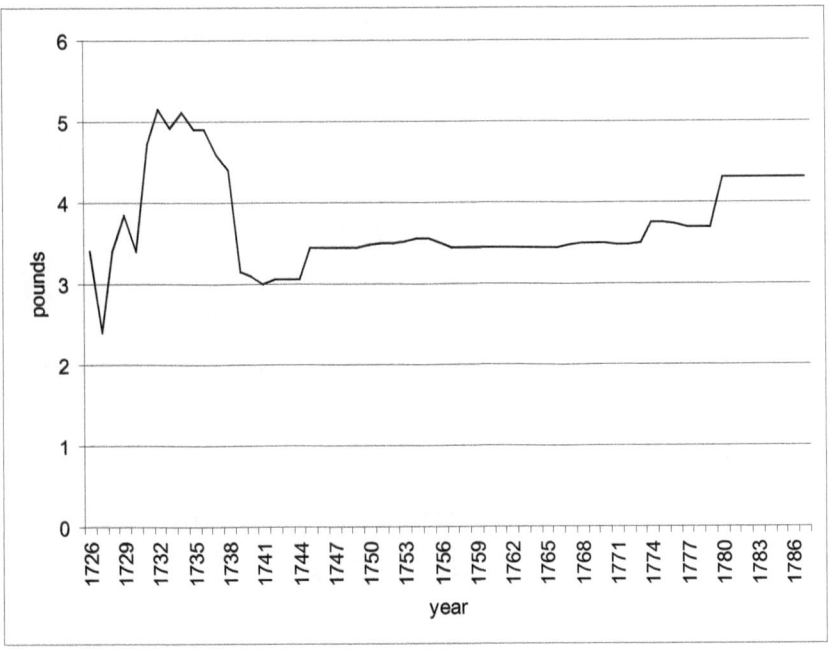

Figure 17. Ellard's and Kelynge's charity expenditure, Campton, 1726–87

charity in the market town. £2 was divided between fourteen men and fourteen women, and of the latter, eleven were widows.

Expenditure for Ellard's and Kelynge's charity increased between 1711 and 1734, with a fall thereafter until 1741 when it reached a plateaux, and thereafter increased slightly to 1787 (*see* figure 17). Sums distributed by the charity ranged from 1s. to 5s. *per annum*; small sums indeed. Despite this, the payments must have been valued by the beneficiaries as an addition to their meagre household income, and in terms of the status, respectability and recognition it conferred. The number of beneficiaries varied between twenty-two and thirty-six in any one year (*see* figure 18), figures that compare favourably with those in receipt of occasional poor relief and outnumber pensioners. In the 1760s there were nine poor relief pensioners and twenty-three occasional recipients, and twenty-five charitable beneficiaries; in the 1780s the figures were ten, twenty-eight and thirty-six respectively; and by the 1780s twenty-four people were allocated a pension, fifty-eight were given some form of occasional relief and fifty parishioners were listed as charitable beneficiaries. Only a minority of people received both poor relief and money from this charity in any one year: in 1767, for instance, one-fifth of charitable beneficiaries (five of twenty-three) were also in receipt of

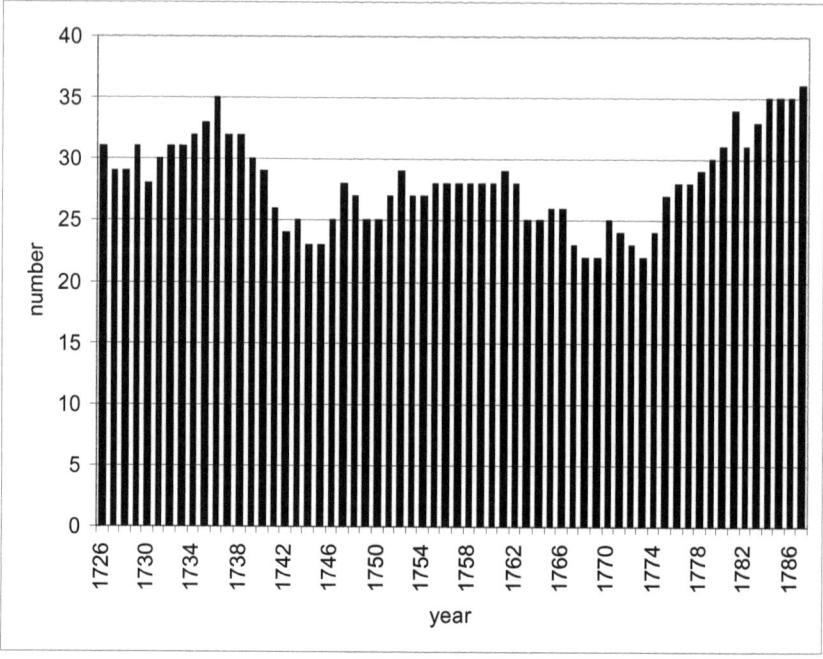

Figure 18. Number of recipients of Ellard's and Kelynge's charity, Campton, 1726–87

weekly regular pensions, three of whom were elderly widows.[82] Although not all beneficiaries were paid continuously and it was common for individuals to experience breaks in the money that they received from the charity, a significant minority were beneficiaries for a considerable length of time, with almost one-quarter receiving relief for twenty years or more. The longest durations were of forty-one, forty-three and forty-seven years (*see* table 16). This is in marked contrast with poor relief pension payments, with around half of all pensions lasting between six months and three years.

The familial characteristics of charitable beneficiaries were very different from those of poor relief recipients: 63 per cent were families, 11 per cent were married couples, 10 per cent were lone men, another 10 per cent were lone women, and the final 6 per cent were female-headed lone parent families. Only one woman, Widow Rogers, could be identified as elderly.[83] This means that more than four-fifths of the families of beneficiaries were headed by men. Fathers and their sons might also be in receipt of charitable funds at the same time, for example Thomas Lincoln, Sr, who received charitable

[82] Ibid. BLARS, P18/25/14.
[83] Charitable beneficiaries were linked with the family reconstitution and overseers' accounts.

## Table 16
### Duration of Ellard's and Kelynge's charity payments, Campton, 1726–87

| Years | number | % |
|---|---|---|
| 1 | 15 | 10.7 |
| 2 | 7 | 5.0 |
| 3 | 14 | 10.0 |
| 4 | 5 | 3.6 |
| 5 | 10 | 7.1 |
| 6 | 6 | 4.3 |
| 7 | 12 | 8.6 |
| 8 | 7 | 5.0 |
| 9 | 4 | 2.9 |
| 10–14 | 17 | 12.1 |
| 15–19 | 9 | 6.4 |
| 20 or more | 34 | 24.3 |

*Source*: Campton charity records, BLARS, P18/25/1–15.

payments between 1726 and 1757 and his son, Thomas Lincoln, Jr, who obtained payments in the overlapping period of 1753–5. Of the women, two-thirds were widows and it was they who regularly received the highest sums. In 10 per cent of cases the annual charitable payment had been transferred to widows upon the death of their husbands.

Occasionally, a reason is given for the payment: Elizabeth Nutkins, for instance, was an orphan, while in 1740 William Godfrey was given additional payment because he was sick, as was Widow Thorowgood in 1729. During the late 1720s and early 1730s there were some qualifications on benefit from the charity; a number of those listed were described as 'certificate people' who could only partake of the sacrament money. Decisions were sometimes recorded whether to start or stop payments to individuals: in 1755 there was a memorandum to the effect that 'Lincoln Junr Certificate to have it no more' while 'Hatwell Junr and Robt Coleman to be added next year'. In 1766 Widow Woodcock and James Waller were only to receive a charitable payment if they resided in Campton; such statements reinforce the point that welfare was exclusive to a parish's own poor. In December 1775 an additional sum of £2 10s. was raised and paid to the poor as the 'penalty for The Honble Mrs Osborn not being buried in Woollen according to Act of Parliaments'. Holding local public office did not disqualify John Derrick, who was clerk of the parish, from receiving charity in 1760, 1761 and 1762.

Overseers' accounts overlap with the charity lists for the period 1767–87 and linkage between the two reveals that 37 per cent of individuals received both charity and poor relief at some point in their lifetimes. This indicates that for the majority of charitable beneficiaries, however, poor relief was never forthcoming and that this charity provided an alternative avenue of 'makeshift' welfare. For those who did get parish assistance, more than half (53 per cent) received either some form of sporadic occasional relief (33 per cent) or regular weekly relief (20 per cent) at the same time. In 40 per cent of cases charity preceded any relief from the parish, again indicating an alternative form of welfare assistance before a request to the parish authorities for poor relief. In only 8 per cent of cases did any poor relief precede charitable payments, and this was only ever occasional relief.

The evidence presented indicates that charity and parochial poor relief, in Campton at least, relieved relatively separate groups of people and that charity offered an alternative, but far less valuable, resource. The Campton charity prioritised male heads of household, most of whom were in middle age, although it rewarded a small core of widows more highly. For many, charitable payments were given for periods far more lengthy than parish pensions, a situation that was possibly due to the small size of the annual pay-outs. It is likely that the recognition of need conferred by membership on this list made it easier for some to go on successfully to request more valuable poor relief later in life, while the poverty of a small group was such that charity and poor relief, either occasional or regular, meant that they received both at the same time. This was indeed a small makeshift in monetary terms, but a much larger one in terms of the hierarchy of resort and in terms of local status and belonging. In Shefford it would appear that there was far more charitable relief and the difference between two contiguous communities reinforces the fact that charitable relief was highly variable from place to place.

A wide range of other makeshift activities, by-employments and resources were available in Bedfordshire to further supplement the family incomes of the labouring poor. However, when their monetary value is quantified it becomes clear that very few of these could supplement income to a large degree and that, moreover, it was the poorest who had to resort to a multiplicity of activities of low value.[84] One such activity was to contribute to a friendly society to insure against sickness, temporary unemployment or the costs of burial; such societies were increasing in number rapidly during this period.[85] The Eversholt labourer Thomas Smart paid 15*d.* a month into a local society, of which he had been a member since 1800.[86] In Bedfordshire just four to five per cent of the population were recorded as members in 1803–4, but by 1835 it has been estimated that at least one parish in four had

---

[84] Williams, 'Economy of makeshifts'.
[85] M. Gorsky, 'The growth and distribution of English friendly societies in the early nineteenth century, *EcHR* li (1998), 489–511; Harris, *Origins of the British welfare state*, ch. vi.
[86] *The Bedfordshire farm worker in the nineteenth century*, ed. N. E. Agar (BHRS lx, 1981), 64–8.

some sort of friendly society.[87] In 1803–4 there were four friendly societies in Shefford, with a total of 146 members. This would equate to 31 per cent of the town's inhabitants, but it is more likely that some members subscribing to the town's societies lived in neighbouring parishes, possibly including Campton.[88] This was certainly the case in the northern Bedfordshire parish of Sharnbrook, where the friendly society also embraced other smaller parishes nearby.[89] In 1834 Dr Hunt commented that, 'There are no savings banks, and few benefit clubs or friendly societies in rural villages, but recourse may be had to such institutions in the market towns in the neighbourhood; but in these times very few young agricultural labourers in Bedfordshire save enough from their earnings to subscribe to such funds.'[90] In 1816 one of the Shefford friendly societies was held at the King's Arms and had its rules confirmed and filed by quarter sessions.[91] The parish of Westoning had a society called the Amicable and Brotherly Society with nineteen members and an age limit of forty-one years. They met once a month in the Chequers Inn and each member had to put in the box 2s. 6d. and spend 6d. The fund covered sickness and death: when ill a member would receive a small weekly sum and attendance from an apothecary; if he died £5 would be paid for his funeral.[92] The household budgets for Westoning in the 1830s reveal that 44 per cent of male household heads were members of friendly societies and that a weekly pay-out in times of sickness or unemployment of 7s. would have replaced three-quarters of the earnings of the head of household. William Aldridge, for instance, earned 10s. a week for forty-one weeks' jobbing and 7s. a week for four weeks from his club.[93]

The parish authorities even paid the odd subscription for members living in Campton and Shefford. The parish could see the economic sense in assisting parishioners to keep up their subscriptions since there would be cash pay-outs in cases of death, unemployment or sickness. There were a number of issues relating to friendly societies that made them of limited importance in comparison with the poor law, however. Pay-outs were restricted in duration for bouts of illness or temporary unemployment and, once exhausted, men could find themselves having to turn to the parish. Furthermore, many friendly societies only insured men, and other groups of expensive, long-term paupers, such as widows with children, would have to rely upon the parish instead. In addition, there is evidence to suggest that the sums paid out by friendly societies were inadequate during the agricultural depression, since by the 1820s and 1830s the overseers' accounts frequently mention 'topping

[87] *Abstract of the poor*, 1803–4, 6–7; Godber, *History of Bedfordshire*, 420.
[88] *Abstract of the poor*, 1803–4, 4–5; *Abstract of census returns*, 1801.
[89] Godber, *History of Bedfordshire*, 420.
[90] *Poor law report*, 506.
[91] Quarter sessions minutes, BLARS, QSM 26, 49 Mich Sess 1816.
[92] Godber, *History of Bedfordshire*, 420.
[93] Williams, 'Economy of makeshifts', 45.

up' the money coming from a man's club. In 1826–7, for instance, eight men had their pay-outs topped up by between 3s. and 4s. per week. Earnings also had to be sufficient to contribute in the first place and, as Dr Hunt suggested, the very poorest could not afford them. Martin Gorsky has highlighted that friendly societies were generally limited in areas of high poor law spending, such as Bedfordshire.[94]

Another makeshift was exemption from paying the poor rate: a minority of ratepayers were excused or defaulted on their rates; and a further group had their rates paid on their behalf by the parish; and another, much larger, group were never rated nor received relief.

Common rights could be very valuable indeed, but access to legal common rights in Campton and Shefford was also restricted. In the year before the enclosure of these communities only around 4 per cent of all agricultural labourers owned common rights dwellings.[95] None the less, labourers and their families would have had some access to self-provisioning on wastes and enclosure would have eliminated or curtailed such informal but customary 'rights', such as gathering fuel.[96] In Campton and Shefford in 1797 the 'rich common of 70 acres' was enclosed.[97] Keith Snell has found a strong association between the extent of parliamentary enclosure in certain counties (including Bedfordshire) and expenditure on poor relief. He has also argued that rising levels of poor relief expenditure and increasing numbers of unemployed labourers dependent upon the parish of Eaton Socon, in Bedfordshire, can be partly accounted for by enclosure.[98] Poor relief expenditure in Campton and Shefford rocketed in the years immediately following enclosure, but since this was also a time of harvest failure and rapid price inflation, it is difficult to tease out the relative impact of enclosure. After enclosure, labourers might have access to small pieces of land on which to grow their own food, but it would appear that self-provisioning in this way was also limited. Dr Hunt commented that cottages in the agricultural parishes in the immediate neighbourhood of Bedford only had very small gardens, although the practice of letting small additional portions of gardening ground (between one to two roods) was 'becoming general'.[99] In

---

[94] Gorsky, 'English friendly societies'.
[95] L. Shaw-Taylor, 'Labourers, cows, common rights and parliamentary enclosure: the evidence of contemporary comment c. 1760–1810', *P&P* clxxi (2001), 95–126, table 1 at p. 108, and 'Parliamentary enclosure and the emergence of an English agricultural proletariat', *JEcH* lxi (2001), 640–62.
[96] Snell, *Annals of the labouring poor*, ch. iv; Humphries, 'Enclosures, common rights, and women'.
[97] A. Young, 'Minutes concerning parliamentary enclosures in the county of Bedford', *Annals of Agriculture* xlii (1804), 22–33 at p. 27. The Enclosure Act for Campton and Shefford was in 1797 and the Award in 1799: W. E. Tate and M. E. Turner, *A domesday of English enclosure acts amd awards*, Reading 1978, 55–9.
[98] Snell, *Annals of the labouring poor*, 195–7, appendix C at pp. 207–9.
[99] *Poor law report*, appendix C, 499.

the central Bedfordshire parish of Westoning only one-fifth of labouring families grew their own garden produce, worth just 2.3 per cent of annual income. In some adjoining parishes, however, there were cottage allotments, and in other parishes some families had access to small pieces of waste by the side of the road on which they could grow barley, wheat and potatoes. The labourers who did cultivate gardens may have been able to produce a substantial amount of food. For instance, the labourer Thomas Smart said that his garden, which was less than a rood in size, was 'a great deal of use to me' and that on the land he could grow eighteen bushels of potatoes, which were sufficient for his family for the year (husband, wife and seven children). Some labourers might have been able to buy and fatten pigs for themselves or for market. The duke of Bedford provided a rood of ground for each cottager in Cople; the vicar Henry Pearse commented that '[the cottager] is both amused and employed by it … He is supplied with vegetables for his family, which would otherwise cost him 1s. per week. He is able also to keep a pig, and to pay his moderate rent, about 10s. per rood'.[100] However, Thomas Smart complained that he could not afford to buy a pig in the first place. It would even seem that pig-keeping and poor relief were two makeshifts that could not be exploited simultaneously; in the early 1830s families who owned a pig could be refused poor relief.[101] Gleaning was another form of self-provisioning, and one which Peter King has estimated could contribute between 3 and 14 per cent to the average labouring family's annual income, but in central Bedfordshire parishes in the 1830s gleaning was valued at only 10s. a year, which was equal to one week's work for an agricultural labourer and a maximum of 2.3 per cent of income.[102]

Some labourers resorted to petty crime in order to eke out a living: there were opportunities for poaching rabbits, hares, fish and game, individually or as part of a 'clutch of poachers'.[103] Poachers would have enjoyed a ready local market for their hauls, or swapped rabbits for beer in pubs, as well as providing meat for the table at home. Poaching rabbits was seasonal, however, and the autumn season was a short one, starting in September and coming to an end when frosts drove the rabbits to ground.[104] Furthermore, poaching carried a heavy financial cost if one were caught: fines were £5 per offence and three months imprisonment with hard labour. George Saby was not only fined £5 for each of his five offences, but he also lost his job.[105]

[100] Ibid., 371.
[101] Williams, 'Economy of makeshifts', 37–8, 40.
[102] King, 'Customary rights', 474; Williams, 'Economy of makeshifts', 35.
[103] *Whitbread's notebooks*. The index lists cases of poaching (51 entries). The quotation is from entry 491.
[104] R. Samuel, 'Quarry roughs', in R. Samuel (ed), *Village life and labour*, London 1975, section 4 at pp. 207–27.
[105] *Whitbread's notebooks*, poaching entries, George Saby, entries 764, 768.

Make-work schemes could also provide opportunities for illegal activity. Federick Fuller, for instance, was charged with stealing the parish stones at Wilden, while in January 1821 six men paid Shefford's overseers a joint sum of 7s. because 'Pebbles Stolen out of the Field when set to Dig Gravel'.[106] Stephen Whitbread, a Shefford blacksmith, was brought to quarter sessions 'accused of cutting down trees sticks, green stubbs and poles, property of Hy. Tingey, at Shefford Hardwick for which [the justice] has fined him 20/'.[107] It seems that some of the very poor might have resorted to begging in Shefford, since the vestry resolved in March 1828 that 'The constables have orders to apprehend all Vagrants found begging in this Town.'[108] A good reputation was another makeshift: being known for poaching reduced the chances of employment by local farmers and a good reputation was also critical to being able to buy a pig on credit.[109]

It is clear that labouring families in Campton and Shefford and the wider county of Bedfordshire, as all over England, put together a living through a multiplicity of sources. As well as income from earnings, a diversity of other non-wage income contributed to family economies and families employed numerous, and frequently overlapping, survival strategies to get by. The details of the mixed economy of welfare and the makeshift economy, and their relative importance, were always specific to locality. In Bedfordshire and the south-east more generally the most essential element of the makeshift economy – earnings – came under tremendous pressure in the early nineteenth century. After 1815 there was widespread unemployment of adult men and boys in field work and parishes stepped in to top up labouring incomes and to provide make-work schemes. In addition, while women and other children remained highly active in the labour market, the lace and straw trades also offered reduced earnings after the Battle of Waterloo. At the same time, access to and resources for self-provisioning contracted sharply. Charity provided little material aid in Campton, but what little it did provide was given to families and a few widows. Receipt conferred the status of being an object of charity as well as respectability. Far more charity was probably available in Shefford, however, which might account for lower parish spending. The mixed economy of social welfare was broader in Shefford. Friendly societies were a growing additional resource in this period, but membership was contributory and payouts were limited in duration and largely restricted to household heads. This was a period of worsening economic conditions exacerbated by a contraction in the wider economy of

---

[106] Quarter sessions records, BLARS, QSR/14, 19, 27 [n.d.].
[107] Ibid. QSR/14/1782/40 [n.d.].
[108] Shefford vestry minutes, ibid. P70/8/1.
[109] Williams, 'Economy of makeshifts', 42.

makeshifts, which must have made poor relief increasingly essential to those labouring people who qualified. Such a situation underscores the fact that poor relief became the central plank of the makeshift economy during the early nineteenth century.

# Conclusion

This book has sought to provide a highly detailed study of the poor and their families during the 'crisis' period of the old poor law, its findings based upon the detail available from the assembly of pauper biographies. Campton and Shefford have been placed 'under the microscope' in order to explore the nature and scope of poor relief in a period of increasing economic and social strain.[1] Micro-history and the local have been used as the site for the consideration of much wider issues, questions that can only be addressed adequately by analysis at the parochial, familial and individual level.

A number of conclusions can be drawn about the role of poor relief at the local level. The first is that the growth of social welfare, which has been identified by other historians for the later seventeenth and eighteenth centuries, continued. Expenditure on the poor in Campton and Shefford rose rapidly from the later eighteenth century, as did the number of both pensioners and occasional recipients. The most valuable form of relief was the regular weekly cash pension. Although the proportion of relief spent on pensions declined, the commitment of both communities to pension payments remained high, accounting for at least 70 per cent of parish spending. Overseers up-rated top pensions and pushed more pensioners into higher pension brackets. The welfare safety net was thrown ever wider, to incorporate male heads of families during the economic crises of 1799–1802 and 1815–22 and unemployed men and boys after 1813, without squeezing out the elderly poor and lone parents, both categories which were deemed the most deserving recipients of pensions. Yet the strain was evident from the 1810s onwards, when overseers particularly targeted relief in kind for cuts and sought to contain costs through medical contracts and infirmary subscriptions. Pension sums also fell back a little from the 1820s. Countering this trend was the amount spent on medical assistance, which actually rose in both communities. The poor law had become one of the most important sources of medical assistance for the poorest part of society and a significant employer of medical and caring services.

The second, and related, conclusion concerns the rather thorny issue of the level of generosity of the old poor law. Historians have generally fallen into the two broad camps of 'optimists' and 'pessimists', with optimists such as Richard M. Smith, Tim Wales, Peter Solar, David Thomson and Susannah Ottaway pointing to substantial levels of assistance to the elderly poor and the relatively high proportion of the aged receiving benefits, whereas Pat Thane

[1] Reay, *Microhistories*, 258.

and Steven King draw a far more negative picture of the restricted nature of relief.[2] There was a further regional dimension, with the north and west providing far less than the south and east.[3] The value of relief in Campton and Shefford can be measured in a number of ways. The first is the nature of relief which in Campton and Shefford was certainly all-encompassing. The second is the proportion of inhabitants in receipt of relief, which could be substantial, particularly at times of economic crisis such as the turn of the century. Another measure is the proportion of spending allocated to the most valuable form of relief, regular weekly pensions, which remained very high, and nominal pension sums were up-rated until the 1820s. The likelihood of receiving relief depended upon family circumstances, however, and the elderly and lone parents (primarily women) were far more likely to receive pensions than couple-headed families, and more generous ones at that. Pensions to married couples with children were limited in duration and were only ever supplementary, worth, at most, 29 per cent of their neighbours' incomes (measured in adult-equivalents). Pensions to lone parents generally lasted longer and were worth more, at up to 37 per cent, but this figure is still at a supplementary level. Like married couples, widows, deserted wives and widowers were clearly expected to contribute to their family economies either through their own earnings or those of their children. Indeed, the earning power of children could be crucial to these households.[4] The presence of the straw-plaiting and hat-making trades in Bedfordshire provided such opportunities for women and children. Lone men and women were somewhat in the middle of the range and could expect sums worth up to 45 per cent. It was the elderly who were most favoured by the parish authorities: pensions to old men, women, and couples were worth up to 62 per cent of the incomes of other local inhabitants and pension durations could be lengthy. They also received assistance tailored to their individual needs, including fuel and care. Such 'extras' added 8 per cent to their incomes (bringing it up to 70 per cent of neighbours' incomes). Nevertheless, pensions were rarely worth 100 per cent of the incomes of independent labouring families. Although relatively 'generous', even the pensions paid to the elderly fell short, so they must have depended upon other sources to supplement their parish pensions. If they did not, then they must have had to eke out that parish pension and must have led a meagre existence. This would appear to undermine somewhat the notion that relief was very generous. Yet, when this level of relief is

---

[2] Thane, *Old age*; King, *Poverty and welfare*; Smith, 'Ageing and well-being'; Solar, 'Poor relief'; King, 'Poor relief reappraised'; Solar, 'Poor relief: a renewed plea'; Thomson, 'The decline of social welfare'; Ottaway, *Decline of life*; Wales, 'Poverty, poor relief and the life-cycle'.
[3] King, *Poverty and welfare*, chs vi–vii.
[4] Wall, 'Economic collaboration', 90–1.

compared with that available in the north-west and what was available after 1834, when relief expenditures halved, it does appear 'relatively generous'.[5]

One of the most surprising findings of this book is the lack of support to couple-headed families. This is not what was believed by contemporaries, such as Thomas Malthus and the architects of the New Poor Law, Nassau Senior and Edwin Chadwick, who saw relief to able-bodied males as central in the operation of the poor law.[6] It is also in marked contrast to the views of many economic historians, who have argued that there was a marked shift in relief towards male heads of households after 1795.[7] All forms of allowances to married couples with children – child allowances, scaled relief, allowances-in-aid-of-wages and unemployment relief – were relatively short in duration and low in cost to the parish. Pensions to families were largely restricted to the periods 1799–1802 and 1815–22. The findings of this book do not confirm George Boyer's argument that the major function of poor relief in rural parishes from 1795 to 1834 was the payment of unemployment benefits to seasonally unemployed agricultural labourers.[8] This form of assistance was one function of poor relief in Campton and Shefford after 1813, but it was never the main function and the unemployed were relatively inexpensive when compared to pensioners. The major function of relief was to provide a substantial proportion of the incomes of the elderly poor and to provide large supplements to the family economies of lone parents.

Such decisions were made by the parish vestry, but while the vestry continued to be an important decision maker at the parochial level, magistrates were increasingly influential in the 'politics of the poor rate' at a regional level. Samuel Whitbread was a particularly active magistrate in the locality as well as a reforming member of parliament, each of his roles informing the other. It is highly likely that Whitbread's approach to poor relief in east Bedfordshire created a more uniform response by parish officers in a number of parishes under his jurisdiction and raised expectations among the labouring poor. A high proportion of paupers appealing to Whitbread had outcomes that were favourable to them. Scaled relief and child allowances were not frequently resorted to in either Campton or Shefford, but the issuing of a scale by Bedfordshire magistrates in 1800 might also have fostered a sense of entitlement to a minimum income by the poor. The 'politics of the poor rate' might also have been 'democratised' to some extent as Shefford's parochial officers increasingly rated down the social scale and even ratepayers who were not from the 'better sort' made it onto the vestry in Shefford. Furthermore, one-fifth of ratepayers would also be paupers at

---

[5] King, *Poverty and welfare*, chs vi–vii.
[6] Blaug, 'The myth of the old poor law', and 'The poor law reexamined'.
[7] See, for instance, Huzel, 'The labourer and the poor law', and the discussion in chapter 2 above.
[8] Boyer, *Economic history*, 15.

some point and, of these, the poor law and ratepayer careers overlapped in half of the cases. There was an attempt to restrict relief to settled 'inhabitants' by using the settlement laws to remove those 'likely to become chargeable' (before 1795) and those who actually became so after 1795.

It is also clear that poverty and the 'politics of the poor rate' had a gendered element: very large numbers of those regularly relived were women, either as unmarried mothers, widowed women with children, or elderly single or widowed women, while the vast majority of ratepayers were men and it was men who constituted the vestry. Poor women had to convince male overseers and vestry members that they were deserving objects of relief. Keith Wrightson has emphasised how the overlapping influences of gender and rank impacted upon women.[9] The poor law offers a window into the micro-politics of gender.[10] The fact that so many women were successful claimants underlines both the likelihood that they would require poor relief due to their poverty and their perceived 'deservingness'. The absence of a male breadwinner pushed women into dependence upon the parish. Elderly women and female-headed lone parent families accounted for the lions' share of high-cost, long-term pensioners in Campton and Shefford. Women headed the families of four-fifths of lone parents and women accounted for 53 per cent of the elderly (19 per cent were men and 28 per cent were couples). This situation changed somewhat with the large increase in the number of men and boys receiving occasional relief after 1815 for unemployment and the rise in the number of elderly men, either alone or married, pushed out of the labour market and onto long-term relief. In the face of a deteriorating economic situation in the south and east, the gendered element of being a proper object of relief shifted to accommodate older men who might, in previous decades, have still been able to do some work and remain independent of the parish. Whilst elderly infirm men past work had always qualified for relief, these men now qualified for regular assistance before they were completely worn out. The line between the able-bodied and the infirm had become blurred. In some south-eastern counties this situation continued under the New Poor Law, despite the law's insistence upon not relieving the able-bodied man.[11]

There operated in both Campton and Shefford 'mixed economies of social welfare', similar in many respects to those found by other historians for other localities. Charity provided some assistance in both communities, but rather more in the market town than in its neighbouring rural and agricultural parish. Even though Campton's Ellard's and Kelynge's charity gave out very little, receipt must have at least conferred status and some notion

---

[9] Wrightson, 'The politics of the parish', 20.
[10] L. Jordanova, 'Gender', in P. Burke (ed.), *History and the historians in the twentieth century*, Oxford 2002, 120–40.
[11] Thomson, 'The decline of social welfare'; Goose, 'Workhouse populations'.

of 'belonging'. Access to formal rights of common and informal customary rights existed before enclosure in 1797, although the evidence suggests that few of the labouring poor would have had access to them. Nevertheless, enclosure largely extinguished access to common and wastes, and at a time of rapid inflation and harvest failures. Other survival strategies which contributed towards the wider 'economy of makeshifts' were also contracting. In this context, the poor law became more central and essential in the lives of the labouring poor under the old poor law.

The life-cycle is central to any analysis of poverty and its relief. Around 85 per cent of all regular recipients in Campton and Shefford were elderly individuals or couples, families, lone parents or orphans. That poverty during parenthood was far more likely to be relieved by local overseers if one belonged to a broken family than an intact one would suggest, however, that a significant level of poverty was not recognised under the old poor law: Rowntree found that couple-headed families with more than four children accounted for 22.16 per cent of those in primary poverty in York in 1899, whereas 'death of chief wage-earner' accounted for 15.63 per cent. The disparity might be accounted for, at least in part, by the fall in adult mortality rates after 1870 which must have reduced the number of broken families in York by 1899.[12] Nevertheless, it would seem that overseers in Campton and Shefford showed less sympathy to the poverty of couple-headed families than to lone parent ones.

Finally, what light has been thrown on the urban-rural differences evident in the operation of the old poor law in rural Campton and Shefford, a market town? John Howlett suggested in 1792 that there were a number of important differences between town and country parishes.[13] He commented on the propensity for towns to spend less per head on poor relief than country parishes. Certainly, in terms of spending on the poor *per capita* of population, Shefford usually spent around half that of Campton, due to the town relieving far fewer of its residents. In Bedfordshire more generally market towns usually (but not always) spent less per head than rural parishes. In terms of spending *per pauper* in Campton and Shefford the difference narrowed considerably. Recipients in Shefford were not necessarily treated less generously. Howlett also argued that in rural parishes the number of paupers was twice that of towns. Campton did relieve a far greater number of inhabitants than Shefford: the rural parish gave poor relief to between 14.7 and 46.2 per cent of its population (including dependants), while Shefford gave assistance to between 10.6 and 17.3 per cent. However, spending was not one-third higher in Campton than in Shefford, which was a further suggestion that he made. Finally, Howlett argued that in country parishes around one half of the residents were given either regular or occasional poor

---

[12] Rowntree, *Poverty: a study of town life*, 120–1.
[13] Howlett, 'On the population and situation of the poor in England'.

relief; almost half the population did receive relief in Campton in 1801 (but not in Shefford), yet this high proportion was not sustained and it fell to 15–18 per cent thereafter.

There were further differences between the rural parish and the market town. In Shefford there were more occasional recipients and the proportion of funds given in occasional relief was higher. It spent far less in relief in kind than Campton in the 1790s, but, by the end of the period, the two communities were allocating a similar proportion of revenue thus. Shefford also allocated fewer top-rated pensions than Campton and the pensions given to the elderly were generally slightly lower. Yet the durations of pensions in Shefford could be longer than in Campton, despite the town relieving fewer pensioners. The market town also gave a greater amount of non-resident relief, particularly in the form of pensions. Shefford might have been able to relieve fewer of its inhabitants due to its more diversified occupational structure, which offered greater employment opportunities: the town was far less reliant upon agriculture than Campton. The 'mixed economy of welfare' was also broader in Shefford and the town could offer its poor far more in the way of charitable provision. Nevertheless, residents who did manage to secure relief from the overseers in Shefford were likely to receive relief that was slightly less generous.

Placing Campton's and Shefford's poor and their families, ratepayers, parochial officers and the local JP, Samuel Whitbread, 'under the microscope' has been extremely fruitful and rewarding. The poor law operated differently by region and from parish to parish; in the words of John Broad, 'the range of resources available to any individual or family reflected the particular circumstances of the parish community in which they lived'.[14] This book provides a unique insight into the detailed operation of the 'politics of the poor rate' in these two communities. The experience of poverty varied by gender, age, familial circumstances and life-cycle stage, as well as by locality. Recognition of this poverty and its relief was contested and negotiated. Social need and social response do not necessarily go hand-in-hand and understanding the interaction between the two at any one point in time is a complicated task for the historian.

---

[14] Broad, 'Parish economies of welfare', 986.

# Bibliography

### Unpublished primary sources

### Bedford, Bedford and Luton Archives Service

*Bedford Infirmary records*
HO:B/A1, HO:B/V18–19 Annual reports
HO:B/F1 Financial records
HO:B/M1–6 Minutes
HO:B/M4 Foul minutes

*Campton parish records*
P18/12/1–2, X514/1–3 Overseers' accounts
P18/16/1 Settlement records, solicitor's bill for a removal appeal, Henry and Ann Blundell, 1833
P18/21 Surveyors' accounts
P18/25/1–15 Charity records
Campton land tax, 1798
Campton-with-Shefford's baptism, marriage and burial registers
Manuscript, 1841 Census enumerators' books for Campton and Shefford

*Shefford parish records*
P70/8/1 Vestry minutes
P70/11/1–3 Ratepayers' books
P70/12/1–2 Overseers' accounts
P70/12/3–4 Bills and vouchers
P70/13/1–4 Settlement papers
P70/14/1–4 Apprenticeship records
P70/15/1–11 Bastardy records
P70/17 Militia records
P70/18/4/3–55 Letters to the overseers
P70/18/6 Pauper inventories
X465 Charity records
X465/320 Indenture, 1834
Shefford land tax, 1798

*Whitbread collection*
W1/325 Correspondence
W1/736–72, W1/806–25 Medical matters
W1/773–805 Return and letters

QSM/19, 22, 26 Quarter sessions minutes
QSR/19, 27 Quarter sessions records

**Cambridge, Cambridge Group for the History of Population and Social Structure**
Family reconstitution for Campton-with-Shefford and Southill

### Published primary sources

*Abstract of census returns*, 1801, 1811, 1821, 1831, 1841
*The merchants miscellany and travellers complete compendium*, Northampton 1785, in *Pigot and Co's national commercial directory*, London–Manchester 1830
*Pigot and Co's royal national and commercial directory and topography*, London 1839
*Post Office directory of Bedfordshire*, London 1847
*Robson's directory*, London 1839
*The universal British directory*, London 1792

### Official documents and publications (in chronological order)

*A bill to explain and amend so much of an act, made in the fifth year of the reign of Queen Elizabeth, intituled, 'An act containing divers orders for artificers, labourers, servants of husbandry, and apprentices,' as empowers Justices of the Peace at, or within six weeks after, every general quarter sessions held at Easter, to regulate the wages of labourers in husbandry*, PP 1795, xcvii, 97, 9 Dec 1795

*A bill to explain and amend so much of an act, made in the fifth year of the reign of Queen Elizabeth, intituled, 'An act containing divers orders for artificers, labourers, servants of husbandry, and apprentices' as empowers Justices of the Peace to regulate the wages of labourers in husbandry*, PP 1800, cxxvii.127, 13 Feb 1800

*Abstract of answers and returns under act for procuring returns relative to expense and maintenance of the poor in England*, PP 1803–4, xiii.1 C.175

*A bill for promoting and encouraging industry among labouring classes of community, and for relief of necessitous poor*, PP 1807, i.81 C.32

*Select committee on local acts for building houses for the poor, or for better collection of poor rates*, PP 1812–13, iii.463 C.113

*Abridgement of abstract of answers and returns relative to expense and maintenance of poor in England and Wales*, PP 1818, xix.1 C.82

*Commission of inquiry into charities in England and Wales: eighth report*, PP 1823, viii.1 C.13

*Select committee on practice of paying wages of labour out of poor rates: report, minutes of evidence*, PP 1824 vi.403 C. 392

*Abstract return on practice of paying wages of labour out of poor rates*, PP 1825 xix.363 C.299

*List of counties reported on, and not reported on, by commissions of inquiry into charities in England and Wales, 1819–28*, PP 1828, xxi.31 C.389

*Analytical digest of coms.' reports on public charities*, PP 1831–2, xxix.1 C.63

*Royal commission of inquiry into administration and practical operation of poor laws*,

PP 1834, xxvii.1 C. 44, appendix (B.1), 'Answers to rural queries', pts I–V; appendix B (2), 'Answers to town queries', pts I–V; Appendix (C) 'Communications'; appendix D, 'Labour rate'
Select committee on poor law amendment act: twenty-sixth and twenty-seventh reports, PP 1837–8, xviii, pt II.281, C359, report 26
Select committee on poor law amendment act: thirty-seventh, thirty-eighth and thirty-ninth reports, PP 1837–8, xviii, pt III.53 C.439, appendix
General digest of endowed charities for counties and cities mentioned in fourteenth report of charity commissionsrs, PP 1867–8, lii, pt II.1, C.433

## Newspapers and periodicals
*The Times*

## Contemporary books and articles

Batchelor, T., *General view of the agriculture of the county of Bedford*, London 1808
*The Bedfordshire farm worker in the nineteenth century*, ed. N. E Agar (BHRS lx, 1981)
Eden, F. M., *The state of the poor: or an history of the labouring classes in England*, London 1797
Howlett, J., 'On the population and situation of the poor in England', *Annals of Agriculture* xviii (1792), 573–81
Malthus, T. R., *Essay on population*, London 1798; 9th edn. London 1888
—— *The works of Thomas Robert Malthus*, IV: *Essays on population*, ed. E. A. Wrigley and D. Souden, London 1986
—— *T. R. Malthus: the unpublished papers in the collection of Kanto Gakuen University*, ed. J. Pullen and T. Hughes Parry, Cambridge 1997
*Samuel Whitbread's notebooks, 1810–11, 1813–14*, ed. A. F. Cirket (BHRS l, 1971)
Young, A., 'Minutes concerning parliamentary enclosures in the county of Bedford', *Annals of Agriculture* xlii (1804), 22–33

## Secondary sources

Anderson, M., *Family structure in nineteenth-century Lancashire*, Cambridge 1971
Apfel, W. and P. Dunkley, 'English rural society and the New Poor Law: Bedfordshire, 1834–47', *SH* x (1985), 37–68
Armstrong, W. A., 'The influence of demographic factors on the position of the agricultural labourer in England and Wales, c. 1750–1914', *AgHR* xxix (1981), 71–82
—— *Farmworkers: a social and economic history, 1770–1980*, London 1988
Ashby, A. W., 'One hundred years of poor law administration in a Warwickshire village', in P. Vinogradoff (ed.), *Oxford studies in social and legal history*, iii, Oxford 1912, 146–62

Aspinall A. and E. Anthony Smith (eds), *English historical documents, 1783–1832*, viii, London 1959, repr. 1996

Baugh, D. A., 'The cost of poor relief in south-east England, 1790–1834', *EcHR* xxviii (1975), 50–68

Beier, A. L., *Masterless men: the vagrancy problem in England, 1560–1640*, London 1985

Bell, P., 'Early health care in Luton and Dunstable', *Bedfordshire Magazine* xix (Autumn 1984), 229–36

Ben-Amos, I. K., *The culture of giving: informal support and gift-exchange in early modern England*, Cambridge 2008

Berg, M., *The age of manufacturers, 1700–1920*, London 1985

Berry, A., 'Community sponsorship and the hospital patient in late eighteenth-century England', in Horden and Smith, *The locus of care*, 126–50

Black, J., 'Illegitimacy, sexual relations and location in metropolitan London, 1735–85', in T. Hitchcock and H. Shore (eds), *The streets of London from the great fire to the great stink*, London 2003, 101–18

—— 'Who were the putative fathers of illegitimate children in London, 1740–1810?', in Levene, Nutt and Williams, *Illegitimacy*, 50–65

Blaug, M., 'The myth of the old poor law and the making of the new', *JEcH* xxiii (1963), 151–84

—— 'The poor law reexamined', *JEcH* xxiv (1964), 229–45

Bonfield, L., 'Seeking connections between kinship and the law in early modern England', *C&C* xxv (2010), 49–82

Botelho, L. A., *Old age and the English poor law, 1500–1700*, Woodbridge 2004

Boulton, J., *Neighbourhood and society: a London suburb in the seventeenth century*, Cambridge 1987

—— 'Going on the parish: the parish pension and its meaning in the London suburbs, 1640–1724', in Hitchcock, King and Sharpe, *Chronicling poverty*, 19–46

Boyer, G. R., *An economic history of the English poor law, 1750–1850*, Cambridge 1990

Broad, J., 'Parish economies of welfare, 1650–1834', *HJ* xlii (1999), 985–1006

—— 'Housing the rural poor in southern England, 1650–1850', *AgHR* xlviii (2000), 151–70

Brundage, A., *The English poor laws, 1700–1930*, Basingstoke 2002

—— and D. Eastwood, 'The making of the New Poor Law redivivus', *P&P* cxxvii (1990), 183–94

Burnett, J., *Useful toil: autobiographies of working people from the 1820s to the 1920s*, London 1974

Burnette, J., *Gender, work and wages in industrial revolution Britain*, Cambridge 2008

Cannan, E., *The history of local rates in England*, 2nd edn, London 1912

Charlesworth, A., 'The Captain Swing protests of 1830–1', in A. Charlesworth (ed.), *An atlas of rural protest, 1548 to 1900*, London 1983, 151–4

Cooper, D. and M. Donald, 'Households and "hidden" kin in the early nineteenth-century England: four case studies in suburban Exeter, 1821–1861', *C&C* x (1995), 257–78

Cowherd, R. G., *Political economists and the English poor laws*, Athens, OH 1977

Crawford, P., *Parents of poor children in England, 1580–1800*, Oxford 2010

Cunningham, H., 'The employment and unemployment of children in England c. 1680–1851', *P&P* cxxvi (1990), 115–50

Daunton, M. J., *Progress and poverty: an economic and social history of Britain, 1700–1850*, Oxford 1995

—— (ed.), *Charity, self-interest and welfare in the English past*, London 1996

Digby, A., 'The labour market and the continuity of social policy after 1834', *EcHR* xxviii (1975), 69–83

Dunkley, P., 'Paternalism, the magistracy and poor relief in England, 1795–1834', *IRSH* xxiv (1979), 371–97

—— *The crisis of the old poor law in England, 1795–1834: an interpretative essay*, London 1982

Dyson, R., 'Who were the poor of Oxford in the late eighteenth and early nineteenth centuries?', in Gestrich, King and Raphael, *Being poor in modern Europe*, 43–89

Eastwood, D., 'The republic in the village: the parish and poor at Bampton, 1780–1834', *Journal of Regional and Local Studies* xii (1992), 18–28

—— *Governing rural England: tradition and transformation in local government, 1780–1840*, Oxford 1994

Emmison, F. G., *The relief of the poor at Eaton Socon* (BHRS xv, 1933)

Evans, T., *'Unfortunate objects': lone mothers in eighteenth-century London*, Basingstoke 2005

Feinstein, C. H., 'Pessimism perpetuated: real wages and the standard of living in Britain during and after the industrial revolution', *JEcH* lviii (1998), 625–58

Fideler, P. A., *Social welfare in pre-industrial England*, Basingstoke 2006

Finch, J., *Family obligations and social change*, Cambridge 1989

Finlayson, G., *Citizen, state and social welfare in Britain, 1830–1990*, Oxford 1994

Fissell, M. E., 'The "sick and drooping poor" in eighteenth-century Bristol and its region', *Society for the Social History of Medicine* ii (1989), 35–58

—— *Patients, power, and the poor in eighteenth-century Bristol*, Cambridge 1991

Flinn, M. W., 'The Poor Employment Act of 1817', *EcHR* xiv (1961), 82–92

Floud, R. and P. Johnson, *Cambridge economic history of modern Britain*, I: *Industrialisation, 1700–1860*, Cambridge 2004

Fulford, R., *Samuel Whitbread, 1764–1815: a study in opposition*, London 1967

Gash, N., 'Rural unemployment, 1815–34', *EcHR* vi (1935), 90–3

Gestrich, A., S. King and L. Raphael (eds), *Being poor in modern Europe: historical perspectives, 1800–1940*, Oxford 2006

Gillis, J. R., *For better, for worse: British marriages, 1600 to the present*, Oxford 1985

Ginter, D. E., *A measure of wealth: the English land tax in historical analysis*, London 1992

Godber, J., *History of Bedfordshire, 1066–1888*, Bedford 1984

Goose, N., *Population, economy and family structure in Hertfordshire in 1851*, I: *The Berkhamsted region*, Hatfield 1996

—— 'Workhouse populations in the mid-nineteenth century: the case of Hertfordshire', *LPS* lxii (1999), 52–69

—— *Population, economy and family structure in Hertfordshire in 1851*, II: *St Albans and its region*, Hatfield 2000

—— 'Farm service in southern England in the mid-nineteenth century', *LPS* lxxii (2004), 77–82

—— 'Poverty, old age and gender in nineteenth-century England: the case of Hertfordshire', *C&C* xx (2005), 351–84
—— 'Farm service, seasonal unemployment and casual labour in mid nineteenth-century England', *AgHR* liv (2006), 274–303
—— 'The straw plait and hat trades in nineteenth-century Hertfordshire', in Goose, *Women's work*, 97–137
—— 'Working women in industrial England', in Goose, *Women's work*, 1–28
—— (ed.), *Women's work in industrial England: regional and local perspectives* (*LPS* supplement), Hatfield 2007
Gorsky, M., 'The growth and distribution of English friendly societies in the early nineteenth century, *EcHR* li (1998), 489–511
Green, D. R., *Pauper capital: London and the poor law, 1790–1870*, Farnham 2010.
Gritt, A. J., 'The census and the servant: a reassessment of the decline and distribution of farm service in early nineteenth-century England', *EcHR* liii (2000), 84–106.
Hampson, E. M., *The treatment of poverty in Cambridgeshire, 1597–1834*, Cambridge 1934
Harris, B., *The origins of the British welfare state: social welfare in England and Wales, 1800–1945*, Basingstoke 2004
Harris, T. (ed.), *The politics of the excluded*, c. 1500–1850, Basingstoke 2001
Healey, J., 'The development of poor relief in Lancashire, c. 1598–1680', *HJ* liii (2010), 551–72
—— 'Poverty in an industrializing town: deserving hardship in Bolton, 1674–99', *SH* xxxv (2010), 125–47
Hindle, S., 'Power, poor relief, and social relations in Holland Fen, c. 1600–1800', *HJ* xli (1998), 67–96
—— 'The problem of pauper marriage in seventeenth-century England', *TRHS* 6th ser. viii (1998), 71–89
—— *The birthpangs of welfare: poor relief and parish governance in seventeenth-century Warwickshire* (Dugdale Society Occasional Papers xl, 2000), 1–32
—— *State and social change in early modern England*, Basingstoke 2000
—— 'Exhortation and entitlement: negotiating inequality in English rural communities, 1550–1650', in M. J. Braddick and J. Walter (eds), *Negotiating power in early modern society: order, hierarchy and subordination in early modern Britain and Ireland*, Cambridge 2001, 102–22
—— *On the parish? The micro–politics of poor relief in rural England c. 1550–1750*, Oxford 2004
—— '"Waste children?" Pauper apprenticeship under the Elizabethan poor laws, c. 1598–1697', in P. Lane, N. Raven and K. D. M. Snell (eds), *Women, work and wages in England, 1600–1850*, Woodbridge 2004, 15–46
—— '"Without the cry of any neighbours": a Cumbrian family and the poor law authorities, c. 1690–1730', in H. Berry and E. Foyster (eds), *The family in early modern England*, Cambridge 2007, 126–57.
Hitchcock, T., '"Unlawfully begotten on her body": illegitimacy and the parish poor in St Luke's Chelsea', in Hitchcock, King and Sharpe, *Chronicling poverty*, 70–86
—— P. Sharpe and P. King, 'Introduction: chronicling poverty: the voices and strategies of the English poor, 1640–1840', in Hitchcock, King and Sharpe, *Chronicling poverty*, 1–18

—— P. King and P. Sharpe (eds), *Chronicling poverty: the voices and strategies of the English poor, 1640–1840*, London 1997

Hobsbawm E. J. and G. Rudé, *Captain Swing*, London 1969

Holland, M. (ed.), *Swing unmasked: the agricultural riots of 1830 to 1832 and their wider implications* (FACHRC publications), Milton Keynes 2005

Honeyman, K., *Child workers in England, 1780–1820: parish apprentices and the making of the early industrial workforce*, Aldershot 2007

Horden P. and R. Smith (eds), *The locus of care: families, communities, institutions, and the provision of welfare since antiquity*, London 1998

Horrell, S. and J. Humphries, 'Women's labour force participation and the transition to the male-breadwinner family, 1790–1865', *EcHR* xlviii (1995), 89–117

Howkins, A. and N. Verdon, 'Adaptable and sustainable? Male farm service and the agricultural labour force in midland and southern England, c. 1850–1925', *EcHR* lxi (2008), 467–95

Hufton, O. H., *The poor of eighteenth-century France, 1750–1789*, Oxford 1974

Humphries, J., 'Enclosures, common rights, and women: the proletarianisation of families in the late eighteenth and early nineteenth centuries', *JEcH* l (1990), 17–42

—— 'Female-headed households in early industrial Britain: the vanguard of the proletariat?', *Labour History Review* lxiii (1998), 31–65

—— 'Household economy', in Floud and Johnson, *Cambridge economic history of modern Britain*, i. 238–67

—— *Childhood and child labour in the British industrial revolution*, Cambridge 2010

Hunt, E. H., 'Paupers and pensioners: past and present', *A&S* ix (1989), 407–30

Huzel, J. P., 'Malthus, the poor law, and population in early nineteenth-century England', *EcHR* xxii (1969), 430–52

—— 'The demographic impact of the old poor law: more reflections on Malthus', *EcHR* xxxiii (1980), 367–81

—— 'Parson Malthus and the Pelican Inn protocol: a reply to Professor Levine', *Historical Methods* xvii (1984), 25–7

—— 'The labourer and the poor law, 1750–1850', in Joan Thirsk (ed.), *The agrarian history of England and Wales, VI: 1750–1850*, Cambridge 1989, 755–810

*The inhabitants of Cardington in 1782*, ed. D. Baker (BHRS lii, 1973)

Innes, J., 'The "mixed economy of welfare" in early modern England: assessments of the options from Hale to Malthus (c. 1683–1803)', in Daunton, *Charity*, 139–80

Jones, P., 'Clothing the poor in early-nineteenth-century England', *Textile History* xxxvii (2006), 17–37

—— 'Swing, Speenhamland and rural social relations: the "moral economy" of the English crowd in the nineteenth century', *SH* xxxii (2007), 271–90

—— 'Finding Captain Swing: protest, parish relations, and the state of the public mind in 1830', *IRSH* liv (2009), 429–58

—— '"I cannot keep my place without being deascent": pauper letters, parish clothing and pragmatism in the south of England, 1750–1830', *Rural History* xx (2009), 31–49

Jordanova, L., 'Gender', in P. Burke (ed.), *History and the historians in the twentieth century*, Oxford 2002, 120–40

Katz, M. B. and C. Sachsse (eds), *The mixed economy of social welfare*, Baden-Baden 1996

Kent, D. A., '"Gone for a soldier": family breakdown and the demography of desertion in a London parish', *LPS* xlv (1990), 27–42

Kidd, A., *State, society and the poor in nineteenth-century England*, Basingstoke 1999

King, P., 'Customary rights and women's earnings: the importance of gleaning to the rural poor, 1750–1850', *EcHR* xliv (1991), 461–76

—— 'Pauper inventories and the material lives of the poor in the eighteenth and nineteenth centuries', in Hitchcock, King and Sharpe, *Chronicling poverty*, 155–91

—— 'The rights of the poor and the role of the law: the impact of pauper appeals to the summary courts, 1750–1834', in R. M. Smith and S. King (eds), *Poverty, poor relief and welfare, 1650–1929*, Woodbridge 2010

King, S, 'Poor relief and English economic development reappraised', *EcHR* l (1997), 360–8

—— 'Reconstructing lives: the poor, the poor law and welfare in Calverley, 1650–1820', *SH* xxii (1997), 318–38

—— *Poverty and welfare in England*, Manchester 2000

—— 'Making the most of opportunity: the economy of makeshifts in the early modern north', in King and Tomkins, *The poor in England*, 228–57

—— 'The bastardy prone sub-society again: bastards and their fathers and mothers in Lancashire, Wiltshire, and Somerset, 1800–1840', in Levene, Nutt and Williams *Illegitimacy*, 66–85

—— '"It is impossible for our Vestry to judge his case into perfection from here": managing the distance dimensions of poor relief, 1800–40', *Rural History* xvi (2005), 161–89

—— '"Stop this overwhelming torment of destiny": negotiating financial aid at times of sickness under the English old poor law, 1800–1840', *Bulletin of the History of Medicine* lxxix (2005), 228–60

—— 'The clothing of the poor: a matter of pride or a matter of shame?', in Gestrich, King and Raphael, *Being poor in modern Europe*, 365–87

—— 'Sickness and old age', in King, Nutt and Tomkins, *Narratives of the poor*, i. 1–125

—— 'Friendship, kinship and belonging in the letters of urban paupers, 1800–1840', *Historical Social Research* xxxiii (2008), 249–77

—— '"I fear you will think me too presumtuous in my demands but necessity has no law": clothing in English pauper letters, 1800–1834', *IRSH* liv (2009), 207–36

—— T. Nutt and A. Tomkins (eds), *Narratives of the poor in eighteenth-century England*, i, London 2006

—— and C. Payne (eds), 'The dress of the poor, 1700–1900', *Textile History* (special edition) xxxiii (2002), 1–127

—— and A. Tomkins, 'Introduction', in King and Tomkins, *The poor in England*, 1–38

—— and A. Tomkins (eds), *The poor in England, 1700–1850: an economy of makeshifts*, Manchester 2003

Kirby, P., *Child labour in Britain, 1750–1870*, Basingstoke 2003

Kussmaul, A., *Servants in husbandry in early modern England*, Cambridge 1981

Landau, N., 'The laws of settlement and the surveillance of immigration in eighteenth-century Kent', C&C iii (1988), 391–420
—— 'The eighteenth–century context of the laws of settlement', C&C vi (1991), 417–39
Lane, J., *Apprenticeship in England, 1600–1914*, London 1996
Laslett, P., 'The bastardy-prone sub-society', in Laslett, Oosterveen and Smith, *Bastardy*, 217–46
—— 'Introduction: comparing illegitimacy over time and between cultures', in Laslett, Oosterveen and Smith, *Bastardy*, 1–70
—— 'Family, kinship and collectivity as systems of support in pre–industrial Europe: a consideration of the "nuclear-hardship" hypothesis', C&C iii (1988), 153–75
—— K. Oosterveen and R. M. Smith (eds), *Bastardy and its comparative history: studies in the history of illegitimacy and marital nonconformism in Britain, France, Germany, Sweden, North America, Jamaica and Japan*, London 1980
Lees, L. H., *The solidarities of strangers: the English poor laws and the people, 1700–1948*, Cambridge 1998
Leonard, E. M., *The early history of English poor relief*, Cambridge 1900, repr. London 1965
Levene, A., 'Family breakdown and the "welfare child" in nineteenth- and twentieth-century Britain', *History of the Family* xi (2006), 67–79
—— 'Children, childhood and the workhouse: St Marylebone, 1769–81', *London Journal* xxxiii (2008), 37–55
—— 'Parish apprenticeship and the old poor law in London', EcHR lxiii (2010), 915–41
—— 'Poor families, removals and "nurture" in late old poor law London', C&C xxv (2010), 233–62
—— T. Nutt and S. Williams, 'Introduction', in Levene, Nutt and Williams, *Illegitimacy*, 1–17
—— T. Nutt and S. Williams (eds), *Illegitimacy in Britain, 1700–1850*, Basingstoke 2005
Lyle, M. A., 'Regionality in the late old poor law: the treatment of chargeable bastards from "Rural Queries"', AgHR liii (2005), 141–57
McIntosh, M. K., 'Networks of care in Elizabethan English towns: the example of Hadleigh, Suffolk', in Horden and Smith, *Locus of care*, 71–89
Mandler, P., 'The making of the New Poor Law redivivus', P&P cxvii (1987), 131–57
—— 'The making of the New Poor Law redivivus: reply', P&P cxxvii (1990), 194–201
Marshall, J. D., *The old poor law, 1795–1834*, 2nd edn, Basingstoke 1985
Neuman, M., 'A suggestion regarding the origins of the Speenhamland plan', EHR lxxxiv (1969), 317–22
—— 'Speenhamland in Berkshire', in E. W. Martin (ed.), *Comparative development in social welfare*, London 1972, 85–127
—— *The Speenhamland county: poverty and the poor laws in Berkshire, 1782–1834*, New York 1982
Newman Brown, W., 'The receipt of poor relief and family situation: Aldenham, Hertfordshire, 1630–90', in Smith, *Land, kinship and life-cycle*, 405–22

Nutt, T., 'The paradox and problems of illegitimate paternity in old poor law Essex', in Levene, Nutt and Williams, *Illegitimacy*, 102–21

—— 'Illegitimacy, paternal financial responsibility, and the 1834 Poor Law Commission Report: the myth of the old poor law and the making of the new', *EcHR* lxiii (2010), 335–61

O'Day, R., *The family and family relationships, 1500–1900: England, France and the United States of America*, Basingstoke 1994

Ottaway, S. R., 'Providing for the elderly in eighteenth-century England', *C&C* xiii (1998), 391–418

—— *The decline of life: old age in eighteenth-century England*, Cambridge 2004

—— and S. Williams, 'Reconstructing the life-cycle experience of poverty in the time of the old poor law', *Archives* xxiii (1998), 19–29

Oxley, G. W., *Poor relief in England and Wales, 1601–1834*, Newton Abbot 1974

Pelling, M., 'Old age, poverty, and disability in early modern Norwich: work, remarriage, and other expedients', in Pelling and Smith, *Life, death and the elderly*, 74–101

—— *The common lot: sickness, medical occupations and the urban poor in early modern England*, London 1998

—— and R. M. Smith (eds), *Life, death and the elderly: historical perspectives*, London 1991

Postan, M. M., *Fact and relevance: essays on historical method*, Cambridge 1971

Poynter, J. R., *Society and pauperism: English ideas on poor relief, 1795–1834*, London 1969

Rapp, D., *Samuel Whitbread (1764–1815): a social and political study*, London 1987

Razzell, P., C. Spence and M. Woollard, 'The evaluation of Bedfordshire burial registration, 1538–1851', *LPS* lxxxiv (Spring 2010), 31–54

Reay, B., *Microhistories: demography, society and culture in rural England, 1800–1930*, Cambridge 1996

—— *Rural Englands: labouring lives in the nineteenth century*, Basingstoke 2004

Robin, J., *The way we lived then*, Aldershot 2000

Rowntree, B. S., *Poverty: a study of town life*, 2nd edn, London, 1902

—— *Poverty and progress: a second social survey of York*, London 1941

Saito, O., 'Who worked when: life-time profiles of labour force participation in Cardington and Corfe Castle in the late eighteenth and mid-nineteenth centuries', *LPS* xxii (1979), 14–29

Samuel, R., 'Quarry roughs', in R. Samuel (ed.), *Village life and labour*, London 1975, 207–27

Sharpe, P., 'Poor children as apprentices in Colyton, 1598–1830', *C&C* vi (1991), 253–70

—— 'The women's harvest: straw-plaiting and the representation of labouring women's employment, c.1793–1885', *Rural History* v (1994), 129–42

—— *Adapting to capitalism: working women in the English economy, 1700–1850*, London 1996

—— '"The bowels of compation": a labouring family and the law, c. 1790–1834', in Hitchcock, King and Sharpe, *Chronicling poverty*, 87–108

—— *Population and society in an east Devon parish: reproducing Colyton, 1540–1840*, Exeter 2002

Shave, S. A., 'The dependent poor? (Re)constructing the lives of individuals "on the parish" in rural Dorset, 1800–1832', *Rural History* xx (2009), 67–97

Shaw-Taylor, L., 'Labourers, cows, common rights and parliamentary enclosure: the evidence of contemporary comment, c. 1760–1810', *P&P* clxxi (2001), 95–126

—— 'Parliamentary enclosure and the emergence of an English agricultural proletariat', *JEcH* lxi (2001), 640–62

—— 'Family farms and capitalist farms in mid nineteenth-century England', *AgHR* liii (2005), 158–91

—— 'Diverse experiences: the geography of adult female employment in England and the 1851 census', in Goose, *Women's work*, 29–50

Slack, Paul, *Poverty and policy in Tudor and Stuart England*, London 1988

—— *The English poor law, 1531–1782*, London 1990

—— *From reformation to improvement: public welfare in early modern England*, Oxford 1999

Smith, J. E., 'Widowhood and ageing in traditional English society', *A&S* iv (1984), 429–49

Smith, R. M., 'Some issues concerning families and their property in rural England, 1250–1800', in Smith, *Land, kinship and life–cycle*, 1–86

—— 'The structured dependence of the elderly as a recent development: some sceptical historical thoughts', *A&S* iv (1984), 409–28

—— 'Charity, self–interest and welfare: reflections from demographic and family history', in Daunton, *Charity*, 23–49

—— 'Ageing and well-being in early modern England: pension trends and gender preferences under the English old poor law, c. 1650–1800', in P. Johnson and P. Thane (eds), *Old age from antiquity to post-modernity*, London 1998, 64–95

—— (ed.), *Land, kinship and life-cycle*, Cambridge 1984

—— and S. King (eds), *Poverty, poor relief and welfare, 1650–1929*, Woodbridge 2011

—— and N. Tadmor (eds), 'Kinship in Britain and beyond from the early modern to the present', *C&C* xxv (2010), special issue, 3–190

Snell, K. D. M., *Annals of the labouring poor: social change and agrarian England, 1660–1900*, Cambridge 1985

—— 'Pauper settlement and the right to poor relief in England and Wales', *C&C* vi (1991), 375–415

—— *Parish and belonging: community, identity and welfare in England and Wales, 1700–1950*, Cambridge 2006

—— and J. Millar, 'Lone-parent families and the welfare state: past and present', *C&C* ii (1987), 387–422

Sokoll, T., 'Early attempts at accounting the unaccountable: Davies' and Eden's budgets of agricultural labouring families in late eighteenth-century England', in T. Pierenkemper (ed.), *Zur ökonomik des privaten houshalts, haushaltsnechnungen als quellen historicher wirtschaftsund sozialforschung*, Frankfurt–New York 1991, 34–58

—— *Household and family among the poor: the case of two Essex communities in the late eighteenth and early nineteenth centuries*, Bochum 1993

—— 'Old age in poverty: the record of Essex pauper letters, 1780–1834', in Hitchcock, King and Sharpe, *Chronicling poverty*, 127–54

—— *Essex pauper letters, 1731–1837*, Oxford 2001

—— 'Writing for relief: rhetoric in English pauper letters', in Gestrich, King and Raphael, *Being poor in modern Europe*, 91–111

—— 'Large families, wheat prices and the allowance cycle: poverty and poor relief in the agricultural community of Ardleigh, 1794–1801', in R. Wall and O. Saito (eds), *Social and economic aspects of family life-cycle*, forthcoming

Solar, P. M., 'Poor relief and English economic development before the industrial revolution', *EcHR* xlviii (1995), 1–22

—— 'Poor relief and English economic development: a renewed plea for comparative history', *EcHR* l (1997), 369–74

Stapleton, B., 'Inherited poverty and life–cycle poverty: Odiham, Hampshire, 1650–1850', *SH* xviii (1993), 339–55

Styles, J., *The dress of the people: everyday fashion in eighteenth–century England*, London 2007

Tate, W. E. and M. E. Turner, *A domesday of English enclosure acts and awards*, Reading 1978

Taylor, G., *The problem of poverty, 1660–1834*, London 1969

Taylor, J. S., *Poverty, migration, and settlement in the industrial revolution: sojourners' narratives*, Palo Alto, CA 1989

—— 'A different kind of Speenhamland: nonresident relief in the industrial revolution', *JBS* xxx (1991), 183–208

—— 'Voices in the crowd: the Kirkby Lonsdale township letters, 1809–36', in Hitchcock, King and Sharpe, *Chronicling poverty*, 109–26

Thane, P., 'Women and the poor law in Victorian and Edwardian England', *HWJ* vi (1978), 30–51

—— *Old age in English history: past experiences, present issues*, Oxford 2000

Thomas, E. G., 'The old poor law and medicine', *Medical History* xxiv (1980), 1–19

Thomson, D., 'Workhouse to nursing home: residential care of elderly people in England since 1840', *A&S* iii (1983), 43–67

—— 'The decline of social welfare: falling state support for the elderly since early Victorian times', *A&S* iv (1984), 451–82

—— 'I am not my father's keeper: families and the elderly in nineteenth century England', *Law and History Review* ii (1984), 265–86

—— 'The overpaid elderly', *New Society*, 7 Mar. 1986, 408–9

—— 'Welfare and the historians', in L. Bonfield, R. M. Smith and K. Wrightson (eds), *The world we have gained: histories of population and social structure*, Oxford 1986, 355–78

—— 'The welfare of the elderly in the past: a family or community responsibility?', in Pelling and Smith, *Life, death and the elderly*, 194–221

Tomkins, A., 'Paupers and the infirmary in mid-eighteenth-century Shrewsbury', *Medical History* xliii (1999), 208–27

—— 'Women and poverty', in H. Barker and E. Chalus (eds), *Women's history: Britain, 1700–1850*, London 2005, 152–73

—— *The experience of urban poverty, 1723–82*, Manchester 2006

—— 'Men's paupers letters', in King, Nutt and Tomkins, *Narratives of the poor*, i. 205–97

Trumbach, R., *Sex and the gender revolution: heterosexuality and the third gender in enlightenment London*, London 1998

Verdon, N., 'The rural labour market in the early nineteenth century: women's

and children's employment, family income, and the 1834 poor law report', *EcHR* lv (2002), 299–323
—— *Rural women workers in nineteenth-century England*, Woodbridge 2002
Wales, T., 'Poverty, poor relief and the life-cycle: some evidence from seventeenth-century Norfolk', in Smith, *Land, kinship and life-cycle*, 351–404
Wall, R., 'Leaving home and the process of household formation in pre-industrial England', *C&C* ii (1987), 77–101
—— 'Some implications of the earnings, income and expenditure patterns of married women in populations in the past', in J. Henderson and R. Wall (eds), *Poor women and children in the European past*, London 1994, 321–35
—— 'Economic collaboration of family members within and beyond households in English society, 1600–2000', *C&C* xxv (2010), 83–108
Walmsley, J., 'Provision for the non able-bodied poor in the eighteenth and early nineteenth centuries: some evidence from three Bedfordshire parishes', *The Local Historian* xx (1990), 9–19
Wells, R., *Wretched faces: famine in wartime England, 1793–1801*, Sutton 1988
Williams, M., '"Our poor people in tumults arose": living in poverty in Earls Colne, Essex, 1560–1640', *Rural History* xiii (2002), 123–43
Williams, S., 'Caring for the sick poor: poor law nurses in Bedfordshire, c. 1770–1834', in P. Lane, N. Raven and K. D. M. Snell (eds), *Women, work and wages, c. 1650–1900*, Woodbridge 2004, 141–69
—— 'Malthus, marriage and poor law allowances revisited: a Bedfordshire case study, 1770–1834', *AgHR* lii (2004), 56–82
—— 'Earnings, poor relief and the economy of makeshifts: Bedfordshire in the early years of the New Poor Law', *Rural History* xvi (2005), 21–52
—— '"A good character for virtue, sobriety, and honesty": unmarried mothers' petitions to the London Foundling Hospital and the rhetoric of need in the early nineteenth century', in Levene, Nutt and Williams, *Illegitimacy*, 86–10
—— 'Poor relief, labourers' households and living standards in rural England, c. 1770–1834: a Bedfordshire case-study', *EcHR* lviii (2005), 485–519
—— 'Practitioners' income and provision for the poor: parish doctors in the late eighteenth and early nineteenth centuries', *Social History of Medicine* xviii (2005), 1–28
Wrightson, K., 'The politics of the parish in early modern England', in P. Griffiths, A. Fox and S. Hindle (eds), *The experience of authority in early modern England*, London 1996, 10–46
Wrigley, E. A., 'Family reconstitution', in E. A. Wrigley (ed.), *An introduction to English historical demography*, London 1966, 96–159
—— 'British population during the "long" eighteenth century, 1680–1840', in Floud and Johnson, *Cambridge economic history of modern Britain*, i. 57–95
—— R. S. Davies, J. E. Oeppen, and R. S. Schofield, *English population history from family reconstitution, 1580–1837*, Cambridge 1997
—— and R. S. Schofield, *The population history of England, 1541–1871: a reconstruction*, 2nd edn. Cambridge 1989
—— and D. Souden, 'Introduction', in *Works of Malthus*, iv. 7–9

## Unpublished theses

Barker-Read, M., 'The treatment of the aged poor in 5 selected West Kent parishes from settlement to Speenhamland (1662–1797)', PhD, Open University 1989

Berry, A., 'Patronage, funding and the hospital patient, c. 1750–1815: three English regional case studies', PhD, Oxford 1995

Hitchcock, T. V., 'The English workhouse: a study in institutional poor relief in selected counties, 1696–1750', PhD, Oxford 1985

Sharpe, P. 'Gender-specific demographic adjustment to changing economic circumstances: Colyton, 1538–1837', PhD, Cambridge 1988

Taylor, S. W., 'Aspects of the socio-demographic history of seven Berkshire parishes in the eighteenth century', PhD, Reading 1987

Thomas, E. G., 'The treatment of poverty in Berkshire, Essex and Oxfordshire, 1723–1834', PhD, London 1971

Thomson, D., 'Provision for the elderly in England, 1830 to 1908', PhD, Cambridge 1980

Williams, S., 'Poor relief, welfare and medical provision in Bedfordshire: the social, economic and demographic context, c. 1770–1834', PhD, Cambridge 1998

## Internet sources

Shave, S. A., 'The welfare of the vulnerable in the late eighteenth and early nineteenth centuries: Gilbert's Act of 1782', *History in Focus, Special Theme 'Welfare'* (on–line journal), 2008, http://www.history.ac.uk/ihr/Focus/welfare/articles/shaves.html, last accessed July 2010

# Index

able-bodied: definition of, 114, 163; and the allowance system, 9, 56, 62, 96, 132, 162; and setting to work, 2, 4–5, 52. *See also* allowance system; New Poor Law; parish work; unemployment, seasonal underemployment; workhouses, poorhouses
administrative costs, 36 n. 6, 39 n. 13, 53
age: employment and unemployment, 23–4, 44, 104, 112, 140–4, 145, 148; individual pauper biographies, 115–16, 122, 128; life-cycle stage, 14–15, 165; profile, 27, 65. *See also* burials; children; elderly; marriage; unemployment, seasonal underemployment; widowhood
agricultural depression, 5, 8–9, 10, 26, 36–7, 58, 131–44, 155–6, 158, 160. *See also* cost of living; employment; unemployment, seasonal underemployment
Agricultural Society, Bedfordshire, 95
agriculture, *see* employment
allotments, *see* gardens, allotments
allowance system, 21, 35 n.1, 36, 56–63, 100, 112–13, 124, 130, 133, 162; food schemes, 58, 100; individual pauper biographies, 115–16; scales, 11, 17, 58, 62; types of schemes, 9–10, 12. *See also* New Poor Law; parish work
allowances-in-aid-of-wages, *see* allowance system
almshouses, 51
Ampthill, 24, 52, 66, 135, 143, 150
Anti-Poor Law campaign, 66
Apfel, W., 66
apprenticeship (pauper), 2, 15, 101–2, 106–7, 121, 144, 145–6; clothing for, 44; individual pauper biographies, 44, 88, 106; and settlement, 80
Armstrong, A., 131
asylums, *see* medical relief
attitudes towards the poor, 8, 35, 66, 91–100, 123–4. *See also* New Poor Law
Auxiliary Bible Society, 93

badging the poor, 95
Barker-Read, M., 5, 150
bastardy examinations, *see* settlement; unmarried mothers
Batchelor, T., 24, 27, 99, 139
Baugh, D., 10
Bedford, 25, 77, 92, 107, 109, 145, 156; bread order, 58; non-resident relief, 88, 89; poor relief, 29–30, 60
Bedford, 5th duke, *see* Russell, F.
Bedford asylum, *see* medical relief
Bedford bridewell, 93. *See also* houses of correction, bridewells
Bedford gaol, 93, 132. *See also* crime
*Bedford Gazette*, 140
Bedford guildhall, 93
Bedford Infirmary, *see* medical relief
Bedfordshire hundreds: 29–30, 58, 60–1, 71, 92, 98, 135
Bedfordshire parishes: Aspley Guise, 123, 146; Biddenham, 84; Blunham, 99; Caddington, 139; Cardington, 26, 55, 112, 121, 148; Clophill, 77, 149; Cople, 157; Cranfield, 52; Dunton, 51; Eaton Bray, 98; Eaton Socon, 98, 127, 134, 139, 140, 146, 149, 156; Eversholt, 60–1, 154; Flitwick, 99; Henlow, 92; Hockcliffe, 83; Humbershoe, 65; Islington, 81; Keysoe, 98; Lidlington, 99, 139; Marston Morteyne, 146; Maulden, 90, 99; Meppershall, 82, 99, 150; Millbrook, 98; Moggerhanger, 99; Northill, 146; St Neots, 60; Sharnbrook, 99, 155; Shillington, 81, 95, 106; Southill, 51–2, 90, 92, 97, 99; Stotfold, 99; Turvey, 139; Warden, 81, 99; Westoning, 136–7, 138, 155, 157; Wilden, 158; Willington, 99, 107
begging, 2, 7, 158
belonging, 85–6, 154, 164. *See also* eligibility, entitlement
Berkshire, 21, 29, 47, 62, 71, 134, 138
Biggleswade, 39, 60
Blaug, M. 10, 21, 60–2, 92

181

# INDEX

boarding out children, 101, 102, 104–6, 116, 144, 146, 147
Botelho, L. A., 6, 11, 149
Boyer, G., 9, 10, 60–2, 75, 136, 162
Braintree, 14, 83
Bristol, 3, 73, 74, 120–1
Bristol parishes: Abson and Wick, 102; Temple, 128
Broad, J., 5, 6, 149, 165
Buckinghamshire, 21, 22, 23, 29, 71, 82, 132
burials (paid for by the parish), 41, 81, 146; age at, 42; individual pauper biographies, 31, 33, 49, 64, 104, 110, 112–13, 116, 128, 142; spending on, 41–2, 44–5, 49; types of recipients, 42. *See also* New Poor Law; vital events

Cambridge, 86, 88
Cambridgeshire, 21, 47, 66, 82, 132, 134
Cambridgeshire parish: Linton, 102–3
care and nursing, 40–1, 44, 46, 130, 161; carers and nurses, 52, 105, 110, 116, 123–4, 144, 146–7; carers and nurses as poor relief recipients, 147; individual pauper biographies, 31, 33, 51, 64, 87, 104, 110, 113, 116, 128. *See also* kin; medical relief
census: ages in, 23–4, 27; household size, 27–9; individual pauper biographies, 117; occupations in, 22, 25, 27, 133, 148, 149; population size, 25–6, 28, 54, 55–6, 72; workhouse, 144
Chadwick, E., 162
charity, 6–7, 8, 31, 50, 65, 72, 119, 148–9, 163; duration of, 152–4; family characteristics of recipients, 152–3. *See also* economy of makeshifts, mixed economy of welfare; Ellard and Kelynge's charity (Campton)
Cheshire, 21
child allowances, *see* allowance system
childbirth, *see* medical relief
children, 15–16, 86, 91, 101–2, 103–7; acts of Elizabeth I (1598–1601), 2, 104; bastard children (individual pauper biographies), 31–2, 41, 51, 90, 104–6, 108, 110, 115–16, 148; burials of children, 42; poverty life-cycle stage, 13, 116, 120, 124–5, 129, 148; as a proportion of the population, 27–9, 56, 124–5; in the workhouse, 15, 51–2. *See also* allowance system;

boarding out children; clothing and shoes; economy of makeshifts; employment; families (couple-headed); fathers (putative of bastards); illegitimacy; lone parents; orphans; unemployment, seasonal under-employment; unmarried mothers
christenings, 33, 40. *See also* vital events
churchwardens, 2 n. 5, 11, 91, 150
Clare, J., 77
clothing and shoes (as relief in kind), 31, 33, 110, 128; for children, 44, 51–2, 101, 104, 105, 106, 110, 116, 145; for the elderly, 44, 115, 140, 142; for families (couple-headed), 44; for infirmary admittance, 48; for lone parents, 44; making of, 43–4, 144, 147–8; types and spending on, 42–5; in the workhouse, 50
Cobbett, W., 77
cohabitation, 109
Colchester, 85, 127, 129, 138
common and customary rights, 6, 7, 156, 164. *See also* enclosure; gardens, allotments; gleaning; pig-keeping
constables, 98, 158
co-residence, *see* household structure
Cornwall, 21
Corporations of the Poor, 4
cost of living: deflation, 5, 40, 41, 68; inflation, 4, 8, 9, 10, 29, 36, 63, 64, 156, 164; volatility, 58. *See also* agricultural depression; harvest failures, economic crises
cottage industry, *see* employment
couples, 117; as charity recipients, 152; elderly, 64, 90, 112, 140, proportion of recipients, 18, 101, 113, 163, 164, value of relief, 64, 161; ratepayers, 125–6; young and middle-aged, 17, 82, 137
crime, 7, 95, 96, 123, 124, 125, 132, 157–8. *See also* Bedford gaol
Cumberland, 21
Cunningham, H., 23

Davies, D., 58–9, 94
deflation, *see* cost of living
dependants ('hidden'), 17, 54, 55–6, 72, 73, 164
deserted wives, 8, 15, 65, 122, 123, 161. *See also* lone parents
Devon, 83, 123

182

# INDEX

Devon parish: Colyton, 7
Digby, A., 66
Dorset, 21, 123
Dorset parish: Corfe Castle, 26
Dunkley, P., 62, 63, 66
Dunstable, 22, 24, 146
Durham, 3

earnings: agriculture, 24, 155–6; parish work, 105–6, 114, 136–8, 141, 147–8; proportion by family member, 148–9; straw-plaiting, 24–5, 51, 149. *See also* economy of makeshifts; employment; family economy; household budgets
East Anglia, 4
Eastwood, D., 29
economy of makeshifts, 1, 16, 19, 110, 121, 131, 148–59, 161, 164; definition of, 7–8; by region, 7–8; role of women and children, 8. *See also* common and customary rights; crime; earnings; enclosure; friendly societies; gardens, allotments; gleaning; kin; pig-keeping; savings banks
Eden, F. M., 12, 24, 58–9, 65
elderly, 12, 17, 33, 111–14, 125, 136, 137, 163; acts of Elizabeth I (1598–1601), 2; appeals for relief, 86–7, 103, 141, 143; burials, 42; as charity recipients, 152; definitions of old age, 14–15, 17, 64, 102–3, 114; duration of poor relief, 33, 57, 64, 112–13; individual pauper biographies, 31–2, 90, 113, 122, 128; kin, 121–4; as pensioners, 3, 4, 56–7, 65, 112–13, 115–19, 131, 140–4; poverty life-cycle stage, 13, 18, 101, 120, 129, 164; as a proportion of the population, 65; ratepayers, 27, 126, 128; in the workhouse, 51. *See also* age; clothing and shoes; generosity and the value of relief; illness; kin; New Poor Law; widowers; widows
eligibility, entitlement, 8, 17, 18, 80, 80–91, 96, 100, 102, 111, 162. *See also* belonging
Ellard and Kelynge's charity (Campton), 150–4, 158, 163–4, 165
employment: agriculture, 23, 25, 27, 137, 148–9; by-employments, 7, 138, 143, 154; hat-making, 21–2, 132, 149, 161; lace-making: children, 21, 24, 26–7, 104, 132, 145, 148–9, 158, regions, 21–2, women, 21, 26–7, 108, 132, 137, 148, 149, 158; seasonal nature of, 4, 131–44, 147, 157, 162; servants: domestic, 27, farm, 23, 145–6; general, 29, 44, 51, 79, 80, 102, 108, 121; spinning, 21, 26–7, 105, 112, 137, 148; straw-plaiting: children, 23–4, 132–3, 137–8, 145, 148–9, 158, 161, Chinese and Japanese imports, 22–3, men, 22, 23, 133, plaiting schools, 145, regions, 21–5, seasonality, 23, 137, women, 21–3, 27, 51, 108, 132, 137–8, 145, 148–9, 158, 161. *See also* agricultural depression; apprenticeship (pauper); earnings; economy of makeshifts; family economy; occupational structure; parish work; unemployment, seasonal under-employment
enclosure, 156, 164. *See also* common and customary rights; gardens, allotments; gleaning; pig-keeping
entitlement, *see* eligibility, entitlement
Essex: allowance system, 10, 132, 134; care work between kin, 123; New Poor Law, 66; non-resident relief, 83; pauper letters, 76, 124, 143; poor rates, 29, 71; proportion on relief, 21; straw-plaiting, 22; unemployed women, 137
Essex parishes: Ardleigh, 14, 74, 78; Terling, 141
examinations, *see* settlement
Exeter, 3, 74

families (couple-headed): appeals for relief, 88; as charity recipients, 152, 158; duration of poor relief, 57, 68, 107, 161, 162; poverty life-cycle stage, 13, 18, 101, 104, 124–6, 129; ratepayers, 103; as recipients of allowances: contemporary views, 59–60, 140, in Campton and Shefford, 17, 58–63, 68, 102, 107, 112–13, 116–17, 130, 160–4, secondary literature on, 9, 12, 15, 102; rewards to (from Bedford Agricultural Society), 95–6; settlement, 81, 82. *See also* allowance system; family economy; household budgets; household structure; lone parents; militia men
family economy, components: employment of women and children, 22–5, 161–2; other resources, 148–50, 154–9, 161–2; poor relief, 7–8, 19, 136–7, 161–2. *See also* charity;

183

earnings; economy of makeshifts; employment; household budgets
family reconstitution, 30–4, 55 n. 61, 115, 122, 125 n. 82. *See also* vital events
farmers, 23, 26, 52, 78–9, 80, 98–9, 129, 137, 140, 158. *See also* occupational structure; property holding
fathers (putative of bastards), 16, 108–9
Fideler, P., 8
Fissell, M., 102, 120–1
Fitzpatrick, J., 2nd earl of Upper Ossory, 93
food, drink and provisions (paid for by the parish): during harvest failures, 58; during illness, 49; individual pauper biographies, 51, 52, 64, 105, 110, 122, 128, 140, 142; procurement, 144, 148; spending on, 45–6; for weddings, 108; in the workhouse, 50, 90
foster families, *see* boarding out children
Fox, C., 94
friendly societies, 7, 8, 42, 47, 88, 154–6, 158. *See also* economy of makeshifts
fuel (paid for by the parish), 4, 44–6, 49, 50, 101, 144, 148, 161; individual pauper biographies, 31, 33, 105, 115

gardens, allotments, 156–7, 164
Gash, N., 131, 136
gender, 1, 12, 14, 16, 65, 101, 111, 129, 163, 165. *See also* deserted wives; employment; family economy; lone men and women; lone parents; masculinisation of relief; unemployment, seasonal under-employment; unmarried mothers; widowers; widows
generosity and the value of relief, 5–6, 17, 40, 71, 160–2; for the elderly, 15, 57, 64–5, 125, 160–1; for families (couple-headed), 57–8, 59, 65, 68, 107, 130, 161; increase in value, 3, 4; for lone men and women, 65; for lone parents, 16, 56–7, 63, 65, 68, 125, 130, 136, 160–2, 164; north and west, 5, 8–9, 161–2; by region, 4, 5–6, 161–2; rural-urban, 38–9, 164–5; settlement, 5, 12; south and east, 4, 5–6, 8–9, 10, 16, 39 n. 12, 56, 64, 66, 161. *See also* household budgets; New Poor Law
Gilbert's Act (1782), 4–5
gleaning, 157. *See also* economy of makeshifts

Goose, N., 22, 25, 149
Gorsky, M., 156

Hampshire, 21
harvest failures, economic crises, 8, 10, 58–9, 63, 94, 156, 160, 161, 164
Hatfield, 24
Herefordshire, 21, 23
Hertfordshire, 21, 22, 24, 27 n. 45, 66, 82, 144, 149
Hertfordshire parishes: Aldenham, 4, 73, 126 n. 84, 127; Ashwell, 52; Berkhamsted, 24; Redbourn, 24
Hindle, S., 10, 11, 69
Hitchin, 81
Hobsbawm, E., 98
Honeyman, K., 106, 145
Horrell, S., 149
hospitals, *see* medical relief
household budgets, 58–9, 65, 123, 136–7, 148–9
household listings, 14, 26, 55
household structure, 27–9, 68, 102, 119–20, 136–7; co-residence, 7, 33, 36, 122–3, 130
houses of correction, bridewells, 95, 108–9. *See also* Bedford bridewell
houses of industry, 4
housing, *see* Whitbread, S.
Howlett, J., 25, 38–9, 164–5
Hufton, O., 7
Humphries, J., 8, 149
Hunt, E. H., 15, 103, 143–4
Huntingdonshire, 21, 82
Huzel, J., 10, 62

illegitimacy: rise of, 102, 107; subsociety, 110–11. *See also* fathers (putative of bastards); lone parents; unmarried mothers
illness, poor relief for, 45–6, 90, 101, 112, 120, 121, 123, 126, 146; acts of Elizabeth I (1598–1601), 2; appeals for relief, 86, 88, 89; elderly men, 140–3; individual pauper biographies, 33, 48, 88–9, 104–5, 110, 115, 127–8, 140–3, 153. *See also* food, drink and provisions; New Poor Law
indemnity certificates, *see* settlement
industrial parishes and regions, 8–9, 15, 22, 23, 82, 84, 106, 145. *See also* north and west
inflation, *see* cost of living

# INDEX

inherited poverty, 101, 119, 130. *See also* kin

Jones, P., 42, 43, 89

Kent, 2, 10, 21, 29, 71, 74, 126 n. 84, 132
Kent parishes: Cowden, 150; Odiham, 119; Wrotham, 150
kin: assistance between, 11, 90, 101, 119–25, 126–7, 130; care and nursing between, 33, 116, 123–4, 130; charity, 152–3; and the economy of makeshifts, 7–8, 121; kin clauses of poor law, 121. *See also* inherited poverty; 'kinship universe'; household structure
King, P., 18, 93–4, 157
King, S., 5, 7, 12, 15, 42, 111, 121, 161
'kinship universe', 120
Kirby Lonsdale, 89

labour rate, *see* allowance system; parish work
Lancashire, 2
Lancaster, 84–5
land tax, 26, 80
Laslett, P., 110–11
Leeds, 83
Leicestershire, 21
Leighton Buzzard, 83
less-eligibility, 95, 96
Levene, A., 106, 145
life-course, *see* life-cycle, life-course
life-cycle, life-course: of the poor, 1, 12, 13–14, 16, 78, 101–19, 121, 148, in Campton and Shefford, 18, 32–3, 63, 129–30, 164, 165; of ratepayers, 78, 125–9. *See also* Rowntree, B. S.
life expectancy, 113
'lifetime' paupers, 116–19, 124, 130. *See also* pauperised life-courses
Lincolnshire, 2, 82
London, 16, 74, 83
London Foundling Hospital, 16
London parishes: Boroughside, 73; St Martin's-in-the-Fields, 3–4; Southwark, 81
lone men and women, 17, 56–7, 64, 65, 116, 124, 152, 162; as charity recipients, 152
lone parents, poor relief for, 15–16, 17, 107–11, 155; as charity recipients, 152; duration of relief, 63–4; individual

pauper biographies, 107–8, 109–10, 111, 115–17; poverty life-cycle stage, 18, 101, 102, 104; settlement, 81, 107–8. *See also* clothing and shoes; deserted wives; generosity and the value of relief; illegitimacy; unmarried mothers; widowers; widows
Luck, L., 23
Luton, 22, 24, 60, 123, 146

Macqueen, T. P., 132
magistrates (JPs): duties, 52, 69, 76–7, 80, 92, 94, 95, 96, 98, 100; orders and adoption of scales, 9, 58, 62; and the 'politics of the parish', 11, 90, 91, 162. *See also* New Poor Law; pauper appeals; 'politics of the parish'; quarter sessions; Whitbread, S.
Maidstone, 150
make-work schemes, *see* parish work
Malthus, Revd T., 59–60, 92–3, 95, 96–7, 162
Manchester, 85
marriage: age at, 63; 'forced' marriages, 108–9; remarriage, 31, 88
masculinisation of relief, 12, 18, 131–44
medical relief, 45–9, 93, 101–2, 144; appeals for, 88; childbirth and lying-in, 40–1, 46, 47, 104, 108, 110, 111, 146, 147; growth of medical relief, 4, 45; hospitals, 36, 46, 47–9, 88, 160, Bedford Infirmary, 33, 44, 47–9, 88, 89, 93, 100, 117, lying-in hospitals, 16; lunatic asylums, 46, 49, 93; surgeon-apothecaries, 33, 46–7, 88, 89, 91, 93, 144, and medical contracts, 36, 46–7, 100, 144, 146, 147, 160; workhouse, 50. *See also* care and nursing; illness; New Poor Law; smallpox
micro-history, 1, 160
Middlesex, 82
Middlesex parish: Stoke Newington, 88
migration and mobility, 82, 120, 121–2, 126, 140
militia men: families, 53, 127
Millar, J., 15–16, 64
mixed economy of welfare, 1, 6–7, 16, 19, 148–59, 161, 163, 165. *See also* charity; economy of makeshifts; friendly societies; New Poor Law
mortality rates, 104, 164

# INDEX

Napoleonic Wars, 8, 18, 36, 68, 97, 134, 143, 144, 158; demobilisation, 8, 131; impact upon straw trade, 22, 24
negotiation, 11, 69, 86–91, 100, 122, 165
Neuman, M., 62
Newman, A., 74
Newman Brown, W., 127
New Poor Law (1834), 1, 5, 8, 62, 66–8; and the able-bodied, 66–8, 133–5, 162, 163; attitudes towards the poor, 91–2, 95, 99, 162; burials, 42; continuance of allowance system, 66–8; continuance of the mixed economy of welfare, 7; and the elderly, 15, 143–4; generosity and the value of relief, 6, 17, 35, 66–8, 162; magistrates, 11 n. 61; medical relief and illness, 66–8; and women, 112, 125, 130
non-resident relief, 25 n. 33, 38 n. 10, 76, 82–91, 100, 106, 122, 165
Norfolk, 4, 12, 13, 21, 66, 73, 118
north and west: application for relief, 11–12, 163; economy of makeshifts, 7–8; non-resident relief, 82–3, 84–5; unemployment, seasonal under-employment, 131–2. See also generosity and the value of relief; industrial parishes and regions
*Northampton Mercury*, 140
Northamptonshire, 21, 47, 82
Northumberland, 3
Norwich, 3, 74, 83
nuclear family hardship, 120
Nutt, T., 16

occupational structure, 25, 27, 78–9, 80, 165. See also employment; farmers; owner-occupiers, property holding
old age, see elderly
Old Age Pensions Act (1908), 103
orphans, 15; acts of Elizabeth I (1598–1601), 2; poverty life-cycle stage, 13, 18, 101, 164; as recipients, 17, 18, 57, 101, 102, 103–5, 116, 145, 153, 164; in the workhouse, 15, 51. See also children
Osborn, Sir G., 26, 48
Ottaway, S: age of dependency, 103; elderly as deserving, 65, 111, 129; gender of recipients, 12, 111, 129, 141; generosity of relief, 5, 15, 160–1; and kin, 122, 124. See also age; elderly
Ouse, river, 93

overseers: applications to, 11–12, 163; attitude towards the poor, 12, 52, 86, 87, 124, 164; charity role, 150; duties, 69, 82, 88, 139, 163; expenditure on the poor, 53, 101, 106, 110, 129, 131, 133, 135, 136, 160; and magistrates, 50–1, 77, 92, 108, 123; pauper letters, 89, 143; and the 'politics of the parish', 11, 79, 90, 91; providing work, 145, 146; as targets of violence, 98–9; and the vestry, 92. See also magistrates; negotiation; 'politics of the parish'; vestry; Whitbread, S.
owner-occupiers, 26. See also property holding
Oxford, 75
Oxfordshire, 21, 47, 59

parish policy, 4, 35–54, 72–3, 78–80, 91–2, 100, 130, 138, 162. See also parish work; 'politics of the parish'
parish registers, see family reconstitution; vital events
parish work: make-work schemes: in Bedfordshire, 18, 36, 90, 97–8, 100, 106, 114, 127, 131–44, 158, types of schemes, 9–10; other parish work, 50, 131, 144–8; setting to work, 2, 4–5, 52, 104, 131, 144. See also allowance system; boarding out children; care and nursing; medical relief
parliamentary papers, 31, 59; *Abstract of the poor* (1803–4), 28–30, 39, 83; *Abstract of the poor* (1818), 28–30, 77, 78; Children's Employment Commission (1843), 24; Children's Employment Commission (1864), 21–2; *Poor law report* (1834), 9, 21, 56, 59–60; 'Rural and town queries' (1834), 9, 18 n. 94, 59, 60–2, 75, 99, 132, 138, 148–9; *Select committee on building houses for the poor* (1812–13), 76; *Select committee on labourers' wages* (1824), 9, 21, 59, 60–2, 132. See also New Poor Law; poor law commission
pauper appeals, 11, 18, 44, 50–1, 52, 93–4, 141, 162. See also pauper letters
pauper biographies: and hidden dependants, 17, 55; longitudinal analysis, 18, 34, 59, 101, 103–4, 110, 130, 147, 160; methodology, 16, 30–4, 59; quantitative analysis, 16,

186

# INDEX

34, 35, 56–7, 160. *See also* ratepayer biographies
pauper letters, 76, 86–91, 100, 103, 124, 143
pauperised life-courses, 18, 42, 101, 115–19, 124, 130. *See also* 'lifetime' paupers
pig-keeping, 157, 158. *See also* economy of makeshifts
Pitt, W., 94
poaching, *see* crime
political economy, 92
'politics of the parish', 1, 10–12, 16, 18, 77–8, 90, 99–100, 129, 162–3, 165
poor houses, *see* workhouses, poor houses
poor law commission, 9, 107, 132. *See also* New Poor Law; parliamentary papers
*Poor law report* (1834), *see* parliamentary papers
poor laws: acts of Elizabeth I (1598–1601), 2, 17, 69, 73, 104, 144; economic impact of, 1, 9–10, 16, 162; expenditure, nominal, 5, 8, 9, 92, 97, 156, in Bedfordshire, 17, 66–8, in Campton and Shefford, 36–8, 40, 134–6; expenditure, *per capita*, 5, 8, 25, in Bedfordshire, 17, 66–8, in Campton and Shefford, 38–9, 164; expenditure *per pauper*, in Campton and Shefford, 38–9, 164. *See also* administrative costs; north and west; south and east
poor rates, 4, 24, 53, 61, 83, 105, 132, 139; acts of Elizabeth I (1598–1601), 2, 69; in Bedfordshire, 29; paid by the parish, 51, 127; 'politics of the parish', 10; proposals by Whitbread, S., 95, 96. *See also* ratepayer biographies; ratepayers; ratepaying
poor relief: application for, 11–12, 86–91, 163; duration, 101, 165; in kind, 4, 7, 35, 68, 101, 124, 131, 160, 161, 165, expenditure in kind, 17, 19, 39–50; more than one period of relief, 112, 115–19; tailored nature of, 58, 64, 108, 110, 116, 124, 161. *See also* boarding out children; burials; care and nursing; christenings; clothing and shoes; food, drink and provisions; fuel; medical relief; poor rates; rent and lodging; unemployment, seasonal under-employment; weddings; welfare (growth of)
poor relief, number of recipients: in Bedfordshire, 28, 30; in Campton and Shefford, 36–8, 132–4, 164; nationally, 8, 28; as a proportion of population, 21, 28, 30, 54–6, 65, 72–4, 164. *See also* dependants (hidden)
poor relief, occasional relief and recipients, 3, 5, 25, 28, 30; in Campton and Shefford, 17, 35, 68, 101, 109, 131; definition of, 35 n. 2; expenditure on, 16–17, 39–40, 85–6, 90; for illness, 46; individual pauper biographies, 33, 48, 49, 64, 104, 110, 115, 116; number of recipients, 28, 37–8, 54–6, 63, 75, 160, 163, 165; overlap between cash and kind, 42, 44; as a proportion of population, 54–6; ratepayer-paupers, 127–8; for unemployment and seasonal unemployment, 132–40, 142, 151, 154, 164, 165
poor relief, pensions and pensioners: 4, 5, 6, 11, 25; in Bedfordshire, 28, 30; in Campton and Shefford, 35, 91–2; categories, 17, 56–7, 101–30, 131, 160, 162, 163; as charity recipients, 151–2; definition of, 35 n. 2; duration of relief, 101, 112, 115–19; expenditure on, 16–17, 39–41, 42, 44, 63, 160–1, 165; individual pauper biographies, 31, 33, 48, 49, 50–1, 52, 88, 101–30, 147; number of, 37–8, 54–6, 75, 101–30, 160, 165; older men, 140–4, 163; and poverty life-cycle, 18, 101–30, 164; as a proportion of population, 54–6; ratepayer-paupers, 125–9. *See also* allowance system; couples; elderly; families (couple-headed); generosity and the value of relief; lone men and women; lone parents; New Poor Law; non-resident relief; orphans; pauperised life-courses; widowers, widows
population growth, 3, 4, 5, 8, 10, 96; in Campton and Shefford, 26, 38, 54, 72; impact of poor relief upon, 59–60, 63, 97. *See also* Malthus, Revd T.
Potton, 39, 83
Poynter, J. R., 62, 95
prenuptial pregnancy, 108–9
Preston, 23
proletarianisation, 14
property holding, 26, 72, 75, 77–9, 80, 96–7, 98–9, 126. *See also* farmers; owner-occupiers

# INDEX

Puddletown, 141

quarter sessions, 52, 58, 76–7, 92, 94–6, 123, 139, 155, 158. *See also* magistrates; Whitbread, S.

ratepayer biographies, 16, 17, 30–4, 71, 115, 125. *See also* pauper biographies; poor rates; ratepayers; ratepaying
ratepayers, 69–100, 163, 165; appeals on rating, 76–7; attitudes towards the poor, 12; exemption and defaulting, 70, 75, 76–7, 80, 100, 103, 126, 127–9, 156; family circumstances, 18, 32, 33–4, 71, 103, 125–6; number of, 36, 70, 74; proportion of inhabitants paying the rates, 17–18, 69–70, 71–4; ratepayer-paupers, 18, 32, 126–9, 162–3; rates paid by the parish, 51, 127; as vestry members, 91; wealth of, 17–18, 71, 74–6, 162; women as, 91, 126, 127. *See also* poor rates; ratepayer biographies; ratepaying
ratepaying, 17–18, 32, 50, 51, 69–100, 99; duration, 78. *See also* poor rates; ratepayer biographies; ratepayers
regional variation, *see* north and west; south and east
relatives, *see* kin
removals, *see* settlement
rent and lodging (paid for by the parish), 4, 31, 45–6, 51, 87, 89, 90, 105, 110, 141
riots, *see* Swing Riots; unrest
roads (parish work on), *see* parish work
roundsman system, *see* allowance system; parish work
Rowntree, B. S., 13, 63, 116, 124–5, 126, 164
Royal Lancastrian Institution, 97
Rudé, G., 98
rural industry, *see* employment
rural parishes: economy of, 10; Gilbert's Act (1782), 4–5; implementation of parish rating, 69; poor law provision, 4, 15–16, 64; the poverty life-cycle, 13, 15–16, 64; urban/rural differences, 25, 38–9, 59, 60–2, 73–4, 82–3, 155, 164–5; vestry, 91
'Rural and town queries' (1834), *see* parliamentary papers
Russell, F., 5th duke of Bedford, 26, 95, 98, 139, 157; agent, 98; steward,

97. *See also* Agricultural Society, Bedfordshire

St Albans, 24
Salisbury, 3
savings banks, 155. *See also* friendly societies; self-help
scales (parish), *see* allowance system
schooling, *see* employment; Whitbread, S.
*Select committee on labourers' wages* (1824), *see* parliamentary papers
self-help, 7, 95, 96. *See also* friendly societies; savings banks
self-provisioning, *see* common and customary rights; economy of makeshifts; gardens, allotments; gleaning; pig-keeping
Senior, N., 162
settlement: conferment of settlement, 72, 75, 80–1, 96, 100, 102, 110, 145; disputes over, 106; examinations, removals and indemnity certificates, 14 n. 77, 16, 80, 81–2, 89, 107–8, 115, 137 n. 24, 163; laws, 2, 80, 126, 163; within pauper letters, 86, 12. *See also* generosity and the value of relief; non-resident relief; pauper letters
Sharpe, P., 85, 89–90
Shaw-Taylor, L., 22
Shefford: market, 25–6
Shrewsbury, 75
Shropshire, 21, 47
sickness, *see* illness
Slack, P., 3, 6, 55, 71, 73, 128
smallpox, 46, 49, 90, 147. *See also* care and nursing; medical relief
Smith, R. M., 5, 12, 15, 120, 141–2, 160–1
Snell, K. D. M.: apprenticeship (pauper), 106, 145; belonging, 85–6; enclosure, 156; generosity of relief, 5, 40, 44–5; indemnity certificates (settlement), 80; lone-parent families, 15–16, 64; New Poor Law, 99; women's work, 137
Sokoll, T., 14, 74
Solar, P., 15, 160–1
solitaries, *see* lone men and women
Somerset, 1 n.1
south and east: allowance system, 60; charity, 150; economy of makeshifts, 7–8, 158; farm service, 145; Gilbert's Act (1782), 4–5; growth of welfare, 35, 36; migration, 82; non-resident

# INDEX

relief, 83; 'politics of the parish', 11; poor relief, 5–6, 16, 39 n. 12, 161; proportion of the population on relief, 21; Swing Riots, 98–9; unemployment, seasonal under-employment, 8, 36, 68, 129, 131–2, 143, 144, 163; urban centres, 16, 64, 80. *See also* generosity and the value of relief

Speenhamland system and scales, *see* allowance system

Staffordshire, 23

Stapleton, B., 119

'strangers', 90, 100. *See also* vagrancy

Sturges Bourne Acts (1818–19), 78, 95

Styles, J., 42

Suffolk, 6, 21, 29, 66, 71, 150

Suffolk parishes: Cratfield and Poslingford, 12 n. 69; Whitton, 129

Surrey, 82, 132

surveyors of the highways, 91, 132, 139

survival strategies, *see* economy of makeshifts

Sussex, 2, 10, 21, 132

Swing Riots, 98–9. *See also* unrest

Taylor, J. S., 84, 89

Thane, P., 15, 161

Thomson, D., 15, 103, 124, 143–4, 160–1

Toddington, 39, 132, 139

Tomkins, A., 7

Turner, J., 66, 137

'under-class', 119, 130

unemployment, seasonal under-employment: ages of the unemployed, 140–3; and enclosure, 156; friendly society payouts, 154; and illness, 45; individual pauper biographies, 48, 87, 89, 106, 127–8, 157; kin support, 120, 124; under the New Poor Law, 66–8; non-resident relief, 82–3; older men, 15, 18–19, 129, 163; parliamentary papers, 61; poor relief for, 9–10, 12, 56, 100, 126, 131–44, 158, 160, 162, 163; ratepayer-paupers, 127–8; setting to work, 4, 96; in the south and east, 8, 36, 68, 129, 131–2, 143, 144, 163; structural unemployment, 5, 8, 158; unrest and Swing Riots, 98–9. *See also* agricultural depression; allowance system; Napoleonic Wars; parish work; parliamentary papers

unmarried mothers: bastardy examinations, 107–8; cohabitation, 109; generosity of relief, 15–16, 63–4; multiple illegitimate births, 109–10; in pauper letters, 86; poor relief recipients, 15–16, 63–4, 101, 102, 107, 125; subsociety, 110–11. *See also* children; fathers (putative of bastards); illegitimacy; lone parents; marriage; settlement

unrest, 66, 69, 98, 100. *See also* Swing Riots

Upper Ossery, 2nd earl, *see* Fitzpatrick, J.

urban parishes and townships: implementation of parish rating, 2, 69; poor law provision, 15–16, 64; the poverty life-cycle, 13, 15–16, 64; urban/rural differences, 25, 38–9, 59, 60–2, 73–4, 80, 82–3, 155, 164–5. *See also* Workhouse Test Act (1722)

utilitarianism, 92

vagrancy, 7, 53, 90, 158; 'gypsys', 90; Irish vagrants, 90; Scots vagrants, 90. *See also* 'strangers'

Verdon, N., 148–9

vestry: application for relief to, 11–12, 163; costs, 53; decisions on: disorderly persons, 98, parish clothing, 110, 145, responsibilities of kin, 122; policy, 4, 35–6, 72–3, 78–80, 91–2, 99, 100, 130, 137, 138, 162; 'politics of the parish', 10–11, 94, 99, 129, 162; Swing Riots, 99; voting, 77–78, 96. *See also* parish policy

vital events, 25, 30–3, 64, 125 n. 82. *See also* burials; christenings; family reconstitution; weddings

Wales, T., 4, 12, 13, 15, 118, 160–1

Wall, R., 120, 121

Walter, J., 79

Warwickshire, 2, 73

Warwickshire parish: Tysoe, 138

weddings (paid for by the parish), 40–1, 108–9. *See also* vital events

welfare (growth of), 3–4, 12, 16, 17, 35, 68, 135–6, 141, 160

Whitbread, S., JP, MP, 31, 92–7, 100, 162, 165; auditing of poor rates, 72; critic of Revd T. Malthus, 60, 92, 95, 96, 97; education of the poor, 93, 94, 95, 97; housing the poor, 93,

96, 97; less-eligibility, 95, 96; local concerns, 93; minimum wages, 92, 93, 94, 100; National Poor's Fund, 96; in parliament, 92, 93, 94–7, 162; pauper appeals, 18, 44, 50–1, 90, 93–4, 141; poor law, 92, 93, 94–5, 100, 114, 108, 122–3; ratepayer appeals, 76–7, 162; settlement cases, 81–2; views on the vestry, 78; workhouses, 51–3, 93. *See also* magistrates (JPs); 'politics of the parish'

widowers: individual pauper biographies, 31, 49, 115, 116, 127–8; as lone parent families, 44, 63, 65, 116, 125, 161; previously in receipt of relief, 112–13; ratepayers, 126; when came onto relief, 113. *See also* elderly; lone parents

widowhood: age at, 120; in pauper appeals, 86

widows, 111–13; acts of Elizabeth I (1598–1601), 2; age at widowhood, 120; as charity recipients, 150–3, 154, 158; employed, 111–12; individual pauper biographies, 31, 32–3, 104, 115–16, 91, 105; as lone parents, 15, 56, 63, 65, 125, 155, 161; under the New Poor Law, 143–4; pauper letters, 86–7, 88; poverty life-cycle stage, 13, 32–3, 101, 102; previously in receipt of relief, 112–13; proportion of recipients, 12, 101; ratepayers, 78–9, 126; settlement certificates, 82; when came onto relief, 112–13; widow-headed lone parent families, 125. *See also* lone parents; elderly

Wiltshire, 21
Woburn, 24
work, *see* earnings; employment; occupational structure
Workhouse Test Act (1722), 4, 10, 96
workhouses, poor houses: in Bedfordshire, 51–3, 93, 96; in Campton and Shefford, 35–6, 49–51, 90, 105, 110, 136, 148; contracts for, 35; inmates, 12 n. 71, 15, 16; maintenance of the able-bodied, 4, 9; numbers inside, 28, 30–1, 35–6. *See also* Gilbert's Act (1782); Whitbread, S.; Workhouse Test Act (1722)
Wrightson, K., 10, 163
Wrigley, E. A., 22

York, 3, 74, 75, 83, 124, 164
Yorkshire, 84–5
Young, A., 23, 24, 77

www.ingramcontent.com/pod-product-compliance
Ingram Content Group UK Ltd.
Pitfield, Milton Keynes, MK11 3LW, UK
UKHW021329180426
11947UKWH00017B/1531